Politics and the Common Man
An Introduction to Political Behavior

The Dorsey Series in Political Science

Politics and the Common Man
An Introduction to Political Behavior

H. T. REYNOLDS, Ph.D.
Assistant Professor of Political Science
University of Delaware

1974

THE DORSEY PRESS   *Homewood, Illinois 60430*
Irwin-Dorsey International   *London, England WC2H 9NJ*
Irwin-Dorsey Limited   *Georgetown, Ontario L7G 4B3*

First Printing, May 1974

ISBN 0-256-01534-1
Library of Congress Catalog Card No. 74–76457

Printed in the United States of America

For My Mother and Father

Preface

The purpose of this book is to describe and interpret the political attitudes and behavior of the common man. The book considers several aspects of political life from conventional politics to participation in mass movements and violence. It also examines the origins, organization, and changes of opinions as well as how different social and political institutions affect them. The objective is, in short, to see how the average man reacts to and behaves in the political world.

To achieve this goal I have drawn from what I feel is among the best research in psychology, sociology, anthropology, and political science. The theories, ideas, and findings from these disciplines explain a good deal about political man. They give us insights into why people vote the way they do, why they join mass movements, why they accept or reject policies or leaders, why they act peacefully or violently, why they are concerned or apathetic. We need to rely on such a diversity of fields and approaches because these phenomena are quite complex.

What is known about the common man's political attitudes and behavior is often rudimentary compared to what we want or need to know. Thus the book perhaps raises as many questions as it answers. Realizing this possibility, I have tried to cite in both the text and notes some of the outstanding research and literature on various topics so that the interested reader can pursue them in greater detail. Mass political behavior is an exciting area for research and if nothing else I hope to encourage others to study it vigorously.

The sources of political attitudes and behavior are important topics because, I believe, the common man in most democracies does not always get a fair shake from his government. His real and legitimate needs often go unnoticed or unheeded. Public policies provide him with symbolic satisfactions instead of material or substantive rewards. Nor does he have an equal share in governmental decision-making: He tends to be a bystander registering approval or disapproval of what others have decided, but does not take an active part in their deliberations. His opinions are frequently unspoken or unheard. Sometimes, in extreme cases, he behaves violently, or else totally rejects and withdraws from politics. Rather than being an enlightened citizen who thinks and acts independently, the average man seems to be the object of endless campaigns to persuade and manipulate him.

It would, of course, be easy to blame this state of affairs on sinister oligarchies which keep their subjects in servitude. However, this approach is misleading. Certainly power is unevenly distributed and some groups are more powerful than others. But since we live in a democracy, the real question is why people do not or cannot take advantage of the opportunities provided by their political freedom. Why do they stay on the sidelines when they could be active participants?

To answer this question, we have to begin with the man in the street. We must ask about his motivations. What does he think? What does he want? Why does he act the way he does? Knowing the answers does not tell us everything about power in government, but it helps us understand the nature and limits of public participation in modern democracies.

To the extent the book is successful in any of its aims, I owe a debt of gratitude to numerous individuals. I am especially grateful to John Wahlke, Herb Asher, and William Reynolds who contributed many valuable suggestions. I also want to thank Paul Dolan and John Doble for their helpful comments. Mark Bertozzi collected much of the material used in Chapter 7. I appreciate his generosity in making it available to me.

Finally, I thank my wife, Lisa. As always, she has been a source of support and encouragement and I would not have finished the manuscript without her.

April 1974   H. T. REYNOLDS

Contents

xiii

1

Introduction: The Common Man and Politics

In 1970, Richard Scammon and Ben Wattenberg published *The Real Majority*, a widely read book describing American electoral politics.[1] Of particular interest is its appeal to politicians, who see in it a blueprint for winning elections.

The authors' plan for waging a successful campaign is simple: The smart candidate walks firmly in the middle of the road on issues. He is neither too liberal nor too conservative, but stays in the "center" where most of the votes are. A wise candidate supports New Deal social-welfare legislation such as social security, increases in the minimum wage, and aid to education but takes a hard line on crime in the streets, drugs, protest demonstrations, and permissiveness.[2]

In many respects, their advice seems reasonable though it does contain some disturbing implications. For one, they imply that a

---

[1] Richard M. Scammon and Ben J. Wattenberg, *The Real Majority* (New York: Coward-McCann, Inc., 1970).

[2] Ibid., chap. vi.

1

candidate might have to abandon, or at least compromise, his principles in order to get elected. So instead of raising issues that need to be discussed, candidates will avoid them. Elections become devices purely for electing public officials, not for considering alternative solutions to significant problems.

Apart from whatever moral judgments one makes about *The Real Majority,* however, it is a theory of voting which many have found useful to study and follow. The book has been avidly read by politicians, campaign advisors, and public relations consultants —in short, by the people who have the practical job of winning elections. Its appeal is thus more than academic. *The Real Majority,* many believe, contains accurate and useful information about voters' attitudes and behavior.

Since it has had wide acceptance we can meaningfully ask if it is a correct theory of voting. Are Scammon and Wattenberg right? Is theirs good scholarship? Do they correctly understand the current state of public opinion? Do candidates have workable alternative strategies to follow?

We need not answer these questions here. We are discussing *The Real Majority* merely to stress at the outset that the study of public opinion and political behavior has more than academic interest. These topics involve significant practical problems. Men and women from all walks of life—government, journalism, business, and community affairs—turn to social scientists for information and advice about mass political behavior. Occasionally they want to satisfy their curiosity. But more often they have a specific need which they feel requires the attention of an expert in political behavior.

The turbulent events of the 1960s have expanded the demand for this type of expertise. As one example, consider the proliferation of presidential and congressional commissions to study political and social problems such as riots, assassinations, crime, the effects of violence in the mass media, campaign financing, pornography, government reorganization, and drug abuse. These panels have in turn enlisted the social sciences to throw light on why people behave as they do.

The purpose of this book is to examine systematically public opinion and political behavior with a view toward seeing (1) the different ways people become involved in politics; (2) where and how they learn their attitudes and behavior; (3) how they are affected by various social and political institutions and events; (4) how people are motivated to act as they do; and (5) the impact their behavior has on governmental decision making. The book is not limited to a single activity such as voting but instead includes a wide variety of behaviors ranging from alienation to violence. Neither is it concerned with politics per se. Instead, it attempts to describe what social scientists know (or think they know) about many politically relevant behaviors.

POLITICAL ATTITUDES

What Is an Attitude?

Although the term "attitude" is commonly used by laymen and political scientists alike, there is a great deal of ambiguity regarding its definition and measurement. On the one hand, when talking about public opinion people customarily think of attitudes as "real" things—things which exist in an individual's mind and which underlie and motivate his behavior. On the other hand, no one has ever seen or touched an attitude. It is an inferred entity which can be observed and quantified only indirectly.

This suggests that we first of all have to think of an attitude as a state of mind. More precisely, it involves an evaluation of someone or something as when a person says "I like Senator McHennessey." Hence, an opinion is a judgment about an *attitude-object*. We may have many beliefs concerning the object (e.g., Senator McHennessey is honest), but it is the evaluative or affective quality which distinguishes attitudes from other cognitions. Putting these ideas together, we can state a more formal definition of an attitude:[3]

> *An attitude is an individual's readiness or disposition to respond in a favorable or unfavorable manner to some object.*

Psychologists often define an attitude by reference to three components, *cognitive, affective,* and *behavioral.* The cognitive com-

---

[3] Throughout this book the terms "attitude" and "opinion" are treated as synonyms. Many authors, particularly psychologists, like to define opinion as the *expression* (verbal or otherwise) of an underlying attitude. But for our purposes, this usage is too restrictive.

ponent consists of what the person knows about the object; the affective deals with his liking or disliking of it; and the behavioral component refers to how the individual will respond to the object. These components are discussed in different terms in a later section.

Several features of the definition stand out. For one, an attitude is a potential response to a stimulus; it is not necessary that the individual always be consciously aware of his feelings. It is only assumed that if he has an attitude toward some object, then a stimulus (such as a question on a public opinion poll) will elicit a particular response. Moreover, repeated exposure to the same stimulus will produce roughly the same response unless the attitude itself changes. An attitude, then, means an enduring tendency or disposition to evaluate an object in some manner.

We may have attitudes toward a variety of things: politicians, parties, events, and issues, to mention a few. The attitude-object may be simple or complex, though in general the more complicated it is the harder it will be to make generalizations about the corresponding attitudes. Similarly, the expression of an attitude can take many forms such as liking-disliking, desiring-avoiding, agreeing-disagreeing, pro-con, and so forth. What is essential is that there be some feeling of being for or against something.

Finally, most social scientists believe that attitudes can be measured in some fashion. Underlying their belief is the assumption that people favor or disfavor things to differing degrees and that it is therefore possible to rank individuals by how strongly they feel. In addition to asking if a person favors something we can ask him how much he favors it. When a person does not have either a positive or negative attitude (that is, when he neither likes nor dislikes Senator McHennessey) he is neutral or has no opinion. If we were to locate this person on an attitude scale it would be at a point midway between the positive and negative ends.

At this time we can now generalize the definition of attitude to cover the notion of public opinion, a concept which political scientists have found very difficult to define.

Public Opinion.   Public opinion refers to the attitudes toward some object or set of objects which are held by the members of a society. Obviously not everyone has to have the *same* attitude. Sometimes the public will be in substantial agreement; sometimes it will be sharply divided; and sometimes it will be fragmented. Very often there will be widespread apathy. In fact, determining what the public as a whole wants or feels on any given issue is frequently very difficult to do. For this reason we should perhaps use the term "public opinions."

Also, one should be careful not to think of public opinion as a material phenomenon or a mystical force with an existence of its own which can be studied separately from the individuals comprising the society. Nor can public opinion be determined from the results of an election. Public opinion is simply a shorthand term useful in discussing the collective feelings of many people.

By the same token, political decisions do not flow directly from public opinion or the "will of the people." There is no obvious and direct connection between mass attitudes and governmental decision making. True, politicians usually try to gauge and anticipate public demands. But public opinion is not a physical entity which impels them to behave in one manner or another. In fact, public leaders often find in the public what they want to find. Public opinion is related to particular times, places, and objects: what political consequences it has in any given context is always an open question.[4]

Although the definitions of attitudes and public opinion are quite straightforward, the phenomena they label are complex. Analyzing attitudes is a tricky process. Thus, to help understand attitudes and their role in political life, we will first examine different ways of analyzing attitudes.

Different Ways of Analyzing Attitudes

Direction. Since the evaluation of an object is the main component of an attitude, the most obvious way to describe an opinion is in terms of whether or not the individual favors the object. If he agrees with, likes, or is for something, his attitude is in a positive direction; if he disagrees, dislikes, or is against the object his attitude is in a negative direction. Hence, direction tells how or in what way a person feels about an object. There are a variety of methods for determining the direction of a person's attitudes, the simplest being to ask him more or less directly what his opinion is.

---

[4] For more on this point, see Chapter 9.

Intensity and Salience.   An attitude can also be described by a measure of how strongly an individual holds his position. One person may be moderately in favor of a policy while another is strongly for it. Both attitudes are in the same direction but they differ in intensity.

Closely related to intensity is the concept of salience. Salience refers to how important an attitude object is to an individual. He may favor public aid to parochial schools, for example, and yet not really care much about the issue.

Salience and intensity are key concepts in the study of political behavior. For many people, in America as well as in other countries, politics is seen as far removed from the cares of everyday life. To them, political events seem hard to influence and control. So it is not surprising that many of the major issues of the day arouse little concern among much of the public. Current events are usually salient to those who are in some way directly involved or who can see a connection between the event and their own needs and interests. Not everyone worries much about reciprocal trade legislation. Those who do are mainly importers and exporters and economists or, perhaps, workers who feel their jobs are threatened by foreign competition. The rest of us may have opinions but we probably do not feel too strongly about them.

Attitude intensity and salience have important implications. One is that policy makers normally have plenty of leeway in formulating and carrying out public policy. If intensity is low enough, decisions can sometimes run counter to the expressed will of the majority. Public opinion polls consistently show that a majority of Americans favors some attempt to control firearms; yet Congress just as consistently refuses to enact meaningful gun control legislation. Although the majority favors gun controls it apparently does not feel sufficiently intense to cajole Congress into action. At the same time, those opposed to the regulation of firearms, the so-called Gun Lobbyists, who deeply believe such laws threaten their liberties, put intense pressure on congressmen to prevent the passage of gun control legislation.

On the other hand, if large numbers of people feel intensely about an issue, problems of another kind can arise. Consider the data in Figure 1.1. A sample of residents in Detroit were asked their opinions of a court order requiring the busing of some chil-

Figure 1.1
COMPARISON OF WHITE AND BLACK ATTITUDES
TOWARD SCHOOL BUSING TO ACHIEVE INTEGRATION

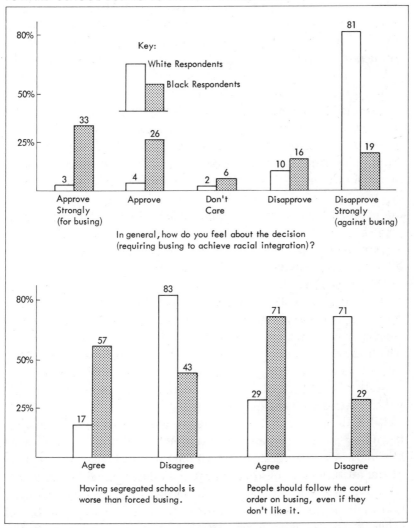

Source: *The 1972 Detroit Survey of Attitudes toward Busing and Other Attitudes.* (See Appendix.)

dren between Detroit and suburban counties to achieve racial integration in the schools. The figures suggest that white and black respondents differ sharply and that many of them feel quite strongly about the matter. In a community such as Detroit where people are divided into two hostile camps on an issue, serious cleavages and conflicts may arise. Unless it is mitigated by other factors, the polarization can disrupt normal political processes and lead to political instability and even violence.

Intensity is important for methodological reasons as well. We can frequently get people to respond to public opinion questionnaires. But even though the respondents answer the questions we should not automatically assume that they have much emotion invested in their responses. This notion helps explain fluctuations in attitudes which are sometimes found in public opinion polls. Many individuals switch back and forth in their preferences simply because they are not very concerned with the topic. Therefore, despite their objective and scientific appearance, opinion surveys often measure only weakly held attitudes.[5]

Dimensionality.   So far we have been discussing attitudes and attitude-objects as if they could be described by a single scale or continuum. However, when dealing with complex phenomena it is usually necessary to be more precise. There are many attitudes which cannot be adequately measured by a single dimension but instead require several *dimensions* or *components*. In these cases, we talk about multidimensional attitudes. Perhaps an example will further clarify this point.

What does it mean when someone asserts that "the country is becoming more conservative?" Presumably he is referring to a set of widely held attitudes which are changing. But what is the nature of the attitudes in question? What is a conservative? Being a conservative may mean opposition to or prejudice against minority groups. It might mean intolerance of dissent, or any number of other things. Conservativism as a label for an attitude toward political life as a whole is multidimensional. Generally, it cannot be characterized by a single component. Rather, we need to think in terms of the different types or dimensions of conservatism.

---

5 See Philip E. Converse, "Attitudes and Non-Attitudes: Continuation of a Dialogue," *The Quantitative Analysis of Social Problems,* ed. Edward R. Tufte (Reading, Mass.: Addison-Wesley Publishing Co., 1970), pp. 176–86.

The data presented in Table 1.1 shows that while a man may be conservative in one sense he may be liberal in another. In particular, three types of attitudes are presented—social welfare legislation (i.e., federal health insurance), civil liberties (i.e., the rights of the accused), and foreign affairs (i.e., the war in Vietnam). Table 1.1*a*, for example, indicates that about a third of the conservatives on foreign affairs are liberal with regard to federal health insurance. Similarly, about 23 percent of the liberals on the Vietnam question are conservative on the issue of health insurance. Overall, the tables reveal only a modest relationship between attitudes. Thus, conservativism, like many other attitude syndromes such as alienation and authoritarianism, involves several dimensions. When discussing conservativism it is essential to state exactly how the term is being used.

Knowing that attitudes are multidimensional can help us solve a lot of sticky problems. What are we to make of a man who maintains that he is against higher taxes but at the same time demands increased spending for schools, hospitals, and public parks? Should we classify him as a conservative or a liberal? One answer for the

Table 1.1
RELATIONSHIPS BETWEEN POLITICAL ATTITUDES

(a)

Attitude toward Federal Health Insurance†	*Attitude toward the War in Vietnam**		
	Liberal	*In Between*	*Conservative*
Liberal	54%	28%	33%
In Between	23	36	24
Conservative	23	36	43
	100%	100%	100%
	(382)	(549)	(331)

(b)

Attitude toward Federal Health Insurance†	*Attitude toward the Rights of the Accused†*		
	Liberal	*In Between*	*Conservative*
Liberal	49%	33%	34%
In Between	24	36	25
Conservative	27	31	41
	100%	100%	100%
	(317)	(421)	(425)

Table 1.1 (continued)

(c)

Attitude toward the Rights of the Accused‡	Attitude toward the War in Vietnam*		
	Liberal	In Between	Conservative
Liberal	39%	23%	19%
In Between	32	43	31
Conservative	29	34	50
	100%	100%	100%
	(361)	(570)	(338)

* "There is much talk about 'hawks' and 'doves' in connection with Vietnam, and considerable disagreement as to what action the United States should take in Vietnam. Some people think we should do everything necessary to win a complete military victory, no matter what results. Some people think we should withdraw completely from Vietnam right now, no matter what results. And, of course, other people have opinions somewhere between these two extreme positions." For convenience, those advocating military victory are classified as "Conservative," and those favoring withdrawal are considered "Liberal."

† "There is much concern about the rapid rise in medical and hospital costs. Some feel there should be a government health insurance plan which would cover all medical and hospital expenses. Others feel that medical expenses should be paid by individuals and through private insurance like Blue Cross." Those favoring a government program are classified "Liberal" while those favoring private plans are considered "Conservative."

‡ "Some people are primarily concerned with doing everything possible to protect the legal rights of those accused of committing crimes. Others feel that it is more important to stop criminal activity even at the risk of reducing the rights of the accused." Those favoring protection of the rights of the accused are classified "Liberal"; those in favor of stopping crime regardless of the rights of the accused are considered "Conservative."

Note: Figures in parentheses refer to the number of cases.

Source: *The CPS 1970 American National Election Study.* (See Appendix.)

apparent contradiction is that his attitudes stem from at least two dimensions, fiscal policy and social welfare legislation. He is conservative on the former and liberal on the latter.

Stability. Stability refers to how long a person holds an attitude of a given intensity and direction. Psychologists typically regard attitudes as learned predispositions which exist for relatively long periods of time. However, some research (especially voting studies) shows that many political attitudes are quite unstable.

Some interesting data come from a study in which the same respondents were periodically reinterviewed over a period of four years. Philip Converse's analysis of these data indicates that people frequently change their minds on such important matters as civil rights, social welfare legislation, the relationship of government to free enterprise and foreign policy. Although the content of these issues remains fairly constant over time, Converse found a high degree of turnover in opinion every two years. Many of the respondents in the study seem to fluctuate considerably in the direction of their preferences.[6]

There are several reasons for instability. Many issues are not salient or important to the public. So people naturally change their minds occasionally. In addition, short-term forces, a political campaign, for example, sometimes create a temporary interest in a topic. Once the force is gone, the matter recedes in importance and people stop paying attention to it. Instability may also be the product of survey research techniques. As Converse discovered, if people are repeatedly asked their views on issues of little concern to them we should not be surprised by the seeming instability of their preferences.[7]

Information Content (Cognitive Component). As a general rule, attitudes are related to information about the attitude-object. If a person favors a particular candidate, he usually has more information about that candidate than he does about the opponent. Furthermore, he will normally have more *favorable* than unfavorable information about his choice.[8] People tend to be selective in what they know about politics. In other words, opinions are based on at least some minimal level of information which may or may not be entirely accurate and representative of the object.

Beliefs. Closely related to the information content of attitudes are beliefs. Beliefs about an attitude-object refer to two kinds of thoughts. First, individuals associate many qualities and characteristics with the object. Suppose that we are dealing with attitudes toward Senator McHennessey. An individual may impute several attributes to the senator: "he is old," "he is experienced," "he is resourceful," "he is crooked," "he is handsome." These are beliefs

---

[6] Ibid., pp. 168–76.

[7] Ibid., pp. 176–80.

[8] Don D. Smith, "Cognitive Consistency and the Perception of Others' Opinions," *Public Opinion Quarterly*, Vol. 32 (Spring 1968), pp. 1–5.

about the senator. One psychologist maintains that attitudes toward an object are really a function of one's beliefs. Change the beliefs and the attitude itself will change.[9] A second type of belief concerns the estimation of an attitude-object's relationship with other positively or negatively valued objects. A person may like Senator McHennessey not only because the senator has fine qualities but also because the senator works for legislation favored by the individual.[10]

This means that the same attitude position can result from different sets of beliefs. Many southern whites and northern blue-collar workers no doubt have similar negative attitudes toward blacks. Yet in the case of the Southerners, the attitudes may be a product of stereotyped beliefs (e.g., blacks are lazy, shiftless) while the workers may believe their jobs are being threatened by blacks insisting on job equality. In discussing the causes and cures of prejudice one has to recognize this type of phenomena, because a policy designed to mitigate the effect of prejudice may work on one group but not on the other.

Much political science research has tended to oversimplify attitudes, especially in connection with complicated objects such as parties, candidates, and issues. But it is difficult to analyze these attitudes and the relationships among them unless we realize that they are based on numerous beliefs.

Functions.   Still another way of describing attitudes is in terms of the functions they serve for the individual. The concept of function is extremely important in social science. Something is functional if it aids in maintaining the stability, equilibrium, or integrity of the system of which it is a part. Loosely speaking, an attitude can be said to be functional for an individual if it helps him to understand and get along in the world; it is dysfunctional if it hinders or prevents his adjustment to his environment.

---

[9] Martin Fishbein, "An Investigation of the Relationships between Beliefs about an Object and the Attitude toward That Object," *Human Relations,* Vol. 16 (1963), pp. 233–39 and "The Relationships between Beliefs, Attitudes, and Behavior," *Cognitive Consistency,* ed. Shel Feldman (New York: Academic Press, 1966), pp. 199–223.

[10] Milton J. Rosenberg, "An Analysis of Affective-Cognitive Consistency," *Attitude Organization and Change,* ed. Milton J. Rosenberg, et al. (New Haven, Conn.: Yale University Press, 1960), pp. 15–64.

The idea of function turns out to be a very significant and useful tool in studying public opinion. It has been argued that attitudes serve a variety of functions.[11] One example is social adjustment. Some people hold particular attitudes in order to be compatible with their friends and neighbors; they may take a certain position on the war in Vietnam, for instance, merely in order to minimize disagreements and disputes with people they like and respect. This suggests that even though they may rationalize their opinions by giving reasons for their views, their attitudes are not based on a reasoned analysis of the merits of the issue. Rather, they stem from a need to be socially accepted. And what is more, efforts to change them by rational persuasion are probably fruitless until the function the attitudes perform is itself changed.

Centrality and Constraint.   Until now we have been speaking of attitudes as isolated phenomena. Now it is necessary to stress their interrelatedness. Taken together, all of the attitudes an individual has can be referred to as a belief system.[12] The centrality of an attitude refers to how closely it is tied into the person's larger system. Another way of looking at centrality is as follows: suppose that we are able to change a particular attitude. What effect will this change have on other attitudes? If an attitude is in some sense basic or central to the individual's belief system, then altering it will presumably cause changes in other attitudes. If, on the other hand, the attitude is on the periphery of the individual's attitude system, then changing it will produce few additional alterations. Converse uses the term "constraint" to describe these relationships among attitudes.[13]

An *ideology* can be thought of as an especially closely related or constrained set of attitudes and beliefs. Although we are accustomed to talking of liberalism and conservativism as popular ideologies,

---

[11] Daniel Katz, "The Functional Approach to the Study of Attitudes," *Public Opinion Quarterly*, Vol. 24 (1960), pp. 163–204; and M. Brewster Smith, Jerome S. Bruner, and Robert W. White, *Opinions and Personality* (New York: John Wiley & Sons, Inc., 1956).

[12] Milton Rokeach, *The Open and Closed Mind* (New York: Basic Books, Inc., 1960), chap. ii.

[13] Philip E. Converse, "The Nature of Belief Systems in Mass Publics," *Ideology and Discontent*, ed. David E. Apter (New York: The Free Press, 1964), pp. 207–9.

many students of politics feel that well-defined and structured ideologies are relatively rare among mass publics. Using data gathered in the early 1950s, Converse reports that less than 4 percent of this sample of voters can be classified as "ideologues"—that is, people who see politics in terms of a well-defined conservative-liberal ideology.[14] For most people, the constraint among attitude elements is relatively low. They view political issues as discrete, isolated matters and do not apply a general standard of performance in evaluating parties and candidates. More important, they have difficulty relating what happens in one situation to what happens in another, as when a man fails to see that increases in the defense budget may come at the expense of other programs he favors. Unlike a staunch liberal who believes "exorbitant" military expenditures waste the taxpayer's money and undermine vitally needed domestic programs, the nonideologue does not discern a pattern but evaluates policies one by one without seeing their interrelatedness.

There is some evidence that Americans have become more ideological in recent years. Since the evidence for this trend is still tentative (most of it has not even been published), one cannot say how much change has occurred. But the population does appear more politicized now than it did in the 1950s.

The absence of widespread ideologies among the electorate is critical in understanding American politics. Without an ideology voters have difficulty voting rationally because they do not have an abstract and general dimension against which to measure the performance of their representatives. They are not able to say Senator McHennessey is a good liberal or conservative, for the terms liberal and conservative have no meaning to them. This does not mean voters do not take policy issues into account when voting; it only suggests that it is harder for them to do so.

Another implication of these remarks about constraint is that people frequently have inconsistent attitudes, such as a loyal Democrat supporting a Republican for office. Two attitudes are *consistent* if they logically imply each other—other things being equal. (Being a loyal Democrat does not normally imply supporting a Republican.) To the extent that constraint is low it is easy to find incon-

---

14 Ibid., pp. 214–19.

sistent attitudes, and a change in one of them will not necessarily produce a change in the others. When people are made aware of the inconsistencies, however, they are often motivated to resolve the imbalances in one manner or another.

Difficulties in Measuring Political Attitudes

It is worth pausing here to mention some difficulties in measuring attitudes. Normally the direction and intensity of attitudes are measured by paper-and-pencil tests or questionnaires. An individual answers a series of questions or statements and his responses, one hopes, indicate his attitudes toward the various objects.

Of course, the trick is to ascertain the individual's true feelings. Since we do not have direct access to the attitude, we have to rely on the individual's responses to various stimuli (e.g., asking for his reaction to a candidate). But unknown to the investigator, the stimuli may be directed at the wrong attitude-object or the response may be distorted or mismeasured in some way so that we finally end up with a misrepresentation of the opinion. In measuring the attitudes of large numbers of people the possibilities for such errors proliferate.

By the same token, because someone responds to a stimulus we cannot automatically assume that he has an opinion. Some people give substantive answers—even if they do not have an opinion—simply because they feel they should answer in order to appear intelligent or because they think the investigator wants a response. In this case, we may be simply recording what Converse calls non-attitudes.[15]

Also, the answers we receive depend in large part on the stimuli or, more simply, on our phrasing of the questions. This has been vividly demonstrated by Converse and Schuman who show that a person's apparent position on the war in Vietnam is affected by the wording of the question he is asked.[16] A Gallup poll conducted in the summer of 1966 showed 70 percent of the respondents favoring bombing oil storage depots in North Vietnam, a position considered

---

[15] Converse, "Attitudes and Non-Attitudes," pp. 176–80.

[16] Philip E. Converse and Howard Schuman, " 'Silent Majorities' and the Vietnam War," *Scientific American*, Vol. 222 (June 1970), pp. 17–25.

at the time to be hawkish. Yet less than eight weeks later, Converse and Schuman report, another Gallup poll indicated that a majority of the sample approved of submitting the Vietnam problem to the U.N. and accepting "the decision, whatever it may be." Superficially, there appears to be inconsistency and instability in preferences. But as the authors note, the differences are more apparent than real because the responses were made to totally different questions.

Furthermore, attitudes are complex phenomena, as we have seen. Most of the public opinion polls that one comes across in the media do not deal with intensity or dimensionality. They are concerned mainly with a simple presentation of the direction of attitudes. A Gallup poll, for instance, may ask someone if he favors impeaching President Nixon. Yet the poll rarely measures the individual's intensity of feeling or his readiness to do something about his beliefs. So although a poll may show a majority in favor of impeachment, it usually does not indicate how much people care about the matter. The cry for impeachment, in other words, may not be heard in Congress. Nor do most polls tell how much public opinion has been swayed by short-term influences such as the Watergate revelations. It is quite difficult to measure and analyze the various components of opinions we have been discussing.

These points are raised in order to emphasize the fact that one must be cautious in interpreting the results of public opinion polls and surveys and in making quick generalizations about what the public does or does not want. And obviously it is not a simple job to explain the origins of a person's attitudes, changes in them and their relation to his overt behavior, all of which are keys to understanding politics.

POLITICAL BEHAVIOR

What Is Political Behavior?

In the past, political scientists have defined mass political behavior mostly in terms of electoral behavior such as voting, talking about politics, and campaigning. Certainly in a democracy these are important activities. But recent events in the United States and elsewhere have shown dramatically that people express their political views in a variety of ways. They march, demonstrate, and even commit acts of violence. An increasingly large and diverse number of groups appear willing—and perhaps eager—to resort to direct action to attain their goals. It appears that extremism on both the right and left is becoming a potent political force. At the same time, we have heard of widespread alienation and withdrawal from politics on the part of students, intellectuals, workers, and even the "man in the street." In a word, the manner in which men express their hopes and fears, their frustration and anger, their needs and desires often goes beyond the ballot box.

Until recently, political scientists have not studied the more extreme forms of political behavior. This no doubt stems from an emphasis on democracy and democratic procedures but it is also a reflection of a fairly tranquil postwar America. They have tended to accept as reality those portions of the democratic creed asserting that political expression should occur through regular and peaceful channels. In view of the diverse forms of political expression, however, we must go beyond the study of electoral behavior to examine other activities such as extremism and violence. Of course, most of our attention is on voting, since this is still a significant form of political activity, at least in the Western world. Yet for a complete picture of mass political behavior, it is also necessary to discuss extremism, authoritarianism, apathy, and violence.

How then can we meaningfully define political behavior? One definition is:

> *Political behavior is physical, overt activity in which individuals express politically relevant drives, motives and attitudes.*

For the moment let us avoid stating the exact meaning of "politically relevant." The definition calls attention to the fact that behavior is rooted in several psychological processes, not in just attitudes alone. It is true that political analysts usually turn to attitudes when attempting to explain behavior such as voting. But other psychological factors affect a person's actions.

Moreover, the definition is encompassing enough to include behaviors which are not traditionally or legally prescribed and is exclusive in that it leaves out activities that are not related in some sense to the political psychology of the individual. Needless to say, we will confine ourselves to those behaviors which are sufficiently widespread to be of more or less direct political significance. In other words, sexual behavior ultimately has consequences for every government, but its effects are so indirect that we can discount it for our purposes. Finally, although the definition stresses activity, it does not preclude us from inquiring into the causes of non-participation.

As with attitudes, it is helpful to consider ways of describing behavior. To simplify matters we will use a threefold typology, realizing that it is a simplification and that there are probably other dimensions which could be added.

Dimensions of Political Behavior

Active-Passive. The usual way of representing behavior is by the amount of energy invested in it by the actor. Although political discussions sometimes become heated, talking politics is generally considered less demanding than voting. After all, in order to vote an individual has to get registered, find the polling place, wait in line, make up his mind, and finally wade through sometimes long and complicated ballots. Voting, in turn, is less arduous than holding a public office and certainly less so than taking part in a guerrilla war. So it seems reasonable to locate different behaviors on a passive-active dimension as in Figure 1.2. In this sense, Lester Milbrath uses labels like "spectator" and "gladiatorial" to emphasize the variation in psychological and physical involvement entailed in different kinds of political activities.[17]

Milbrath, as well as others,[18] also stresses the *cumulative* nature of political behavior. To illustrate, consider someone who has participated in a street demonstration. It is likely that this person, who has risked personal injury or arrest, will also have attended rallies, worn buttons, and taken part in discussions—all of which are less hazardous and strenuous than a protest march. In short, doing something at one point along the passive-active scale implies having done less demanding things. On the other hand, a person who only

---

[17] Lester W. Milbrath, *Political Participation* (Chicago: Rand McNally & Co., 1965), p. 18.

[18] For example, see Donald R. Matthews and James W. Prothro, *Negroes and the New Southern Politics* (New York: Harcourt, Brace & World, Inc., 1966), chap. iii.

occasionally talks about politics with his wife is probably not going to get mixed up in a violent confrontation with the police. Obviously, there are exceptions: It is interesting that many people who engage in extremist politics have never voted. On the whole, however, most political behavior is cumulative.

Figure 1.2
TWO DIMENSIONS OF POLITICAL BEHAVIOR

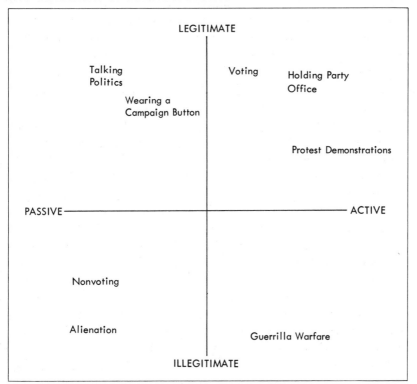

Legitimate-Illegitimate.   Besides being active or passive, behavior can also be legitimate or illegitimate. (See Figure 1.2.) Note at once that this is not totally a matter of legality. According to the democratic creed as expounded in civics textbooks, citizens are encouraged and expected to have an interest in current events, to be informed about issues and candidates, to follow campaigns, and to vote. Complete withdrawal from and rejection of all political life is disapproved. Conversely, even a democracy proscribes certain forms of behavior. Some people believe that individual citizens do not have the right to decide which are just and unjust wars and must always obey government. Being a conscientious objector in wartime is not necessarily illegal, but it does carry a social stigma. Furthermore, conscientious objectors are not entitled to veterans' benefits even though they must perform noncombatant duties. In addition, there are manifestly illegal acts such as assassinations or riots. So it seems sensible to classify behavior according to the prevailing normative and legal standards. The classifications in Figure 1.2 which apply to the United States are only suggestive since they depend on how one views the prevailing social order.

Of course, it is true that laws and norms change and what is acceptable in one era may not be so in another. Not too long ago peaceful protest marches—today accepted as commonplace occurrences—were considered by many to be disruptive, immoral, Communist-inspired and downright illegal. (For some they still are.)

Purposive-Nonpurposive.   In many behaviors having significant political consequences, an actor may be expressing (consciously or not) psychological motivations without having any particular purpose in mind. For other actors the same activities may be related to a specific goal and thus are purposive or instrumental.[19] The point here is the *motivation* of the actor. If he is simply projecting or expressing his opinions or drives without attempting to achieve a particular political objective the activity is, in our usage, nonpurposive; if he does have such an objective it is purposive. We cannot say ahead of time whether or not a behavior is purposive since it depends on the individual's intentions. This is why this dimension does not appear in Figure 1.2.

Take voting as an example. Although there is little evidence, some people no doubt voted for George Wallace because they thought he would bring about desirable changes or as a protest against the liberalism of the two major parties. But others may have voted for him because he provided a satisfactory outlet for the expression of various psychological motives. Others voted for him in order to change the status quo. Therefore, a vote for Wallace, as for any candidate, may result from any of several motives.

Rioting, too, provides a handy illustration. One hotly debated

---

[19] Milbrath, *Political Participation,* pp. 12–13.

question concerns whether riots in the ghetto do anything to promote the interests of blacks. The question itself presupposes a theory about riot behavior, namely that it is purposive. But surely many if not most of the participants become spontaneously involved and have no well-defined objectives. They may be simply responding to their frustration and anger at their political and social system. Or, they may have immediate goals such as grabbing a color television set if the opportunity arises, but do not have any long-range political objectives. Of course, in spite of the motives of the participants, riots nevertheless have enormous political consequences.[20]

The Relationship between Attitudes and Behavior

It seems logical and almost self-evident to expect people to act on the basis of their opinions. If a man is deeply prejudiced against blacks we would expect him to refuse to live next door to them. Nevertheless, in spite of the apparently obvious connection, social scientists have been hard pressed to show empirical relationships between attitudes and behavior. The problem has been especially acute in voting research where it has not been easy to predict how a person will vote even if his attitudes toward issues, candidates, and parties are known.

The classic example of this problem, however, is found in Richard LaPiere's famous and widely cited study of attitudes toward minorities.[21] In the early 1930s, LaPiere spent some time traveling around with a young and obviously educated Chinese couple. When he first approached a hotel clerk for accommodations for the three of them he was surprised by the unhesitating and friendly reception he received. (Remember, this is the 1930s, an era not known for its liberalism on racial matters.) Several months later he telephoned the hotel to ask if they would accept "an important Chinese gentleman." The answer to his inquiry was a flat "no."[22]

This puzzling reaction led LaPiere to conduct a study in which the three visited numerous hotels and restaurants where they were almost always accepted. He later wrote these establishments asking

---

[20] See Chapter 8 for a further discussion of this point.

[21] Richard T. LaPiere, "Attitudes vs. Actions," *Social Forces*, Vol. 13 (1934), pp. 230–37.

[22] Ibid., p. 232.

them if they would accept Oriental customers. Of those places reply-ing, over 90 percent said they would refuse. Obviously, there is a discrepancy between the proprietors' verbal and overt behavior. This study has been used to support the assertion that opinions and behavior frequently do not coincide.

It has been even more difficult to demonstrate that changing an attitude will cause a change in behavior. In a laboratory situation, for example, one can sometimes get people to switch their verbal opinions by presenting them with a series of persuasive communica-tions. Yet in surprisingly few cases is subsequent behavior actually modified.

None of this is to say that behavior and opinions are not con-nected, for in fact they usually are. Rather, we are asserting that the connections are extremely complex and we cannot blithely assume a simple causal relationship between the two. It is always an empirical matter to determine if and how a specific behavior can be predicted from a specific opinion. Many of these topics are considered further in the following chapter, which discusses atti-tudes in more detail.

2

The Psychology of Political
Attitudes and Behavior

To some observers America has become a "sick society." The
sickness, the critics say, involves a conflict between two realities.
On the one hand, Americans are a compassionate people. Our
democratic creed stresses brotherly love, humanitarianism, and
charity. On the other hand, many events as well as social and political institutions belie these values. As a result, the "national consciousness" is characterized by a kind of collective schizophrenia:
we constantly seem to violate our best traditions. This point is well-
illustrated by public reactions to the My Lai massacre of 1968.

On the morning of March 16, 1968 a company of U.S. soldiers
entered the South Vietnamese village of My Lai. Although it had
in the past been used as a staging area for Communist forces, the
hamlet on this day was deserted except for women, children, and a
few old men. Accounts of what happened vary on the details, but
it is clear beyond any doubt that at least 100 unarmed and helpless
civilians were massacred, without provocation, by the American
troops. The atrocity was abhorrent to any reasonable standard of
military conduct. And yet, even in the face of the exposure of the

event and its perpetrators, public reaction was curiously mixed. To be sure, many Americans were appalled. But many others had no trouble reconciling the massacre with their beliefs in the goodness of the American cause in Vietnam. A letter to *Newsweek* said:

> Any "innocent civilian" who thinks he can feed, clothe, shelter and otherwise succor the Communists in their organized subversion and at the same time expect treatment different from that which he received at [My Lai], ought to have his rice bowl examined.[1]

One of the leaders of the massacre, Lieutenant William Calley, was tried and convicted of murder. The evidence against Calley was overwhelming. Still, a poll done for ABC revealed that 77 percent of the sample thought the government was making Calley a scapegoat while only 24 percent thought he should have been found guilty.[2] The American Legion campaigned to raise $200,000 for his defense. Congress and the Pentagon were flooded with protests of Calley's conviction. Remarking on the reaction to the Calley decision, Stephen Lesher wrote that "this response clearly represented every stratum of American society, from redneck to radical chic."[3] Finally, President Nixon, no doubt reacting to rising public sentiment, commuted Calley's life sentence to 20 years.

Without going into the merits of the case, we may question these reactions which raise some interesting questions about public attitudes. My Lai stands in sharp contrast to America's traditional values and institutions. For this reason many citizens, it seems, have difficulty reconciling the massacre with their beliefs. In the public's responses there appears to be a need either to rationalize the action or to deny its importance, both of which help to preserve one's faith in his country. The public's response to My Lai is an example of attitude dynamics—that is, why and how people maintain attitudinal consistency, what conditions produce changes in their attitudes, and how attitudes are related to behavior.

These are important issues. Many 20th-century problems involve attitudes. Public opinion surrounding the My Lai incident is just

---

[1] *Newsweek,* December 22, 1969, p. 4.

[2] *New York Times,* April 17, 1971.

[3] Ibid., April 11, 1971.

one example. Race relations, acceptance of social and economic change, tolerance of dissent, and political participation are just a few of the areas where a knowledge of attitude dynamics can lead to a better understanding of political behavior.

The purpose of this chapter, which is a continuation of the material in Chapter 1, is to describe and explain attitude dynamics. The chapter is divided into three parts. First, we will examine a *functional* approach to attitudes. Although the functional approach contains some ambiguous concepts, it explains why people hold the attitudes they do and why it is often hard to change attitudes. The functionalists help us avoid thinking of attitudes in a simplistic way. Next, we will describe *balance theory* which is mainly concerned with showing how people resolve attitudinal inconsistencies. Since, as we will see, it is not always easy to predict a person's behavior solely on the basis of his attitudes, the concluding section deals with the relationship between attitudes and overt behavior.

THE FUNCTIONS OF ATTITUDES[4]

M. Brewster Smith, Jerome Bruner, and Robert White write:

A pattern of opinions may be for one man a basis of personal serenity in the face of a changing world, for another a goad to revolutionary activity. Opinions, in short, are part of man's attempt to meet and to master his world. They are an integral part of personality.[5]

Attitudes, these authors believe, serve various purposes or *functions*. (Something is "functional" if it helps a person adapt to his environment.) In order to understand attitudes, we can ask how they help people meet and master their needs. What does a particular attitude do for someone? What needs does it satisfy? How does it help him adjust to his environment? Why, in short, does he hold the attitudes he does?

Functionalists have identified several functions of attitudes, four of which are especially important.

---

4 This section relies heavily on Daniel Katz, "The Functional Approach to the Study of Attitudes," *Public Opinion Quarterly*, Vol. 24 (1960), pp. 163–204; and M. Brewster Smith, Jerome S. Bruner, and Robert W. White, *Opinions and Personality* (New York: John Wiley & Sons, Inc., 1956).

5 Smith, Bruner, and White, *Opinions and Personality*, p. 1.

Adjustment (Instrumental) Function

In the first place, attitudes assist in the achievement of goals. Attitudes can be quite useful in attaining goals either because they provide a *means* for doing so or because they have become associated with the attainment of the goal.[6] Some examples will illustrate this point.

Consider a blue-collar worker who began working in the thirties during the depression, a period of high unemployment, low wages, and economic insecurity. His major goal or motive in those days was a steady, well-paying job. Many workers saw the Democratic party as an instrument for the attainment of this goal. Loyalty to the party became associated with the satisfaction of a particular need, economic security. For many workers attitudes toward the Democratic party (though not necessarily to particular candidates) have persisted to this day. No doubt these attitudes are held partly because the party is associated with prosperity and full employment.

Attitudes can also be a means to an end, as in interpersonal relations where holding an attitude may provide social acceptance. "Opinions," Smith, Bruner, and White say, "can play another role: that of facilitating, disrupting, or simply maintaining an individual's relations with other individuals."[7] Whether or not they are aware of it, people in closely knit groups generally share the same opinions. For each individual, having a particular set of attitudes promotes his integration into the group. To the extent that his views differ from those of his friends, he is less welcomed. For example, some people are prejudiced not only because they believe in racial differences, but because their prejudices make them more acceptable to their friends and neighbors. Hence, attitudes facilitate social acceptance. Besides being a goal in itself, social acceptance also leads to the achievement of still other goals. So by having a certain attitude, a person may be successful in several endeavours.

The point is that opinions often help a person attain material or social objectives. Furthermore, he is not apt to change his attitudes unless his goals change.

---

[6] Katz, "The Functional Approach to the Study of Attitudes," pp. 170–71.

[7] Smith, Bruner, and White, *Opinions and Personality*, p. 41.

Ego-Defense Function

People spend a great deal of "energy on living with themselves."[8] They attempt to protect their sense of worth and self-esteem while at the same time trying to control a variety of conflicting emotions, some of which are consciously unacceptable. That part of the personality involved in this process is called by some psychologists the ego. Psychological devices which protect the ego are called ego-defenses.

The functionalists believe that many attitudes have ego-defense functions. One defense mechanism, for example, is *projection,* or the attribution of one's own consciously unacceptable motives to others. To see how attitudes relate to projection, suppose that a person has been socialized to abhor sexual promiscuity, so much so that he can barely tolerate his own "normal" sexual desires. His sexual motives, then, can arouse anxiety: he has sexual urges but has been taught to fear and hate them. Although he may be able to repress his motives from consciousness they still create tension. One way to reduce the tension and anxiety is to project these motives onto someone else. Hence, this individual might, for example, think of a minority group as being sexually permissive. Prejudice against blacks would be a logical consequence of this belief. Negative attitudes or prejudice, in short, aid the individual in living with his consciously unacceptable impulses.[9]

This example is not meant to be a theory of prejudice, and indeed, many of these ideas are hotly debated among social scientists. The point is only that a person's attitude may not be based on reasoned analysis. In arriving at an opinion he may have ignored many "objective" facts. He holds the attitude not because he has studied the situation carefully, but rather because the attitude fulfills a psychological need, one which he may not be aware of. Perhaps many of the reactions to My Lai were based on ego-defense functions. Of course there is no evidence but it seems apparent that the public did not react strictly on the merits of the case.

---

[8] Katz, "The Functional Approach to the Study of Attitudes," p. 172.

[9] See Irving Sarnoff, "Psychoanalytic Theory and Social Attitudes," *Public Opinion Quarterly,* Vol. 24 (1960), pp. 271–74, for a detailed discussion of this point.

Value Expressive Function

Attitudes frequently "have the function of giving positive expression to [the individual's] central values and to the type of person he conceives himself to be."[10] Some self-styled liberals favor the legalization of marijuana not because they believe—after weighing the pros and cons—that legalization is in the interests of health or freedom, but because they regard legalization (or think others do) as the "liberal" position. The attitude in this case is a way of reaffirming one's belief in the kind of person he wants to be; it is a means of establishing and maintaining self-identity. Attitudes which serve this purpose also allow one to alter his self-image to meet changes in his environment.

Knowledge (Object-Appraisal) Function

For many individuals events like the My Lai massacre are mysterious; it is difficult to relate these happenings to their beliefs and experiences with other aspects of American life. But sometimes attitudes help the individual clarify and understand the world. They play a role in satisfying people's need to know, a need that is often difficult to satisfy in other ways.

"We have to stand fast in Vietnam or else we'll be fighting on our own shores next time. I support our policy in Vietnam." The underlying attitude here about the war in Vietnam reflects a need for simplicity. As before, it is not necessarily based on a set of well-founded beliefs about Communist aggression. World politics is complicated. President Nixon traveled to Moscow and Peking at the same time American prisoners of war were sitting in jails in North Vietnam. We spend billions of dollars each year to defend ourselves from aggression and at the same time trade with the very nations we fear. All the while, the Director of the FBI asserts that internal Communist subversion is the nation's most important problem. To a specialist in foreign policy these facts may not be contradictory. But their meaning to the man on the street is not at all clear. By taking certain attitudes (such as a hawkish view of the war in Vietnam) a man can bolster his simplified interpretation of

---

[10] Katz, "The Functional Approach to the Study of Attitudes," p. 173.

the Communist menace: "We are fighting to prevent aggression. Period." This simplistic posture leads to an especially simple understanding of international relations.

The four functions, adjustment, ego-defense, value expressive, and knowledge, do not include all of the possibilities. Nor has this discussion even touched the complexities and nuances of the topic. But for us the specific functions or the ways they work are not as important as the fact that *attitudes serve different needs.*

The ideas of the functionalists can be summarized in a basic proposition:

> *Attitudes emerge in response to psychological needs. In order for an attitude to change, there must first be a corresponding change in the need which the attitude is fulfilling.*

As noted above, prejudice in some people may serve an ego-defense function. If so, then according to the functionalists, it is both pointless and fruitless to attempt to reduce the prejudice by logical, rational persuasion. Prejudice will be reduced when the individual feels more secure, not when he obtains more information. Instead of presenting him with facts and figures about racial equality it might be better to make him aware of his motives and the needs his attitudes are meeting. Self-insight of this sort would presumably change the underlying needs and hence permit a change in attitudes as well.

Some laboratory studies support the functionalist interpretation of attitudes. Daniel Katz, Charles McClintock, and Irving Sarnoff describe interesting experiments in which they tried to change people's prejudices against blacks.[11] First, they determined if the subject's attitudes were related to ego-defense needs. Those subjects whose attitudes serve an ego-defense function were called high ego-defenders. The investigators then used two types of persuasion: (*a*) logical restructuring which "consisted of a rational appeal utilizing facts and reasoned arguments" and (*b*) self-insight procedures which attempted to show the subject the real psychological basis of his

---

[11] Daniel Katz, Irving Sarnoff, and Charles McClintock, "Ego Defense and Attitude Change," *Human Relations,* Vol. 9 (1956), pp. 27–45; and Daniel Katz, Charles McClintock, and Irving Sarnoff, "The Measurement of Ego Defense as Related to Attitude Change," *Journal of Personality,* Vol. 25 (1957), pp. 465–74.

attitudes.[12] (The self-insight appeal, in other words, was designed to make the subject aware of his motives; it did not argue with him on logical grounds.) Katz and his associates hypothesized that for high ego-defenders self-insight would reduce prejudice more than rational persuasion would. The data generally supported their hypothesis.

This approach to attitudes has its critics. Martin Fishbein argues that attitudes are based primarily on beliefs about the object. If a person is prejudiced against minorities it is probably because he has stereotyped beliefs. Change those beliefs and his opinions will change.[13] Of course, a person may acquire stereotyped beliefs precisely because they buttress his functional attitudes.

Another difficulty with the functional approach lies in showing an attitude's relation to a particular need. Empirically it is difficult to identify and measure specific needs and to demonstrate that attitudes satisfy these needs. So while the functional approach is theoretically compelling it is difficult to test in the field. Nevertheless, the functionalists make the extremely worthwhile argument that people hold attitudes for various reasons. Once we understand these reasons we begin to understand why they have the opinions they do and what it takes to change them.

BALANCE THEORY OF ATTITUDES

Basic Ideas

Balance theory (sometimes called consistency theory) is a general name for a family of theories, all of which deal with the interrelationships among attitudes.[14] Since there is so much overlap among them we can treat them together under the label of balance theory.

---

[12] Katz, McClintock, and Sarnoff, "The Measurement of Ego-Defense," p. 466.

[13] Martin Fishbein and Bertram H. Raven, "The AB Scales: An Operational Definition of Belief and Attitude," *Human Relations*, Vol. 15 (1962), pp. 35–44; and Martin Fishbein, "An Investigation of the Relationships between Beliefs about an Object and the Attitude toward That Object," *Human Relations*, Vol. 16 (1963), pp. 233–39.

[14] Fritz Heider, "Attitudes and Cognitive Organization," *Journal of Psychology*, Vol. 21 (1946), pp. 107–12; Theodore M. Newcomb, "An Approach to the Study of Communicative Acts," *Psychological Review*, Vol. 60 (1953), pp. 393–404; Charles E. Osgood and Percy H. Tannenbaum, "The Principle of

Balance theory assumes that individuals strive for consistency in their thoughts and actions. Common to all of these theories is the notion that people, consciously or not, strive to maintain order among their attitudes. Hence, they like to be associated with people who share their beliefs and values and dissociate themselves from people with dissimilar preferences. Similarly, people try to keep their own beliefs and opinions internally consistent.

For example, if I like you, then I expect you to like the things I like and dislike things I dislike. Of course, I can tolerate some inconsistency but, on the whole, if your likes and dislikes do not correspond to mine then my attitude toward you is likely to change. To be more concrete, suppose that I abhor the Nixon administration. Suppose in addition I find out that you, my trusted and respected friend, are an enthusiastic supporter of Nixon's policies. Something, then, is out of balance: I like you but you do not share my dislike of Nixon. If I care about both you and the administration in Washington, then I will—according to balance theory—need to alter one or both of my attitudes. Balance theory provides rules and even formulas for predicting which attitudes will change under what circumstances and by how much.

The tension produced by inconsistent or imbalanced attitudes and cognitions is, for some balance theorists, a fundamental human drive much like hunger and sex. Others do not go this far but nonetheless feel that the effort to avoid attitude imbalance explains a great deal about human behavior. Most of the theories are silent as to whether or not the individual is aware of the inconsistency, but they all agree that he will (consciously or unconsciously) try to restore balance.

We are, of course, dealing with an abstract concept. Psychologists claim to create and measure inconsistency under experimental conditions, but we really never "see" the inconsistency. Its existence is only inferred. One problem with balance theory is the indefiniteness

Congruity in the Prediction of Attitude Change," *Psychological Review,* Vol. 62 (1955), pp. 42–55; Leon Festinger, *A Theory of Cognitive Dissonance* (Stanford, Calif.: Stanford University Press, 1957); Milton J. Rosenberg, Carl I. Hovland, William J. McGuire, Robert P. Abelson, and Jack W. Brehm, *Attitude Organization and Change* (New Haven, Conn.: Yale University Press, 1960); and Milton Rokeach and Gilbert Rothman, "The Principle of Belief Congruence and the Congruity Principle as Models of Cognitive Interaction," *Psychological Review,* Vol. 72 (1965), pp. 128–42.

of the concept. We might, for example, invoke inconsistency to explain a particular phenomenon such as a change in a person's behavior. And yet since we do not directly observe the inconsistency it is possible that some *other* variable really accounts for the phenomenon. As we will see, this reasoning is basic to many criticisms of balance theory. Nevertheless, the idea of balance or consistency among cognitions leads to many useful predictions. Furthermore, many psychological concepts are abstract, but we still find them helpful for understanding behavior.

In a complex world inconsistencies are bound to arise. Sometimes our most cherished beliefs are challenged, as in the My Lai incident. Imbalance occurs when two "cognitive elements" are linked or joined together in some manner as, for instance, the linking of American soldiers with My Lai. A *link* or bond is a statement asserting a connection between two objects.[15] Balance theorists identify two types of links, associative and dissociative. Two objects are *associatively* linked if there is a positive relationship between them. Examples are: A likes B, A favors B, A did B, A endorsed B, and A is associated with B. Similarly, *dissociative* bonds suggest negative relationships: A hates B, A did not do B, A attacked B, A is dissociated from B.

Inconsistency occurs when, for example, a favorably evaluated object is associatively (positively) linked to an unfavorably evaluated object. Suppose that a man favors America's role in Vietnam (the first object). When he discovers by reading the evening paper that some soldiers participated in (the associative link) a massacre (the second object), imbalance occurs.

Figure 2.1 shows the results of various combinations of attitude objects and linkages. Note, for instance, that if two favorably evaluated objects are joined by an associative bond then balance exists (cell IV of Table 2.1a). If, instead, a dissociative link joins these two objects, the result is imbalance (cell IV of Table 2.1b). Suppose, for instance, that someone likes *both* Senator Kennedy and President Nixon. Suppose, in addition, that Kennedy assails Nixon's handling of the economy. Then the two positively evaluated objects have been joined by a dissociative bond. According to balance

---

[15] The discussion of linkages is based partly on Roger Brown, *Social Psychology* (New York: The Free Press, 1965), pp. 550–51.

theory, the individual will sense an inconsistency and will be motivated to change one or both of his opinions. These predictions agree with common sense, although some variations of balance theory provide surprising predictions about *how* the imbalance will be resolved.[16]

Figure 2.1
BALANCE AND IMBALANCE BETWEEN TWO ATTITUDES

(a)

Objects Are Linked by Associative Bonds		
Attitude toward	*Attitude toward First Object*	
Second Object	*Unfavorable*	*Favorable*
	I	II
Unfavorable	Balance	Imbalance
	III	IV
Favorable	Imbalance	Balance

(b)

Objects Are Linked by Dissociative Bonds		
Attitude toward	*Attitude toward First Object*	
Second Object	*Unfavorable*	*Favorable*
	I	II
Unfavorable	Imbalance	Balance
	III	IV
Favorable	Balance	Imbalance

Explanation: The entries in the tables are the results of particular linkages among the two objects. For example, in cell II of Table 2.1a the result of a positive link between a favorably evaluated object and an unfavorably evaluated object is attitudinal imbalance.

We can extend these ideas to include more than two objects as in a preceding example. There my fondness for you and my detestation of the Nixon administration were inconsistent with your approval of it. In this situation there are three objects, you, myself, and the Nixon administration, and three bonds. With three objects, inconsistency occurs if there are an *even* number of associative links. In the above case, there are two associative links, I like you and you like Nixon; hence the inconsistency. (See Figure 2.2a.) We could

---

[16] See, for example, Osgood and Tannenbaum, "The Principle of Congruity in the Prediction of Attitude Change."

Figure 2.2
BALANCE AND IMBALANCE BETWEEN THREE ATTITUDE OBJECTS

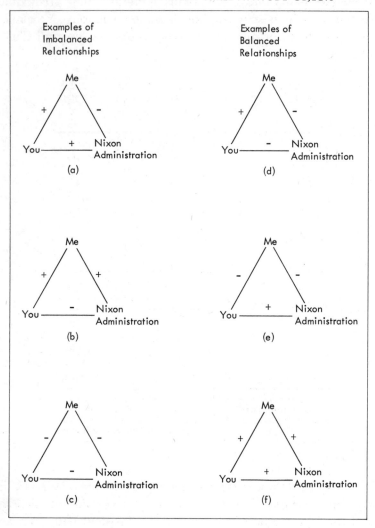

Key: + = associative link
        − = dissociative link
  Note: Interpret Figure (*a*), for example, as "I like you but I dislike the Nixon administration. You like the Nixon administration." According to balance theory, these attitudes are inconsistent.

restore balance by changing one positive bond to negative, or by changing the negative link to positive, thereby creating an *odd* number of positive bonds. For example, I might change my opinion of you or of Nixon. Figure 2.2 illustrates other possibilities. The specific models are not as important as the fact that imbalance arises from the joining of incompatible objects.

One can identify several kinds of imbalance. As in the above cases, inconsistency exists among attitude objects, among interpersonal relations, or among some combination of these. Another important type of imbalance involves attitudes and behavior. A good example is: "I know smoking is bad for my health; yet I smoke."

Causes of Imbalance

Inconsistency can be caused by several factors. In the first place, the world itself changes. Many people formed their opinions of the Vietnam War in the absence of much specific information about the issues involved. Probably few of them had any real understanding of the reasons for our involvement except that the government in Washington said we were fighting to honor our commitments, to maintain our prestige, and to protect the democratic and freedom-loving people of South Vietnam. Then, suddenly, without warning, news of the My Lai massacre appeared. What happened there sharply contradicted what people believed about the war, thereby creating attitudinal inconsistency or imbalance. Hence, in the process of acquiring information we often discover things which do not fit our expectations.

People are sometimes forced into inconsistency by external pressure. Parents may be required to send their children to integrated schools even though they (the parents) oppose integration. In this case, the behavior (sending one's children to an integrated school) is inconsistent with the attitude against integration. If the parents have alternative courses of action available (such as a private all-white school) but do not take advantage of these, the magnitude of the inconsistency will be even greater.

Finally, an individual's own cognitive apparatus is at times fallible. A person is not always logical or rational; he will occasionally have ambivalent feelings. No doubt everyone can tolerate a limited amount of attitudinal imbalance. But as self-generated inconsistencies grow, pressure to resolve the inconsistency increases.

Reactions to Imbalance

Just how does an individual restore balance? There are several ways. The most obvious is to avoid inconsistency in the first place. Some balance theorists claim that the avoidance of situations producing inconsistency is an important human motivation. As will be noted in the chapter on the mass media (Chapter 4), there is some evidence that people seek out information compatible with their views and avoid hearing or seeing opposing viewpoints. The most ardent supporters of President Nixon are not likely to be regular readers of *The New Republic* or *Ramparts,* both of which are quite liberal magazines. By sheltering oneself in this manner, inconsistency does not arise.

Another common response is to denigrate or discount the source of the inconsistency. Those who bring bad news, for example, frequently receive scorn and abuse from the people they serve. Some reacted to My Lai by saying that the press, which they felt could barely be trusted to begin with, distorted and exaggerated the incident and thus damaged the morale of the Armed Forces. This kind of response effectively destroys the links or bonds which are established between two attitudinal objects.

If it is not possible to discredit the source, one can separate or *differentiate* an object into parts. Consider two attitude objects, A and B. Suppose that A, which is strongly liked, becomes positively linked to B, which is strongly disliked. The bond creates attitudinal imbalance. One way to restore the balance is to differentiate between say, A and A' by saying "It's not A but rather A' that is linked to B. Since I don't like A' anyway, there is no problem." A' will usually be a small part or subset of A. More concretely, many Americans considered My Lai an aberration, an isolated incident, which in no manner typified the U.S. policy. Those who committed the atrocity were a minority, millions of other men served with distinction and honor. Psychologically, it is easy to condemn the minority while at the same time preserving one's commitment to the war effort. Whether or not My Lai was an "isolated" event is debatable. What is important here is that many people mentally separated American policy from the massacre and thereby maintained attitudinal balance.

Finally, and of most interest to consistency theorists, people can change their attitudes or their behavior or both to reestablish balance. The change may involve a switch in the *direction* of an opinion—as in changing from being for something to being against it—or simply an alteration in *intensity* of opinion—as in being a little bit less in favor of something than before. Various theorists have developed models and equations for predicting the amount and direction of attitude or behavior change. Since these approaches are quite sophisticated, we cannot deal with them here.[17] Nevertheless, to see how these formulations work we will briefly consider one, Leon Festinger's theory of *cognitive dissonance.*[18]

The Theory of Cognitive Dissonance

Although dissonance theory has been severely criticized, it still remains an important inspiration for research in social psychology. The theory generates a wide variety of predictions—some of them quite surprising—and social scientists have spent considerable time checking them out. Besides providing propositions to test, dissonance theory offers an interesting account of how people resolve cognitive inconsistency.

The principles of Festinger's theory are best understood by referring to an example. Consider the following true case study described by Leon Festinger, Henry Riecken, and Stanley Schachter:

> One day in late September the Lake City *Herald* carried a two-column story, on a back page, headlined: PROPHECY FROM PLANET. CLARION CALL TO CITY: FLEE THAT FLOOD. IT'LL SWAMP US ON DEC. 21, OUTER SPACE TELLS SUBURBANITE. The body of the story expanded somewhat on these bare facts:
>
> Lake City will be destroyed by a flood from Great Lake just before dawn, Dec. 21, according to a suburban housewife. Mrs. Marian Keech, of 847 West School Street, says the prophecy is not her own. It is the purport of many messages she has received by automatic writing, she says. . . . The messages, according to

---

[17] See Brown, *Social Psychology*, chap. xi, for an excellent review.

[18] Festinger, *A Theory of Cognitive Dissonance.*

Mrs. Keech, are sent to her by superior beings from a planet called "Clarion." These beings have been visiting the earth, she says, in what we call flying saucers. During their visits, she says, they have observed fault lines in the earth's crust that foretoken the deluge. Mrs. Keech reports she was told the flood will spread to form an inland sea stretching from the Arctic Circle to the Gulf of Mexico. At the same time, she says, a cataclysm will submerge the West Coast from Seattle, Wash. to Chile in South America.

The story went on to report briefly the origin of Mrs. Keech's experiences and to quote several messages that seemed to indicate she had been chosen as a person to learn and transmit teachings from the "superior beings." A photograph of Mrs. Keech accompanied the story. She appeared to be about fifty years of age, and she sat poised with pad and pencil in her lap, a slight, wiry woman with dark hair and intense, bright eyes.[19]

Mrs. Keech persuaded several people in the community that the end was near. Her adherents, becoming quite organized, made elaborate plans to escape the flood. All of them were publicly committed to the prediction and altered their behavior accordingly. Many of their acts were irrevocable: some quit their jobs; others threw or gave away valuable possessions; Mrs. Keech fasted; and everyone removed metal buttons and zippers from his garments so as not to disturb the intricate electronics of the flying saucer which was to save them. Though Mrs. Keech and her followers acted as discreetly as possible, their behavior was widely observed in the community and attracted considerable attention.

December 21 passed without incident.

The prediction had been unambiguously disconfirmed. Curiously, however, many members of Mrs. Keech's group steadfastly adhered to their belief in the coming millennium. Indeed, the members became *less* secretive and hostile to outsiders; they embarked on a vigorous campaign to proselytize others. After the 21st they began to hold press conferences, had several open houses, and even went Christmas caroling, all in an effort to win support for their cause.

One could easily dismiss Mrs. Keech and her friends as a group

---

[19] Leon Festinger, Henry W. Riecken and Stanley Schachter, *When Prophecy Fails* (Minneapolis: University of Minnesota Press, 1956), pp. 30–31.

of lunatics. True, their beliefs and behavior were extraordinary. Yet, what is of interest to us is their reaction to the prophecy's disconfirmation. The discrepancy between their beliefs and reality was obvious. But rather than cause them to reject the prophecy or at least to cast doubt on it the discrepancy only seemed to reinforce their belief in it. This reaction, which admittedly is an extreme case, is not too dissimilar to what we see in everyday life: in the face of disconfirming evidence people adjust their opinions and behavior in ways which sometimes seem to us as "objective" observers to be peculiar. Festinger's theory of cognitive dissonance was developed partly to explain these phenomena.

The Elements of Dissonance Theory. "*. . . two elements are in a dissonant relation if considering these two alone, the opposite of one element would follow from the other.*"[20] In other words, "I believe the world will end on December 21" is dissonant with my knowledge that the world has not ended. Or, as in a previous example, "I know smoking is bad for my health" and "I don't smoke." If two objects are not linked in the subject's mind, they have an irrelevant relationship.[21]

As with other balance theories, dissonance produces an uncomfortable tension which people try to avoid or reduce. It is a "motivating factor in its own right"—just like hunger or thirst.[22]

The amount or magnitude of dissonance is a function of the importance to the individual of the elements in question. If two attitudes are important to a person, then the amount of dissonance will be greater than if he does not care about them. Consequently, the pressure to reduce the dissonance depends on its magnitude: the greater the amount of dissonance, the greater the tension to reduce it. For Mrs. Keech and her followers, the issues involved matters of life and death. Hence, dissonance was at a maximum and, according to Festinger's theory, its reduction was very important.

Resolving Dissonance. The psychological discomfort produced by dissonance can be reduced in several ways. As was suggested above, one can attempt to avoid dissonance-producing situations.

---

[20] Festinger, *A Theory of Cognitive Dissonance,* p. 13. Italics his.
[21] Ibid., pp. 10–11.
[22] Ibid., p. 3.

Some investigators find that individuals seek out information supporting a choice they have just made and avoid adverse information.[23] People who had just purchased an automobile, for example, sought out information that supported their choice over other cars.[24]

Another strategy is to change one's social environment. Recall that Mrs. Keech and her disciples made, in effect, a public and full-fledged commitment to their belief in the world's doom. The flood never came and the easiest action from one point of view would have been to abandon the whole idea. But to the believers this step would have been too painful because some of their acts were irrevocable. Changing them would bring embarrassment and ridicule. To escape this dilemma Mrs. Keech and a few of her most ardent followers sought to increase their social support by winning others to their cause. Proselytizing in this manner is an attempt to reinforce the original belief. Friends who are in agreement can console and convince one another. Thus in changing one's social milieu one can lessen the effects of dissonance by having the support and reassurance of friends; the discrepancy between beliefs and reality becomes less clear.[25]

Most of us do not make predictions about the end of the world. But whether we are aware of it or not we often go through a similar process of adjusting our environment to be more compatible with our opinions and behavior. Festinger's is one explanation of why we do this.

Still another and obvious way to reduce dissonance is to change one's behavior. If the prophecy does not come true, you quit the group. If you discover that smoking is bad for your health, you quit smoking.

Often, however, it is not easy to change behavior. The behavior may bring pleasure, as with smoking. In these cases, it may be easier

---

[23] Judson Mills, Elliot Aronson and Hal Robinson, "Selectivity in Exposure to Information," *Journal of Abnormal and Social Psychology,* Vol. 59 (1959), pp. 250–53; J. S. Adams, "Reduction of Cognitive Dissonance by Seeking Consonant Information," *Journal of Abnormal and Social Psychology,* Vol. 62 (1961), pp. 74–78; Arthur R. Cohen, *Attitude Change and Social Influence* (New York: Basic Books, Inc., 1964), pp. 78–79.

[24] Danuta Ehrlich, Isaiah Guttman, Peter Schönbach, and Judson Mills, "Postdecision Exposure to Relevant Information," *Journal of Abnormal and Social Psychology,* Vol. 54 (1957), pp. 98–102.

[25] Festinger et al., *When Prophecy Fails,* pp. 27–28.

to change one's beliefs or attitudes to make them conform with behavior rather than vice versa.

The idea that attitudes may conform to behavior leads to some interesting implications. Social scientists, along with most everyone else, usually think attitudes determine behavior. Normally this supposition seems justified. Festinger tells us, though, that a change in behavior can often bring about a subsequent change in opinions.

To see how, consider a case we might come across in any city election. Mr. Barren decides more or less on the spur of the moment to vote for Richard Vari for city councilman. He is proud of his decision and tells his friends and co-workers about it. Later, while talking with some people Barren learns that Vari favors a city sales tax, which Barren has always opposed. Now Barren's behavior and attitude are, in a sense, inconsistent. It is impossible to change his behavior for he cannot negate his vote. Nor does he want to admit he was wrong in voting for Vari since to do so might cast doubt on his abilities as the neighborhood political pundit. One way out of this dissonance is to change his opinion of a sales tax. Barren is then heard to say, "Well, a sales tax will probably help us get a new fire station. Besides, property taxes are already too high."

Most political scientists look at voting as the result of attitudinal forces. Dissonance theory suggests that we can under some circumstances consider political attitudes to be dependent upon behavior. Whatever consistency there is between behavior and attitudes may result from efforts to reduce dissonance. The extent to which dissonance determines attitude change is an empirical matter subject to future investigation. Nevertheless, some evidence supports Festinger's idea.

Forced Compliance.   Many studies of dissonance deal with forced compliance behavior. Suppose that we force or induce a subject holding a particular opinion to engage in an activity which is inconsistent or dissonant with that opinion. What effect will this have on the individual's behavior and attitudes? Based on the results of an interesting experiment, Festinger and J. M. Carlsmith supply a totally unexpected answer.[26]

A naïve subject performed a long, repetitive, and monotonous

---

[26] Leon Festinger and James M. Carlsmith, "Cognitive Consequences of Forced Compliancy," *Journal of Abnormal and Social Psychology*, Vol. 58 (1959), pp. 203–10.

task. After completing the task the subject was asked to lie about it by telling another subject (who was really working for the experimenter) that the task was quite enjoyable. For taking part in the deception the subject was told he would receive a reward. Some subjects expected to get $20 while others expected only $1. Festinger and Carlsmith reasoned as follows.

Subjects who obtained $20 were well rewarded for their lying. Consequently, they should not experience much dissonance between their behavior (lying) and their opinion of the task which was presumably negative. These subjects had simply been paid to do a job. Thus, according to dissonance theory, they would not be motivated to change their opinions. The $1 subjects, on the other hand, were in a different situation. True, they had been rewarded. But the reward was a pittance, not enough to justify the lie. Hence, these subjects would experience dissonance and could reduce it only by changing their *own* opinions of the task.

A postexperimental questionnaire revealed that the $1 subjects did indeed like the task more than those earning $20. Festinger and Carlsmith cite the difference as evidence for their theory.

Although other studies have modified Festinger and Carlsmith's approach in several ways, they still produce the same conclusion: to the extent that an individual cannot attribute his discrepant behavior to anyone or anything but himself he will feel dissonance which he will try to reduce by modifying his privately held opinions.[27] These laboratory findings have interesting practical implications.

Mr. Evans who lives in a small Georgia community of 5,000 was horrified when he learned that a federal judge in Atlanta ordered

---

[27] See, for example, T. C. Brock, "Cognitive Restructuring and Attitude Change," *Journal of Abnormal and Social Psychology*, Vol. 64 (1962), pp. 264–71; T. C. Brock and A. H. Buss, "Dissonance, Aggression and Evaluation of Pain," *Journal of Abnormal and Social Psychology*, Vol. 65 (1962), pp. 197–202; Jack Brehm and Arthur Cohen, *Explorations in Cognitive Dissonance* (New York: John Wiley & Sons, Inc., 1962), pp. 73–78. It should also be noted that this line of research has been sharply criticized on several grounds. As with most aspects of dissonance theory, there are alternative explanations for Festinger and Carlsmith's results. See, for example, Natalia P. Chapanis and Alphonse Chapanis, "Cognitive Dissonance: Five Years Later," *Psychological Bulletin*, Vol. 61 (January 1964), pp. 1–22; and Milton J. Rosenberg, "When Dissonance Fails: On Eliminating Evaluation Apprehension from Attitude Measurement," *Role Playing, Reward, and Attitude Change*, ed. Alan C. Elms (New York: Van Nostrand Reinhold Co., 1969), pp. 66–91.

the immediate integration of the local schools. Since the school board reluctantly complied, Mr. Evans' children will have to attend an integrated elementary school unless he does something. Like Mr. Evans, most members of the community bitterly oppose school integration, and some people have banded together to form an all-white private school. Evans is in a quandary; he would like to join them but he thinks the tuition, $40 a month, is more than he wants to pay. (He could afford it if he cut down expenses elsewhere.) Besides, the school is several miles from his home, so it will be a headache getting his children to and from school. As a result, he decides to send them to the integrated public school.

Mr. Evans is in a dissonance-producing situation. He opposes integration and has an alternative, the private school, by which he can avoid integration. Yet he chooses not to take this option. In this situation, it is hard for him to blame anyone else. After all, many other parents have handled the situation by sending their children to the private school. He simply chooses not to make the sacrifice of money and time. Therefore, he can attribute his behavior which is inconsistent with his attitudes only to himself. According to dissonance theory, then, Mr. Evans' opinions about school integration might change to the point where he at least gracefully accepts integration.

This example illustrates the principle that public policies such as legislation or court orders can have a significant impact on attitudes. As long as an individual sees his behavior as partly attributable to himself and as not totally determined by the external force his attitudes may undergo modification. If behavioral inconsistencies can be completely attributed to or blamed on the external source, then no dissonance will arise. Here the person simply rationalizes the inconsistency: "I had no choice. If I had a choice I would act differently." But often the individual himself is partly to blame and cannot rationalize his behavior in this manner.

In short, dissonance theory suggests that moderate coercion can cause attitudes to change. Seen in this light, the aphorism "You can't legislate morals" requires at least slight modification.

These ideas are largely speculative since most studies supporting them have been carried out in laboratory settings. Nevertheless, there is some "real life" evidence in support of the theory. Morton Deutsch and Mary Collins find that people living in integrated public housing have more favorable opinions of blacks than do whites living in segregated public housing.[28] Festinger interprets their finding to mean that "Living in [the] integrated project forced whites into contact with Negroes, and undoubtedly, rules of ordinary, polite neighborly behavior functioned on many occasions to produce overt behavior which was dissonant with private belief."[29] The dissonance was reduced by developing more friendly attitudes toward blacks.

A Critique of Dissonance and Balance Theory

The problem with this interpretation—and with much of the dissonance and balance theories in general—is the indeterminacy of the main variable, dissonance or imbalance. We may observe a change in attitudes but how do we know dissonance produced the change? The changes might reflect new knowledge or beliefs about blacks or—as the functionalists propose—simply a need to get along with one's neighbors. There are, in other words, numerous alternative explanations for the findings. Without additional evidence we have to be somewhat skeptical about dissonance theory. We certainly need additional research.

At a more fundamental level, some psychologists challenge the central premise of balance theory, that people strive for cognitive consistency and feel psychological discomfort when their attitudes and behavior are inconsistent. According to these psychologists a person's tolerance of imbalance is greater than is suggested by an approach like dissonance theory. Individuals tolerate, even enjoy complexity, variety and ambiguity; they can live quite happily with contradictions in their beliefs and opinions. The amount of inconsistency tolerated by an individual may depend entirely on situational factors and in some cases this amount is large.[30]

---

[28] Morton Deutsch and Mary Evans Collins, *Interracial Housing* (Minneapolis: University of Minnesota Press, 1951), chaps. viii and ix.

[29] Festinger, *A Theory of Cognitive Dissonance*. But another study has indicated that if the pressure is *in*sufficient, a person's attitudes may simply harden instead of change. See Susan A. Darley and Joel Cooper, "Cognitive Consequences of Forced Noncompliance," *Journal of Personality and Social Psychology*, Vol. 24 (1972), pp. 321–26.

[30] Salvatore Maddi, "The Pursuit of Consistency and Variety," *Theories of Cognitive Consistency: A Source Book*, ed. Robert P. Abelson et al. (Chicago: Rand McNally & Co., 1968), pp. 267–74; Jonathan L. Freeman, "How Important Is Cognitive Consistency?" *Theories of Cognitive Consistency: A Source Book*, ed. Robert P. Abelson et al., (Chicago: Rand McNally & Co., 1968), pp.

An interesting example of this phenomenon is supplied by Irwin Silverman.[31] He studied the reactions of his university colleagues to Senator Edward M. Kennedy's automobile accident in which Mary Jo Kopechne was killed. Kennedy's car plunged off a bridge into water off Chappaquiddick Island, a small island off the Massachusetts coast. The senator delayed reporting the accident for about 11 hours. When rescuers arrived at the scene Miss Kopechne was found drowned. Senator Kennedy was criticized on numerous grounds, especially his delay in reporting the mishap, a delay which a few people say cost the girl her life. The mass media thoroughly covered the story including the numerous insinuations of misconduct on the senator's part.

The interesting point, however, is that while many in Silverman's sample distrusted Kennedy's explanations and deplored his actions, their opinions did not change. In spite of their misgivings and doubts about the accident, they continued to think highly of Senator Kennedy. Silverman concludes that "people are not particularly compelled toward resolution [of cognitive imbalance]."[32] His point, then, is simply that balance theories do not completely explain attitudes and behavior.

Theories of cognitive balance have been criticized on these and other grounds. Despite these objections, however, models such as dissonance theory contribute to our understanding of attitude organization and change. People's desire for balance affects their behavior in many circumstances. Knowing how and why people maintain consistency thus helps us understand many types of political attitudes and behavior.

ATTITUDES AND OVERT BEHAVIOR

In concluding this chapter, we switch directions. Balance theory tells us people strive for consistency. Frequently, however, social

---

497–503; and William J. McGuire, "The Current Status of Cognitive Consistency Theories," *Cognitive Consistency*, ed. Shel Feldman (New York: Academic Press, 1966), pp. 1–46.

[31] Irwin Silverman, "On the Resolution and Tolerance of Cognitive Inconsistency in a Natural-Occurring Event: Attitudes and Beliefs Following the Senator Edward M. Kennedy Incident," *Journal of Personality and Social Psychology*, Vol. 17 (February 1971), pp. 171–78.

[32] Ibid., p. 177.

scientists observe apparent inconsistencies between attitudes and behavior. Recall from Chapter 1 La Piere's travels around the country with an Oriental couple. They were accommodated without incident by over 200 restaurants and hotels. LaPiere later wrote these establishments asking if they would serve a "distinguished" Oriental gentleman. Surprisingly almost every proprietor said no. The lack of consistency between the proprietors' verbal and overt behavior has been widely cited as evidence that behavior is not always logically related to attitudes.

Discrepancies between behavior and attitudes pose a serious problem for social science. We expected behavior to be based on attitudes. Yet we often find that they are *not* related in any logical way. Allan Wicker recently reviewed 46 studies dealing with behavior-attitude consistency. The vast majority of these studies found very little congruence, leading Wicker to conclude that attitudes are only weakly related to overt behavior.[33] At least as measured by conventional techniques, opinions and behavior do not seem logically related.

The studies included in Wicker's survey covered a wide range of topics including race relations, child care, job performance, cheating, and political participation. The relationship between attitudes and behavior toward minority groups has received special attention: most of the research indicates that it is very difficult to predict a person's behavior toward minorities knowing only his attitudes.[34]

Still other studies show that changes in attitudes are not always followed by changes in behavior. Irving Janis and Seymour Fesh-bach tried to change the attitudes of a group of high school freshmen toward dental hygiene by giving them a "fear-arousing" communi-

---

[33] Allan W. Wicker, "Attitudes versus Actions: The Relationship of Verbal and Overt Behavioral Responses to Attitude Objects," *Journal of Social Issues,* Vol. 25 (1969), p. 65.

[34] See, for example, James A. Green, "Attitudinal and Situational Determinants of Intended Behavior toward Blacks," *Journal of Personality and Social Psychology,* Vol. 22 (April 1972), pp. 13–17; Gordon H. DeFriese and W. Scott Ford, "Verbal Attitudes, Overt Acts, and the Influence of Social Constraint in Interracial Behavior," *Social Problems,* Vol. 16 (1969), pp. 493–505; Melvin L. DeFleur and Frank R. Westie, "Verbal Attitudes and Overt Acts: An Experiment on the Salience of Attitudes," *American Sociological Review,* Vol. 23 (December 1958), pp. 667–73.

cation. Using a message which graphically depicted the consequences of tooth decay, the investigators found that fear-arousing appeals were effective in changing beliefs and attitudes about dental hygiene, but had little effect in changing actual tooth-brushing habits.[35] Other research along similar lines supports this observation.[36]

An Example from Voting

In political life, too, attitudes and behavior are often not related —or, at least, not related in the way some political scientists think they should be. The data in Table 2.1a show the relationship between attitudes toward federal aid to education and voting preferences. Responses to the question about federal aid to education have been labeled for convenience "Liberal" and "Conservative." (See Table 2.1.) A vote for Humphrey is considered a "Liberal" behavior while a vote for Nixon is "Conservative"—labels which seem reasonable given the ideological proclivities of the two men. (Wallace voters have been ignored.) One can see that although on aid to education the liberals generally supported the liberal candidate, Humphrey, about one third of them voted for Nixon, the conservative. Conversely, about a third of the conservatives voted for Humphrey. Thus, about one third of the sample *seemed* to act inconsistently. How do we explain this phenomenon along with other cases of attitude-behavior inconsistency?

The problem can be analyzed in several ways. For one thing, we may have picked the wrong issue. Since political scientists are so immersed in politics, they often implicitly assume that everyone shares their interests. They "know" federal aid to education is an important issue so they feel the voters should also think it important. Yet many voters probably do not know or care too much about the question of aid to education. Even if they have an attitude on

---

[35] Irving L. Janis and Seymour Feshbach, "Effects of Fear-Arousing Communications," *Journal of Abnormal and Social Psychology*, Vol. 48 (1953), pp. 78–92.

[36] Leon Festinger, "Behavioral Support for Opinion Change," *Public Opinion Quarterly*, Vol. 28 (1964), pp. 404–17; E. Fleishman, E. Harris, and H. Burtt, *Leadership and Supervision in Industry* (Columbus: Ohio State University Bureau of Educational Research, 1955).

the issue, it will not by itself cause them to vote for one candidate over another. Furthermore, a complicated behavior like voting is not likely to be based on just one attitude. Most behaviors are no doubt determined by the interaction of several attitudes. Hence, on the basis of the one issue in Table 2.1a it is premature to say the voters are acting inconsistently. The general point is simply that before we say a person's behavior and attitudes are inconsistent we have to be certain we have identified all of the relevant issues.

Another possibility is that we have not considered enough issues. If, for example, we add a question on federal aid for health care to the question on education we get fewer inconsistencies. (See Table 2.1b.) Of those who are liberal on two issues, almost 80 percent

Table 2.1
RELATIONSHIP BETWEEN POLITICAL ATTITUDES
AND PRESIDENTIAL VOTING BEHAVIOR

(a)

	Relationship between Attitudes and Behavior One Attitude		
	Attitude toward Federal Aid to Education*		
Behavior (Vote in 1968)	Liberal Response	Neutral	Conservative Response
Liberal (Humphrey)	70%	55%	34%
Conservative (Nixon)	30%	45%	66%
	100%	100%	100%
	(310)	(44)	(467)

(b)

	Relationship between Attitudes and Behavior Two Attitudes		
	Attitude on Federal Aid to Education* and Health Care†		
Behavior (Vote in 1968)	Liberal on Both Issues	Mixed	Conservative on Both Issues
Liberal (Humphrey)	77%	48%	20%
Conservative (Nixon)	23%	52%	80%
	100%	100%	100%
	(232)	(214)	(209)

Table 2.1 (continued)

(c)

Relationship between Attitudes and Behavior Three Attitudes			
Attitudes toward Federal Aid to Education,* Health Care,† and Economic Security‡			
Behavior _(Vote in 1968)_	_Liberal_ _on Three_ _Issues_	_Liberal_ _on Two_ _Conservative_ _on One_	_Conservative_ _on Two_ _Liberal_ _on One_	_Conserva-_ _tive on_ _Three_ _Issues_
Liberal (Humphrey) ..	88%	53%	41%	19%
Conservative (Nixon)	12%	47%	59%	81%
	100%	100%	100%	100%
	(142)	(119)	(129)	(156)

*Some people think the government in Washington should help towns and cities provide education for grade and high school children; others think this should be handled by the states and local communities. . . . Which are you in favor of?

† Some say the government in Washington ought to help people get doctors and hospital care at low cost; others say the government should not get into this. . . . What is your position?

‡ In general, some people feel that the government in Washington should see to it that every person has a job and a good standard of living. Others think the government should let each person get ahead on his own.

Responses favoring a greater governmental role are considered "liberal."

Note: Figures in parentheses refer to the number of cases.

Source: _SRC 1968 American National Election Study._ (See Appendix.)

voted for Humphrey, the liberal candidate; only about 20 percent were inconsistent. Also, among the conservatives on education and health care only about 20 percent voted for Humphrey. (The respondents having mixed opinions—that is, one liberal, one conservative—tended to divide their votes evenly as we would expect.) Adding another issue, economic security, reduces the inconsistency still further, especially among the liberals. (See Figure 2.1c.) Less than 20 percent of those with all liberal or all conservative opinions vote inconsistently.[37] The point is that a person may be liberal on one issue, but conservative on two others. We cannot expect to predict his vote knowing _only_ his position on one issue.

---

[37] Note, however, that the number of respondents with opinions on all three issues is a relatively small percent of the total sample. As we will see in Chapter 6, surprisingly few people have opinions on all important social and political issues.

Still another explanation for the results of Table 2.1*a* is that our thinking is too simplistic: we need to know more about an individual than simply his opinion of federal aid to education. At the very least, we should ask how he defines the situation. What are his beliefs about the issue and the candidates? What seems inconsistent or illogical to us may seem entirely sensible to another person. For example, we as social scientists may regard Nixon as the conservative choice. But do others?

Martin Fishbein argues that behavior depends partly on beliefs.[38] A liberal who votes for Nixon may believe that Nixon shares his liberalism. Hence, a vote for Nixon is not at all inconsistent, and, in fact, makes good sense. People do not have the same beliefs or perceptions about political objects as social scientists. Once we take into account their beliefs we may find many fewer inconsistencies than before.

In this regard, it is important to keep in mind the type of objects about which we are talking. We often measure feelings toward liberals *in general* and then try to determine behavior (e.g., a vote) toward a *specific* liberal candidate. The problem is that an individual may not believe that the candidate is liberal; in fact, he may think the candidate is really conservative. A more fruitful approach, Fishbein suggests, is to ascertain the person's beliefs about the candidate and then see if he behaves consistently with these beliefs. If, for example, a person who is liberal thinks Hubert Humphrey *is* conservative, we cannot call him inconsistent for voting for someone else.

We also need to know how an individual views the behavior itself. Some people think voting is a waste of time; others take it quite seriously. Their attitudes toward voting no doubt affect the impact of other attitudes. A man who thinks voting is pointless may not weigh the candidates' positions on aid to education as carefully as a person for whom the vote is sacred. In addition to attitudes toward the behavior, an individual's actions will also be influenced by the expected consequences of his acts and alternative behaviors.

Behavior takes place in a social environment. Few people are able to transcend completely the influence of their friends and neighbors. Although a person may privately favor Nixon, peer group

---

[38] Fishbein, "An Investigation of the Relationship between Beliefs about an Object and the Attitude toward That Object," pp. 233–39.

pressure may cause him to give public support to Humphrey, thereby creating the appearance of inconsistency. Melvin DeFleur and Frank Westie found that subjects in an experiment made significant use of their perceptions concerning the possible approval or disapproval of face-to-face or reference groups.[39] Generally speaking, then, when the "group's opinion" (i.e., the opinion of the majority of the group) opposes an individual's privately held attitude, behavior may be inconsistent; when the individual and the group have the same opinion, behavior and attitudes will probably be consistent.

Finally, attitude-behavior consistency depends on individual capabilities. A person may fail to see the inconsistency of his actions; he may not know how to translate his attitudes into behavior, or he may not have the opportunity to behave consistently.[40] According to many political scientists, the average voter is not interested in politics and has only vague impressions of where the major parties and candidates stand on issues. Consequently, he is unable to relate his own issue preferences to his voting decisions.[41] In short, some individuals do not have the awareness or skills to see the implications of their behavior.

In summary, inconsistency between attitudes and behavior results from several factors. Many inconsistencies are probably more apparent than real. They arise from the shortcomings of the observer rather than the actor. In particular, we need to know what attitudes are important to the individual, what his beliefs are, how he views the behavior itself, what social pressures he is exposed to, and what his level of skills is.

---

[39] DeFleur and Westie, "Verbal Attitudes and Overt Acts," pp. 667–73.

[40] Howard J. Ehrlich, "Attitudes, Behavior, and the Intervening Variables," *The American Sociologist*, Vol. 4 (February 1969), pp. 29–34.

[41] See Chapter 6 for a further discussion of this point.

3

Political Socialization: What and How Children Learn about Politics

Wallace Lambert and Otto Klineberg, two psychologists, asked children in 11 nations what nationality apart from their own they would most and least like to be. The responses from the United States are interesting. Not surprisingly, most American children wanted to be Europeans or Canadians, people with whom they share an ethnic and cultural heritage. The *least* desirable nationality was Russian. Although this choice was not common among 6-year olds, it was the predominant response among 10- and 14-year-old youngsters. Almost 60 percent of the 14-year-olds spontaneously mentioned Russian as the national group they would least like to be. Russian was mentioned more frequently than Chinese, Japanese, Hindu, or African.[1]

One doubts that this result is happenstance. Another study showed that even kindergarten students considered that among 20 flags, the American flag was the most attractive, and the Russian

---

[1] Wallace E. Lambert, and Otto Klineberg, *Children's Views of Foreign Peoples: A Cross-National Study* (New York: Appleton-Century-Crofts, 1967), pp. 33, 249.

flag the least.[2] Obviously, children develop rudimentary political attitudes at an early age. They sense that the Russians are the villains in the cold war and want nothing to do with them. What is important, however, is that these basic predispositions and notions about one's own country and foreign peoples are likely to persist throughout life. Our earliest impressions leave, as it were, "scratches on our minds."[3]

One of the most important tasks facing political science is to explain the origins and development of fundamental attitudes like these. To do so, we must begin with children, for it is a truism that "The political self . . . is made, not born."[4] The process of making the political self, a process called socialization, begins early in life and continues through adulthood. Socialization means the learning of the values, customs, and manners of one's society. A person learns about his social group so that he can function within it. Socialization includes every aspect of a person's development from the formation of his personality to the learning of specific skills. Since socialization is obviously a large topic, we will deal only with a subtopic, the development of political attitudes and roles in children and adolescents.

Socialization explains the origins of people's opinions, beliefs, and values. By looking at their childhoods we discover why people became liberal or conservative, prejudiced or tolerant, politically active or passive, Democrat or Republican. The study of the socialization process, in short, is a first step toward understanding individual political behavior.

Socialization is important for another reason. It explains stability and instability in social systems as a whole. In order to survive, a social and political system needs citizens who have the skills to perform the necessary functions of the society, who know and accept its customs, norms, and roles, and who are loyal to its institutions and practices. If its citizens are not trained in these

---

[2] Edwin D. Lawson, "Development of Patriotism in Children: A Second Look," *Journal of Psychology*, Vol. 55 (1963), pp. 279–86.

[3] Harold R. Isaacs, *Scratches on Our Minds: American Images of China and India* (New York: John Day, 1958), quoted in Lambert and Klineberg, *Children's Views of Foreign Peoples*, pp. 224–25.

[4] Richard E. Dawson and Kenneth Prewitt, *Political Socialization* (Boston: Little, Brown and Co., 1969), p. 19.

respects the system will be unstable and will eventually collapse. So by providing trained and loyal citizens, socialization contributes to the maintenance of the system. Without this training political relations would be unpredictable, chaotic and each generation would likely be at war with the next. Furthermore, governmental institutions such as the presidency or the Supreme Court would lack acceptance and thus could not govern.

But if socialization accounts for social continuity, it also explains, at least in part, social change. The evolution of society results partly from imperfect socialization or the failure of at least some members to learn or accept the traditions and practices of preceding generations. Values or customs may be irrelevant to contemporary needs or they may conflict with other values or customs; the socializing agents may be ineffective teachers. Whatever the reason, many individuals do not learn or accept everything their forefathers were taught. In this way, society adapts and progresses. Thus, socialization affects both the stability and evolution of societies.

Our concern in this chapter is with the individual child: how he learns to be a good citizen, to play a role in politics, to have political preferences, and to translate these preferences into behavior. We start by looking at what children learn and later discuss how they learn these things.

WHAT CHILDREN LEARN

A growing child encounters many different aspects of politics. He learns about his country, its friends and enemies, its institutions, its laws, and its leaders. He learns about his role in politics. He learns to like and trust some public figures and to dislike and distrust others. He develops attitudes, however rudimentary, toward the issues and events of the day. A child's political development entails numerous attitudes and behavior.

Attitudes toward the Political System

Patriotism.   One of the first concepts a child develops is a sense of "we-they." He discovers that he is in some way different from other people; he belongs to groups which are defined by race, religion, and community. Four-, five-, and six-year-old children, as a study by Harold Stevenson and Edward Stewart shows, are not only aware of racial differences but also believe in and use racial stereotypes.[5] In the same fashion, children develop an awareness of neighborhood and community and, by the time they are in grade school, of national identity. The exact age at which a child learns his nationality varies but it certainly occurs by the time he is 10 or 11. At that age he distinguishes his nation from other nations and from other geographic units such as states or provinces.

A child comes to know and love the nation through its symbols like the flag and national anthem and through various rituals like the pledge of allegiance.[6] He usually has positive feelings about his country's symbols. We have already seen, for example, that American children like the American flag best, the Russian flag the least. Another earlier study also indicates that as children grow older they increasingly prefer the American flag to others.[7] These early attachments to the nation are primarily emotional, and are not based on much factual information. As the following dialogue with a second-grade boy indicates, young children have very little substantive knowledge of their country:

What is a nation?
A nation is a state, isn't it? Certain places in it are important.

Can you name a nation?
Washington, New York.

You see the flag up there. What does the flag mean?
Well, I don't quite know. It just stands up there, and you say something to it. We put out hands over our heart and say the pledge of allegiance to the flag.

What does it mean when you pledge allegiance?
Well, we're pledging to the flag.

What do you pledge to the flag?
To give us freedom.

---

[5] Harold W. Stevenson and Edward C. Stewart, "A Developmental Study of Racial Awareness in Young Children," *Child Development,* Vol. 29 (1958), pp. 399–409.

[6] Robert D. Hess and Judith V. Torney, *The Development of Political Attitudes in Children* (Garden City, N.Y.: Doubleday and Co., Inc., 1967), chap. 2.

[7] Eugene L. Horowitz, "Some Aspects of the Development of Patriotism in Children," *Sociometry,* Vol. 3 (1940), pp. 329–41.

What does the flag stand for?
It stands for freedom and for peace.[8]

Later, as they grow older, children acquire information about their country, what it is, and what it stands for. Six-year-olds, according to Lambert and Klineberg's study, evaluate their own and foreign nations in simple and objective terms (e.g., "It's big") whereas the 14-year-olds had more subtle impressions.[9] They base their likes and dislikes on such things as the personality traits and habits of foreigners. Many of them, for example, believe Russians are "aggressive" or "uncultured."

Along with their growing awareness, children also develop a sense of loyalty to the nation. Initially, their patriotism is simple and naïve. It reflects their immediate concerns and needs. Another second grader compares the United States with Britain:

> Well, I wouldn't like to be an Englishman because I wouldn't like to talk their way, and I'd rather be an American because they have better toys, because they have better things, betters stores, and better beds and blankets, and they have better play guns, and better boots, and mittens and coats, and better schools and teachers.[10]

When they learn more about the international system and their country's role in it, patriotism takes on a more "realistic" and perhaps chauvinistic tone. Citing a study of French elementary school children, Fred Greenstein and Sidney Tarrow report that nationalistic sentiments develop at an early age. Most of the boys and girls in the sample did not want to live outside of France except occasionally. They felt Frenchmen should be willing to die for their country if called on to do so, and a sizable portion (38 percent) felt that traitors should be shot.[11]

We previously mentioned that attitudes like loyalty are enduring predispositions. Although a person's opinions of his country may change over time and always depend on situational factors, building

---

[8] Hess and Torney, *The Development of Political Attitudes in Children,* p. 33.

[9] Lambert and Klineberg, *Children's Views of Foreign Peoples,* p. 224.

[10] Hess and Torney, *The Development of Political Attitudes in Children,* p. 32.

[11] Fred I. Greenstein and Sidney G. Tarrow, "The Study of French Political Socialization: Toward the Revocation of Paradox," *World Politics,* Vol. 22 (1969), p. 108.

a sense of patriotism in children is considered a primary function of many social institutions. Schools have the main responsibility in this respect but other formal and informal organizations (e.g., Boy Scouts, Little Leagues) are also important.

Political Institutions and Processes. No less important are attachments to political institutions. In the 1950s and early 1960s, one would occasionally come across a billboard saying "IMPEACH EARL WARREN," who was at that time Chief Justice of the Supreme Court. These billboards, especially common in the South, reflected bitterness and antagonism toward the Supreme Court's rulings on desegregation. Interesting, though, is that the attacks were directed against Warren, not the Court itself. Few of the billboards said "ABOLISH THE SUPREME COURT."[12] People in this country apparently make a distinction between an institution and its particular incumbents. And although they are not hesitant to criticize officeholders, they have a basic respect and sympathy for the offices.

Children's impressions of political institutions, like their views of the nation, are both naïve and favorable. They tend to personify the government, identifying it with authorities such as the President or the mayor of their town. They think of the government not as a set of institutions and roles, but more simply as a group of men most of whom act wisely and benevolently. Upon reaching adolescence, they become more knowledgeable and cynical.

Children also develop idealized and positive attitudes toward law and toward compliance with law. Elementary school children usually think that laws are inevitably just and that punishment always comes to the wrongdoer. Laws, they believe, are the work of good, generous, almost divine men who are acting on everyone's behalf. In short, they generally trust the system of laws.[13] People become more cynical and calculating in their reactions to the law as they

---

[12] It should be added, however, that people's opinions of the Supreme Court are colored by their party politics. Democrats have more favorable impressions of the Court, except when a Republican occupies the White House. In the latter case, Republicans and Democrats feel about the same. Nevertheless, attitudes toward the court are generally favorable although specific decisions may be widely criticized. See Kenneth M. Dolbeare and Phillip E. Hammond, "The Political Party Basis of Attitudes toward the Supreme Court," *Public Opinion Quarterly,* Vol. 32 (1968), pp. 16–30.

[13] Hess and Torney, *The Development of Political Attitudes in Children,* p. 59.

grow older. They learn that violations are not always punished, and, more important, that laws can be used as tools in attaining different goals. Thus, along with knowledge of political institutions in general, age increases one's understanding of law.

Besides inculcating attitudes toward the nation and its major institutions socialization affects our reactions to specific political processes. This point can be illustrated by discussing people's attitudes toward electoral politics.

In many democracies elections are regularly held without trouble. The losers grumble but they accept defeat. The winner is given his chance to do what he can while everyone plans for the next election. In other countries, however, elections are often merely preludes to turmoil or violence. The losers refuse to accept the outcome. Both sides often turn to "other means" to settle their differences. Part of the problem stems from the nature of the stakes being fought for. Despite what the contestants think, the issues in our elections are usually not as serious as those involved in elections elsewhere. For example, an election between Nixon and McGovern in America does not involve the same range and intensity of conflict as would an election between the Communists and President Thieu in South Vietnam. In the latter case, the losing side would probably not accept the results, no matter how fairly the elections were conducted.

There is another reason why elections work more smoothly here than elsewhere. People in this country have been taught and encouraged to accept the "rules of the game." Children learn at an early age to respect various political ideals and practices. They are taught to work "within the electoral system" and to accept its results. Even first and second graders overwhelmingly believe that the losers of elections should accept defeat gracefully. These attitudes are crucial in a democracy because the winners have the leeway and legitimacy to govern.[14]

This orientation to elections contrasts sharply with attitudes in other countries where democratic practices are relatively new. In Burma, for instance, people are uncomfortable with political controversy:

---

[14] David Easton and Robert D. Hess, "The Child's Political World," *Midwest Journal of Political Science,* Vol. 6 (1962), pp. 236–37.

The problem of enmity is peculiarly great because to Burmese the socialization process does not provide the individual with explicit rules for handling conflicts. The individual is only taught that violence and disagreement are bad and dangerous, and cooperation and unanimity are good. There is little recognition that honest differences can arise and that conflicts can be conducted in orderly and law-like ways. Within the society or within its politics there is little room for the concept of the opponent who is still the friend, and of a loyal opposition.[15]

In these circumstances electoral politics may flounder because the citizens have not been trained to compromise, to moderate or postpone their demands, to cooperate with their opponents, and to accept defeat at the polls. Elections work only if all the participants agree to abide by the rules and the outcomes. Where the socialization process does not lead to such acceptance, elections will probably not be a very effective means for settling conflicts.

Similarly, other political institutions and practices acquire legitimacy partly through the socialization process. Some social scientists go so far as to say that socialization experiences create "personality types" or "national characters" conducive to one kind of political system or another. For example, many observers believe that the instability and collapse of the Weimar Republic in Germany during the 1920s can be traced to the "authoritarian character" of Germans in that period. The authoritarian structure and discipline of the German family, as well as the strict discipline of the school system did not prepare Germans for the tolerance and compromise required by a viable democracy. As a result, the Weimar Republic lost support and was ultimately replaced by the Nazi regime. The evidence for this proposition is inconclusive but it does seem clear that a child's education and family experiences to some extent affect his acceptance of political institutions and processes.[16]

---

[15] Lucian W. Pye, *Politics, Personality and Nation Building* (New Haven, Conn.: Yale University Press, 1962), p. 207.

[16] Alex Inkeles and Daniel J. Levinson, "National Character: The Study of Modal Personality and Sociocultural Systems," Vol. IV, *The Handbook of Social Psychology*, ed. Gardner Lindzey and Elliot Aronson, 2d ed. (Reading, Mass.: Addison-Wesley Publishing Co., 1969), pp. 464–71. Also see Gabriel Almond and Sidney Verba, *The Civic Culture* (Princeton, N.J.: Princeton University Press, 1963), chap. 12.

Political Authorities.   Along with a child's opinions of the government, he develops attitudes toward political authority. Americans have traditionally been suspicious of power. The separation of power outlined in the Constitution reflects this distrust. Today, many adults are skeptical and cynical about the integrity, competence, and motives of public officials. Their distrust has been accentuated by the Watergate scandals, but it has been present during much of the post-World War II era.

Surprisingly, then, many studies find that children have favorable, uncritical, even adoring attitudes toward political authorities.[17] A child, according to Robert Hess and Judith Torney, sees political authorities as "powerful, competent, benign, and infallible and trusts them to offer him protection and help."[18] The president seems to be an especially popular figure since American boys and girls think of him as a "benevolent leader:"

> I think that he [the president] has the right to stop bad things before they start. (Fifth-grade girl)
>
> The president deals with foreign countries and takes care of the U.S. (Eighth-grade girl)
>
> The president does good work. (Sixth-grade boy)
>
> The president makes peace with every country but bad. (Fifth-grade boy)
>
> The president gives us freedom. (Eighth-grade girl)[19]

These positive images of the president transcend geographic and ethnic lines and carry over to other major political figures like mayors, policemen, and congressmen. Of course, not all children are uncritical. As they get older, they develop suspicions and dislikes. Moreover, studies of lower class children produce different

---

[17] Fred I. Greenstein, *Children and Politics* (New Haven, Conn.: Yale University Press, 1965), chaps. 2–3; Fred I. Greenstein, "More on Children's Images of the President," *Public Opinion Quarterly*, Vol. 25 (1961), pp. 648–54; Fred I. Greenstein, "Children's Images of Political Leaders in Three Democracies: The Benevolent Leader Revisited," paper presented at the annual meeting of the American Political Science Association, New Orleans, La., September 1973; and Robert D. Hess and David Easton, "The Child's Changing Image of the President," *Public Opinion Quarterly*, Vol. 24 (1960), pp. 632–44.

[18] Hess and Torney, *The Development of Political Attitudes in Children*, p. 242.

[19] Greenstein, *Children and Politics*, pp. 38–39.

results. Dean Jaros and his colleagues discovered that poor white children living in Appalachia have less favorable attitudes toward authorities than do children in national samples.[20] Still, the differences are not great and there is surprising homogeneity in the attitudes among diverse groups of children. For instance, one study, based on an admittedly small sample, finds relatively insignificant differences between white and black youngsters.[21] This same study, incidentally, also turns up evidence that a major national scandal like Watergate and all the accompanying adult skepticism of politicians does not tarnish children's idealizations of political authorities.[22]

Children in other countries express similarly positive sentiments toward their leaders. The child in France is perhaps a bit more distrusting but he, too, has a generally high regard for public officials. British children adore the Queen and, to the extent that they are aware of him, the Prime Minister as well.[23] In each nation, an absence of much concrete information tempers what they think of authority. Until a child is about 10 or 11 his ideas are quite naïve and uninformed and based mainly on analogies with familial authorities.

What children learn about political authorities and how they feel about them depend on circumstances. Just why they have idealized images of political figures is still a matter of debate and research. Perhaps their parents consciously or unconsciously shelter them from the seamy side of politics and teach them instead to respect and obey public officials. Or children may observe that the president or mayor is treated deferentially and hence, through imitation, adopt similar attitudes. Or finally, they may develop favorable opinions of authority in their families—opinions based on both awe and admiration—which they generalize to external figures.[24]

---

[20] Dean Jaros, Herbert Hirsch, and Frederic J. Fleron, Jr., "The Malevolent Leader: Political Socialization in an American Sub-Culture," *American Political Science Review,* Vol. 62 (1968), pp. 564–75.

[21] Greenstein, "Children's Images of Political Leaders in Three Democracies," passim.

[22] Ibid., pp. 18–19.

[23] Ibid., pp. 11–26.

[24] Imitation and generalization are discussed in the next section of this chapter.

We can conclude at this point, however, that children begin to acquire knowledge and opinions of public leaders at an early age. For the most part these attitudes are favorable. These opinions change over the years, becoming more realistic and critical but still constituting the basis upon which adults judge and react to the political world.

Political Roles

Interest and Efficacy.   Some citizens are quite active in politics, taking part on a day-to-day basis. Others stay out of politics altogether while still others are occasional participants. These differences in political participation are explained by several factors. One of the most important, it appears, is what a person experiences as a child and young adult.

Not everyone is interested in politics. True, interest increases slightly with age, but even upon graduation from high school or college many young people do not care much about public affairs. Belonging to a family or a peer group in which interest is high probably contributes substantially to the development of political interest in the individual. Formal education may also increase political interest.

Another characteristic related to participation is efficacy, or a feeling of confidence in one's abilities to have an impact on politics. One occasionally hears someone say, "What's the use? Why bother to vote? Politicians don't listen anyway." In political science terminology, this person is not efficacious or lacks political self-confidence. By contrast, a person who declares "I'm going to call the mayor and raise hell!" is politically efficacious or confident. As with interest, efficacy depends partly on socialization.

Gabriel Almond and Sidney Verba's five-nation study, *The Civic Culture,* concludes that political confidence is a product of one's family and school experiences. Respondents in the study who felt free as children to participate in family or school decision making tended as adults to feel efficacious. Conversely, those who were excluded from taking part did not have much confidence. In other words, children who were permitted to take part in group discussions and so forth became more efficacious as adults than those who were not so permitted.[25]

---

[25] Almond and Verba, *The Civic Culture,* chap. 12.

There is debate over which institution, the school, or the family is most important in instilling confidence in the individual. Probably both are important.[26] At any rate, political self-confidence grows somewhat as a child goes from elementary to secondary school, but even many adults are not very efficacious. Whether a person is efficacious or not seems to depend on whether or not he has been rewarded for being politically active.

If the socialization process does not enhance one's political self-confidence, it at least tries to impart a modicum of citizenship, especially its duties. The good citizen, a child is taught, follows public affairs and votes regularly; he listens to both sides of an argument and carefully weighs the issues before acting. It is paradoxical, though, that children are not always encouraged to demand or expect results from their efforts. Hess and Torney find, for example, that in American schools civics courses often stress passive rather than active involvement in politics. The school curriculum, they say, impresses upon the child "the necessity for obedience and conformity" and "under-emphasizes the rights and obligations of a citizen to participate in government."[27]

Active versus Passive Roles. As a consequence of his early training, a person acquires an active or a passive orientation toward government. Many of these ideas are summarized in a significant and interesting study conducted by Edgar Litt.[28] Litt studied the effects of social class and formal education on socialization. He chose three communities with different socioeconomic characteristics: upper middle class, lower middle class, and working class. Within each area he analyzed the contents of all the civics textbooks used by a major secondary school. He also interviewed educational and community leaders and administered questionnaires to civics classes. Litt was especially concerned with what students were taught about the nature of political power, about the democratic process, and about their participation in it. Were the students encouraged to

---

[26] David Easton and Jack Dennis, "The Child's Acquisition of Regime Norms: Political Efficacy," *American Political Science Review*, Vol. 61 (1967), pp. 25–28; Hess and Torney, *The Developmeent of Political Attitudes in Children*, passim; and Kenneth P. Langton, *Political Socialization* (New York: Oxford University Press, 1969), chap. 6.

[27] Hess and Torney, *The Development of Political Attitudes in Children*, pp. 126, 248.

[28] Edgar Litt, "Civic Education, Community Norms and Political Indoctrination," *American Sociological Review*, Vol. 28 (1963), pp. 69–75.

be active or passive? Did they get a "realistic" view of politics? Did they understand the role of power and conflict in the political process?

The results are revealing for what they tell us about political learning in the United States. The curriculums of the three schools differ significantly. Working-class school children are not encouraged to be politically active; they are given a bland, stereotyped, and artificial description of politics. The textbooks show the government acting mechanically and impersonally. These books do not depict the conflict and power inherent in political relationships. Upper class children, by contrast, get more realistic lessons. They see politics as group conflict in which people seek and use power to achieve various goals. Furthermore, their training fosters a sense of political efficacy and an obligation to participate.

According to Litt, then, children in the three communities learn different roles. Those in the working-class community receive "training in the basic democratic procedures" but without much emphasis on political participation.[29] The middle-class school provides instruction in the elements of democratic government which is "supplemented by an emphasis on the responsibilities of citizenship, not on the dynamics of public decision-making."[30] Only in the upper class community are children socialized to assume leadership roles. These children discover the true bases of political power and how it is used, and can therefore be expected to have a realistic understanding of politics.[31]

Malcolm X recalls an incident which although involving a different context vividly illustrates how schools affect children's perceptions of themselves and what they feel they can become. Malcolm has just told his guidance counselor that he wants to be a lawyer when he grows up:

> Mr. Ostrowski looked surprised, I remember, and leaned back in his chair and clasped his hands behind his head. He kind of half-smiled and said, "Malcolm, one of life's first needs is for us to be realistic. Don't misunderstand me, now. We all here like you, you know that. But you've got to be realistic about being a nigger. A

---

[29] Litt, "Civic Education, Community Norms . . .," pp. 73–75.

[30] Ibid., p. 74.

[31] Ibid., p. 74.

lawyer—that's no realistic goal for a nigger. You need to think about something you *can* be. You're good with your hands—making things. Everybody admires your carpentry shop work. Why don't you plan on carpentry? People like you as a person—you'd get all kinds of work."[32]

Although Malcolm X overcame this experience to become a major political figure, in general the family, the school, and the community combine to give a child role expectations and predispositions. They teach him what to expect and what to demand. Socialization encourages some to be interested, self-confident, and active, while it discourages participation on the part of others.

These data and conclusions have two implications. First, the recruitment of leaders to fill positions in government and the political parties begins at an early age. As a result of differential training some individuals acquire the values, attitudes, and expectations needed for leadership. They develop a sense of political effectiveness as well as the essential skills and interest. When they become adults they are prepared and ready to fill government, party, and community offices. Others learn more passive roles; they may expect to vote but are otherwise only moderately interested in politics. These generalizations are not meant to imply that childhood socialization determines who will lead and who will follow. We are saying, however, that once a person develops a particular political orientation, he is apt to keep it for life.

The second and related implication deals with political participation among social groups. People in the upper classes are politically more active than those in the lower classes.[33] There are several reasons for the differences but data from socialization research, especially those like Litt's, go a long way toward explaining these differences. To a limited extent, child-rearing practices and formal education differ by class.[34] As we have pointed out, middle- and

---

[32] Malcolm X, *The Autobiography of Malcolm X* (New York: Ballantine Books, 1965), p. 36. Reprinted by permission of Grove Press, Inc. Copyright © 1964 by Alex Haley and Malcolm X.

[33] See Chapter 5.

[34] For a survey of findings regarding class differences in child rearing, see Edward Zigler and Irvin L. Child, "Socialization," Vol. III. *The Handbook of Social Psychology*, ed. Gardner Lindzey and Elliot Aronson, 2d ed. (Reading, Mass.: Addison-Wesley Publishing Co., 1969), pp. 483–501.

lower class children have family and school experiences tending to make them less politically involved. Conversely, upper class youngsters acquire activist orientations. This role training, beginning early in life and continuing into adulthood, partly explains different rates of political participation among social classes.

Political Attitudes

We now move from general feelings about the political system and one's place in it to a comparison of parents' and the children's attitudes toward specific objects such as parties, candidates, and issues. Probably the best documented finding is that children generally have the same party identification as their family, especially if the family's preferences are homogeneous. This agreement declines with age, but even so, most high school and college students have nearly the same party identification as their parents. Table 3.1, which contains data on a national sample of high school seniors and their parents, illustrates this point. It shows a moderately strong

Table 3.1
RELATIONSHIP BETWEEN PARENTS' AND STUDENTS'
PARTY IDENTIFICATION

Students' Party Identification	Parents' Party Identification		
	Democrat	Independent	Republican
Democrat	66%	30%	13%
Independent . .	27	53	36
Republican . . .	7	17	51
	100%	100%	100%
	(914)	(443)	(495)

Note: Figures in parentheses refer to the number of cases.
Source: M. Kent Jennings, *Student-Parent Socialization Study*. (See Appendix.)

relationship between parent and child. Most defections in party identification are not to the opposite party but to the Independents. Very few students from Democratic families become Republicans, and only about 13 percent of those coming from a Republican background are Democrats. Most switchers are Independents. Similar conclusions have been reached in numerous other studies conducted since 1950.[35]

Party identification is not a universal attribute. The French do not identify with parties as readily as Americans. Philip Converse and Georges Dupeux speculate that this is because politics is less salient in the French home and children simply do not have the same opportunity to learn a party affiliation.[36]

In contrast to party identification, agreement between parents and children on issues is sometimes quite low. High school and college students do not share the opinions of their parents on specific matters such as economic policy, foreign aid, the handling of the Vietnam War, tolerance of dissent, and civil rights.[37] In addition, students appear to be generally more liberal, particularly in race relations and tolerance of dissent.[38] In short, on public policy and political personalities there are considerable disparities between the views of parents and their children. Whether these differences represent a "generation gap" is another matter.

Political Rebellion?

Many political scientists do not think children rebel against their parents' politics. True, the late 1960s seemed to be a period of fresh awakenings, a time when youth challenged many of society's

---

[35] M. Kent Jennings and Richard G. Niemi, "The Transmission of Political Values from Parent to Child," *American Political Science Review*, Vol. 62 (1968), pp. 169–84. Also see David O. Sears, "Political Behavior," Vol. V. *The Handbook of Social Psychology*, ed. Gardner Lindzey and Elliot Aronson, 2d ed. (Reading, Mass.: Addison-Wesley Publishing Co., 1969), pp. 374–80 for a discussion and list of references.

[36] Philip E. Converse and Georges Dupeux, "Politicization of the Electorate in France and the United States," *Elections and the Political Order*, ed. Angus Campbell, et al. (New York: John Wiley & Sons, Inc., 1966), pp. 277–81.

[37] Jennings and Niemi, "Transmission of Political Values"; R. W. Connell, "Political Socialization in the American Family: The Evidence Re-examined," *Public Opinion Quarterly*, Vol. 36 (1972), pp. 323–33; and Lucy N. Friedman, Alice R. Gold, and Richard Christie, "Dissecting the Generation Gap: Intergenerational and Intrafamilial Similarities and Differences," *Public Opinion Quarterly*, Vol. 36 (1972), pp. 334–46.

[38] Paul B. Sheatsley, "White Attitudes toward Negroes," *Daedalus*, Vol. 95 (1966), pp. 217–38; and Jennings and Niemi, "Transmission of Political Values," pp. 164–84.

cherished beliefs and practices. We heard of the "counterculture," "alternative life-styles," the "Woodstock nation." Certainly young people were suddenly more aware and more critical of injustices than anyone thought. They seemed willing to act militantly, even violently, if necessary, to achieve their goals. Many authors and journalists saw the youth "movement" as the hope (or bane) of the future.

On closer inspection, however, the gap between parent and child seems to represent a failure of the socialization process rather than deliberate rebellion. There are several reasons for thinking so. Generally speaking, politics is not an important topic in most American households. If an adolescent challenges parental authority he usually does so in areas the mother and father think are important. Grades in school, dress, staying out late are matters which concern parents. Defiance of the rules in these respects is tantamount to defiance of the parents' authority and so could be called rebellion. But if a teen-ager claims to be for McGovern over Nixon, or if he favors an end to "imperialistic foreign aid" his parents will probably not be overly upset because they simply do not care that much about the candidates or foreign aid. Consequently, a young person's political attitudes and behavior are usually not a conscious rebellion against his parents' values.

Furthermore, since the parents themselves are not overwhelmingly interested in specific issues (like foreign aid), and hence do not teach their children about them, the youngsters have to learn about them on their own. It is not clear where they hear about issues, but their schools, their peer groups, and their limited exposure to the news media probably all play a part. In any event, learning about specific issues of politics seems to occur in default of—rather than in defiance of—parental guidance.

Finally, the most spectacular instances of "rebellion"—sit-ins, protest marches, campus demonstrations—seemed to be joined by students who were actually quite close to their parents' values. The "hard-core" activists frequently came from liberal and politicized families. Children from politically conservative or apolitical backgrounds were less apt to be involved. A study of Chicago students illustrates this point.

Richard Flacks interviewed a sample of 50 college students drawn from mailing lists of peace, civil rights, and student movement groups in the Chicago area.[39] These students were matched on sex, residence, and type of college by an additional 50 students drawn at random from student directories. Flacks is able to classify the students as "activist" and "non-activists."

A preliminary analysis of the interviews revealed that the fathers of the activists were liberal.[40] Among the nonactivist students, for example, most came from homes where the father was a Republican and self-styled conservative; most of the activists, on the other hand, had fathers who claimed to be "highly liberal" or "socialist."[41] Flacks concludes, therefore, that student militancy does not reflect rebellion, but merely an extension of parental attitudes and values. The activists simply try to live up to the "political traditions of their families."[42]

At this point, we might pause to consider whether or not going to college contributes to the generation gap. Some parents and politicians believe that colleges and universities are hotbeds of Communism and radicalism and they worry about exposing their sons and daughters to such alien ideas. The mass media sometimes encourage us to think that college causes youth to reject their parents' values. And certainly many people wonder if college makes students more liberal.

In view of this conventional wisdom, the available data are surprisingly mixed. On the one hand, a few studies have discovered a liberalizing effect of college. Theodore Newcomb's study of Bennington College in Vermont showed that the women became increasingly liberal in their political and social outlooks during their four years at college.[43] After leaving the liberal college environment, however, they tended to revert to their previous opinions. Other studies have supported these ideas.[44]

---

[39] Richard Flacks, "The Liberated Generation: An Exploration of the Roots of Student Protest," *Journal of Social Issues,* Vol. 23 (1967), pp. 52–75.

[40] Flacks, "The Liberated Generation," p. 66.

[41] Ibid.

[42] Ibid., p. 68. Also see Kenneth Keniston, "You Have to Grow up in Scarsdale to Know How Bad Things Really Are," *New York Times Magazine,* April 27, 1969.

[43] T. W. Newcomb, *Personality and Social Change* (New York: Dryden Press, 1943).

[44] See, for example, Eleanor Maccoby, R. E. Matthews, and A. S. Morton, "Youth and Political Change," *Public Opinion Quarterly,* Vol. 18 (1954), pp. 23–29.

On the other hand, most research indicates that college has a negligible impact on political attitudes. At most, it produces greater awareness and tolerance of civil rights and liberties.[45] In Philip Nogee and Murray Levin's study, for example, two thirds of the students did not change their political orientation and of those who did, only 34 percent became more liberal.[46] Rose Goldsen and her colleagues find college to be, if anything, a conservative influence. Although colleges in the period of their study (the early 1950s) may have been more conservative than they are now, their finding that students "became increasingly conservative as they pass through college" is still of interest to us.[47]

At this point, then, it appears that college has a limited effect in terms of making students more liberal or conservative. This is not to say that college does not affect attitudes toward specific issues. While in college a person may learn about inflation, the war in Vietnam, foreign aid, and tax reform. It is likely, though, that his opinions will at least roughly fit in with the basic political orientation he has already acquired during childhood.

As children grow up, they develop attitudes and expectations about various aspects of their political world. They learn patriotism. Most of them come to believe in and support the nation's political institutions and practices, as well as leading public figures. In the course of their family, school, and other group experiences, they acquire confidence and skills for future political activity. Their socialization includes attitudes toward specific events, issues, and people.

A Note on the Persistence of Socialization

What a child learns in his earliest years shapes his adult behavior. Of course, everyone changes as he grows older. A man encounters

---

[45] Philip E. Jacob, *Changing Values in College: An Exploratory Study of the Impact of College Teaching* (New York: Harper & Row, Inc., 1957); Charles G. McClintock and Henry A. Turner, "The Impact of College upon Political Knowledge, Participation and Values," *Human Relations,* Vol. 15 (1968), pp. 163–76.

[46] Philip Nogee and Murray B. Levin, "Some Determinants of Political Attitudes among College Voters," *Public Opinion Quarterly,* Vol. 22 (1958), pp. 449–63.

[47] Rose K. Goldsen, Morris Rosenberg, Robin M. Williams, and Edward A. Suchman, *What College Students Think* (Princeton, N.J.: D. Van Nostrand Co., Inc., 1960).

new experiences, acquires new ideas and skills, and has to adapt to an ever-changing world. Yet his childhood training predisposes him to act in certain ways. His later experiences often merely reinforce the values, attitudes, and behavior taught him by the family, school, church, neighborhood, and mass media.

It is exceedingly difficult to predict how a person will respond in a specific situation if we know only his socialization history. Many factors determine behavior and it is impossible to attribute it to just one cause. Nevertheless, socialization tells us a great deal about how people become what they are and what they are likely to become. This information, together with what we know about their current cognitive and attitudinal structures and situational properties, allows us to make reasonable guesses about their future behavior.

This knowledge has both theoretical and practical uses. But in order to understand socialization completely we need to consider *how* a person is socialized.

HOW CHILDREN LEARN

As Neal Miller and John Dollard say, "Human behavior is learned."[48] Our interest now is seeing how behavior is learned. White, middle-class children have favorable opinions of political officials like the president or mayor. They think of them as "benevolent" leaders. But we might ask, why are these attitudes so favorable? Why do they develop at such an early age? When do they learn about politicians? Do children like political authorities in the same way as they like their parents? More generally, what conditions encourage and discourage the learning of political opinions and behavior?

For the most part, political scientists have spent more of their time describing socialization than explaining it. We have numerous studies showing what children think and do, but very little research on why. Furthermore, until recently socialization literature has been rather atheoretical and isolated from other disciplines. Political science is rapidly changing in this respect, but at this time we still do not have a comprehensive theory for explaining political learning. Consequently, we have to borrow from other fields.

---

[48] Neal E. Miller and John Dollard, *Social Learning and Imitation* (New Haven, Conn.: Yale University Press, 1941), p. 1.

One difficulty in doing so is that the research in these fields is voluminous. Psychology, sociology, and anthropology contain numerous explanatory theories, many of them quite complex. Although some of these approaches overlap, there are too many variations to discuss here. Instead, we will concentrate on only one approach, *social learning theory*. Even this description will be brief, for it is a long and complex theory.

As we will see, learning theory has its critics, many of whom offer reasonable alternative explanations of socialization. Learning theory is not unified, but has several branches and even its advocates disagree among themselves on important points. Nevertheless, many principles of social learning theory are widely accepted, and it is probably the basis of more research than any other approach. Hence, social learning theory is a good place to start the study of political learning.

The Elements of Social Learning Theory

Consider an admittedly artificial situation. Sally Rae and her family are watching television. The six o'clock news shows Senator Sanborn, a Democrat, making a speech to the Veterans of Foreign Wars. Sally, who is 14 and does not follow politics at all, suddenly and almost impulsively says, "Gee, he's good-looking. I'd vote for him." Her father frowns and replies, "Sanborn! He's a bum." The matter is dropped as soon as a commercial comes on and Sally, not being interested anyway, goes upstairs to finish sewing a dress.

Two days later while watching television with her family, Sally again sees Senator Sanborn but she says nothing.

The following week her father is reading *Newsweek*. Senator Sanborn is on the cover. "He doesn't look too honest," Sally says.

Mr. Rae grins. "That's right, honey. Sanborn tries, but most Democrats just can't run things right."

Sally asks if Sanborn is a Democrat.

"Yeah, he's a Democrat all right. And like most of 'em, he doesn't know what he's doing."

The next day Sally tells her older brother that she doesn't like Democrats.

He responds, "Sis, that's the only smart thing you've said all day."

Sally Rae is learning to dislike Democrats.

This description of Sally's experience with politics is, of course, simplified. But it does illustrate a few principles of learning theory.

Sally, seeing Senator Sanborn on the six o'clock news (the cue situation), makes an initial *response*. Since she knows nothing about Sanborn she responds on the basis of her first impression which happens to be favorable. But her response is immediately challenged by her father. Not only does he disagree with what she says, but by disagreeing he is withholding approval. Her father is not rejecting her as a person but neither is he *rewarding* her for saying she would vote for Sanborn. To the extent that Sally seeks or needs approbation her response is not satisfactory to her need.

Two days later a similar cue situation appears. She responds by saying nothing and again her response goes unrewarded.

When she says Sanborn does not "look too honest" she receives mild approval from her father. The same happens in her discussion with her older brother: her responses are rewarded.

In short, Sally is rewarded only for certain responses. Although, as she grows older, other types of factors—such as her intellectual development—will undoubtedly affect her political attitudes, she nevertheless begins to expect reward from some responses and not from others. When this expectation is internalized and motivates her behavior we say she has *learned* the responses. Psychologists call learning of this sort instrumental or operant conditioning.[49]

Let's examine the principles in more detail.

Instrumental Conditioning.   The principle of instrumental conditioning is this: If in a cue situation a response tends to be followed by a stimulus which is rewarding, then an individual will generally make this response and ignore unrewarded responses. In other words, as a response becomes associated with reward, an individual becomes increasingly likely to make that response. Sally Rae finds

---

[49] Good discussions of these aspects of social learning theory are: Albert Bandura and Richard H. Walters, *Social Learning and Personality Development* (New York: Holt, Rinehart & Winston, Inc., 1963); Winfred F. Hill, *Learning: A Survey of Psychological Interpretations* (San Francisco: Chandler Publishing Co., 1963; Sidney W. Bijou and Donald M. Baer, *Child Development.* Vol. I. *A Systematic and Empirical Theory* (New York: Appleton-Century-Crofts, Inc., 1961); Miller and Dollard, *Social Learning and Imitation;* O. Hobart Mowrer, *Learning Theory and Behavior* (New York: John Wiley & Sons, Inc., 1960); Arthur W. Staats and Carolyn K. Staats, *Complex Human Behavior* (New York: Holt, Rinehart & Winston, Inc., 1963); and B. F. Skinner, *Science and Human Behavior* (New York: The Free Press, 1953).

that negative comments about Senator Sanborn and Democrats (response) meet with approval (reward) from her family. Over time she makes a connection between the response and reward. In anticipation of the reward, she makes that response whenever the cue situation arises. Her response is thus instrumental in obtaining reward.

The basic principle is simple but it contains a number of complicated concepts requiring further explanation.

Rewards.   Her family's approval is a rewarding stimulus which strengthens the behavior it follows. That is, the stimulus (approval) makes the occurrence of the response in a similar cue situation more likely. Stimuli such as these are called positive rewards or reinforcers.[50] There are other stimuli (e.g., Mr. Rae's frowns) whose removal strengthens a response. These are called negative rewards or reinforcers. Reinforcement of responses by positive and negative rewards, according to social learning theory, is what causes people to learn.

A stimulus, such as a mother or father's words of approval, which can reward a child is said to have reinforcement value. Negative reinforcement is sometimes called punishment but since usage of this term varies widely among psychologists, we will not use it further.

Some rewards (e.g., food, water) have innate value to an individual. These are primary reinforcers. Other rewards have to be learned. A mother's smile is not a primary reinforcer since to the newborn child it means nothing. But a child gradually associates smiling with food, warmth, cuddling, and so on. As a result, a smile acquires the status of a reward and is called an acquired or secondary reinforcer. Secondary reinforcers are doubtlessly more important in social learning than are primary reinforcers. The smiles and expressions of approval of Sally's mother and father are positive, secondary rewards: their occurrence after a particular response increases the likelihood that the response will be made in the future.

We assume the rewards have meaning for Sally. Some psychologists feel that people have needs or drives and that whatever satisfies or reduces these drives has reward value. Presumably, Sally

---

[50] Though some psychologists object, we will use reward and reinforcer interchangeably.

wants her parents' love. Consequently, symbols of their love (like smiles) help reduce her need or drive for affection.

In summary, a drive in a particular situation produces a series of responses. If the first response goes unrewarded—that is, it does not reduce the drive—its repetition in that situation becomes less likely. If, instead, a response is rewarded, the connection between it and the cue situation is strengthened. The repetition of this response in a similar circumstance is likely. The greater the number of connections between response and reward the greater the likelihood an individual will produce this response. According to Miller and Dollard, "This strengthening of the cue-response connection is the essence of learning."[51]

This principle explains not only what children learn but what they do not learn. Sally Rae is acquiring a generally unfavorable opinion of Democrats. Except for her feelings about Senator Sanborn, however, she is not learning attitudes toward particular people and issues. In many American families, politics is relatively unimportant and political responses, whenever they occur, are simply not reinforced, either positively or negatively. Thus, although children may develop a broad orientation to political life, they probably form most of their political opinions elsewhere, as in the school or the peer group. (This is not to say that the learning process in the school or the group differs in any essential way from that of the home.) This phenomena can account for the lack of correspondence between parents' and children's political preferences, noted earlier.

According to learning theory, unreinforced behavior gradually weakens or becomes less likely to occur. This process is called *extinction*. The extinction of responses is important to an individual because he learns to discard unproductive behavior. Some psychologists argue that this process is essential for a society's economic and social development because the members of a society learn appropriate skills and discard obsolete ones.[52]

Generalization and Discrimination. Cue situations normally vary, if only slightly, from one time to another. Instead of Senator Sanborn, Sally might see Governor Raymond, also a Democrat. If

---

[51] Miller and Dollard, *Social Learning and Imitation,* p. 17.
[52] Staats and Staats, *Complex Human Behavior,* pp. 72–74.

Raymond is similar to Sanborn in appearance and deportment, he will tend to evoke the same responses Sanborn does. Learning in one situation generalizes or transfers to new ones. The less similar the situation, the less generalization occurs. Obtaining a reward in one context for making a response leads one to expect an analogous reward for giving the same response in a slightly different situation.[53]

The "benevolent" leader phenomena discussed previously can be understood as an example of generalization. Greenstein finds that children have favorable, idealistic opinions of public officials, like the president, mayor, and policeman. It is possible that these children have positive attitudes toward their fathers which are generalized or transferred to public officials. In other words, if a child thinks of his father as omnipotent and benevolent, he may impute these characteristics to men who, in the child's eyes, occupy similar positions of authority. The president, mayor, and police-man, then, elicit the same type of response as a parent because they have reinforcement value.

Generalization can also account for Jaros' converse finding that children in Appalachia have less favorable opinions of political authorities. There children, it might be argued, tend to come from homes in which authority is not as highly respected as in more affluent families. Lacking favorable impressions of authority in their immediate environment, the children do not generalize their feelings to the political arena. In short, their responses to public officials are similar to their responses to their parents.[54]

Learning carries over to new situations, but the process does not continue indefinitely. The individual must at some point learn to make discriminations between stimuli. Generalization goes on only as long as responses are rewarded. If a response to a slightly new cue situation is not reinforced, then the strength of that response declines. For example, Sally Rae might be rewarded for her critical remarks about Senator Sanborn, but not for criticizing Governor Raymond. Gradually she would learn to distinguish between the two men.

---

[53] Miller and Dollard, *Social Learning and Imitation,* p. 44.

[54] This interpretation of children's attitudes toward authority has been criticized. (In fact, Jaros et al., "The Malevolent Leader," p. 570, dispute it.) Nevertheless, this explanation has not been directly disconfirmed and it provides a simple and parsimonious explanation of children's attitudes.

Generalization and discrimination are, of course, essential to an individual's development. By generalizing responses, a child does not have to learn a new behavior for each and every situation he encounters. After learning not to hit her little sister, Sally knows not to hit the little girl next door. Discrimination, on the other hand, allows Sally to react differently in different situations. Yelling in one context (such as at a football game) is appropriate and even rewarded behavior while in another (such as at the dinner table) it is not. By dispensing rewards differentially, socializing agents teach children to make distinctions among stimuli.

Conditions Which Facilitate Social Learning. Many stimuli can acquire reinforcement value for an individual. This is particularly true of the people with whom one comes in contact: members of the family, teachers, neighbors, community leaders, and friends. Since there are so many potential influences we might wonder which ones will be the most effective "teachers." Or, more generally, what conditions facilitate social learning? There are many answers but we will consider only two factors: the characteristics of the learning environment and the needs of the individual.

According to social learning theory, responses which are rewarded or reinforced occur more readily than those which are not. This principle assumes, however, that the individual clearly perceives the reward. When a reward is not perceived or it does not immediately follow behavior, learning will be hindered. Learning is also enhanced if there is little or no competition for responses. If two responses both elicit equal rewards neither response is likely to be learned. Suppose that Sally's father is a Republican and her mother is a Democrat. Sally's pro-Republican statements will be rewarded by her father, but not by her mother who will instead reinforce her pro-Democratic remarks. Thus, Sally may end up as neither a Democrat nor a Republican but a neutral.

These remarks illustrate a general principle: Social learning is facilitated by an absence of conflict and competition among rewards. Consequently, groups such as the family which are small, cohesive, intimate, and homogeneous with respect to attitudes and values will be effective socializing agents. They dispense rewards uniformly. Larger groups—a neighborhood, for example—will be less effective because they are more heterogeneous. In short, responses which are uniformly and clearly rewarded will be learned more readily than responses which receive inconsistent or ambiguous reinforcement.

This principle partly explains a phenomenon called cross-pressure. Many people live in "mixed" political environments. They are exposed to different points of view, or, in social science jargon, cross-pressures. For example, a person may have close friends who are staunch Democrats and others who are Republicans. Several studies indicate that people respond to cross-pressure by withdrawing from the controversy. In an election, they tend to refuse to vote for anyone or to delay making up their minds until the last minute.[55] Learning theory accounts for these reactions in terms of the competition among reinforcers. Since conflicting messages come from both sides, no response receives consistent, unambiguous reinforcement, and consequently no response—whether it be pro-Democratic or pro-Republican—is strengthened. In a sense, the heterogeneity of opinions mean the individual learns not one but several responses, all tending to cancel each other.

If the learning environment is important, so too are the needs of the individual. Although theories differ on specific matters, psychologists believe a person has various needs or drives. He thus values the rewards or reinforcers contributing to the satisfaction of these needs. If Sally needs affection, then her parents' words of approval, smiles, hugs, and so forth will have reinforcement value. It is possible, however, that at a particular time Sally feels especially secure. She may even have an excess or surfeit of approval. In this case, her parents' affection has less reinforcement value and will not facilitate learning.

The principle is simply that the reinforcement value of something (e.g., a word of approval) depends partly on its availability. If it is in short supply (*deprivation* condition) its value for the individual is high and will strengthen behavior. If the reinforcer is abundantly available, however, the individual is *satiated,* and his responses will not be strengthened.[56]

To the extent that an individual needs the rewards a socializing agent (such as a parent or teacher) has to offer, his learning will be influenced by that agent. This is why it is pointless to say one socializing agent is more important than another. Instead, we need

---

[55] See Chapter 6.

[56] Bijou and Baer, *Child Development,* p. 65.

to look at the conditions in the social environment and in the individual which facilitate learning.

Imitation and Learning

So far we have described learning as instrumental conditioning. A person makes a response which is either rewarded or unrewarded. But how does he make the response in the first place? By itself, the theory does not explain where a person initially learns how to make a response. To supplement the principle of conditioning, therefore, many learning theorists add the concept of imitation.[57] Imitation simply means reproducing or copying the behavior of a "model." A model is someone who is imitated, like one's parents or teachers.

At one time or another everyone learns by imitating or following the examples of others. In fact, some psychologists contend that imitation is one of the most important forms of social learning. It is especially significant in the learning of "novel" responses, or responses which the observer has never seen before and hence could not make without a model to follow. Imagine how hard it would be to learn to dance, for example, without having someone to watch.

There are several reasons why an individual imitates a model. These reasons are closely related to the principles of learning as they have been described above. An individual may receive reinforcement for the response he imitates. Or he may see that the model is rewarded for doing something and so he expects a similar reward for doing the same thing. Seeing that her brother is praised for making critical remarks about Senator Sanborn, Sally might logically expect the same treatment if she criticizes the Senator. Furthermore, the model itself may be in a position to dispense rewards as in the case of a small child who is praised for imitating his father's behavior. Finally, psychologists think people can receive vicarious rewards by imitating others. For instance, one student might copy the actions of another student who is very popular, thereby achieving vicarious popularity himself.[58]

---

[57] Bandura and Walters, *Social Learning and Personality Development*, chap. 2; and Miller and Dollard, *Social Learning and Imitation*, chaps. 6–16.

[58] Bandura and Walters, *Social Learning and Personality Development*. See James P. Flanders, "A Review of Research on Imitative Behavior," *Psychological Bulletin*, Vol. 69 (1968), pp. 316–37 for an excellent discussion of imitative learning.

Another effect of imitation is to reduce inhibitions against certain kinds of behavior. For example, a teen-ager has learned not to destroy other people's property. But suppose that he is inadvertently caught up in the midst of a mob vandalizing and ransacking a store. Seeing everyone else rampage through the store may tempt the boy to be destructive himself. Imitation thus has a disinhibiting effect.

As a consequence of imitation a person adds new types of responses to his "behavioral repertoire." The kinds of behaviors which can be learned through imitation seem to be quite extensive. One especially important behavior is aggression. Ethologists such as Konrad Lorenz regard aggression as an instinctive, natural reaction in man. Others feel aggression is the inevitable product of frustration. Learning theorists, however, believe aggression—or at least many aggressive responses—are learned through imitation in the same way as other behaviors are learned. During an experiment conducted by Albert Bandura, children saw human and cartoon figures act aggressively toward an inflated doll.[59] The children tended to reproduce exactly the aggressive behavior of the models. These responses did not occur in a control group which did not observe either model. In addition, still another group of children observed a nonaggressive model and these children imitated the nonaggressive play of this model. Through imitation, the authors think, children either learn various aggressive behaviors or will not be inhibited from displaying learned aggressive responses. As we will see later, imitative learning is used to explain aggression or violence in more realistic settings such as lynch mobs or riots.[60]

Of course, not every aspect of a model's behavior is or can be learned. The relationship of the model to the observer is also important. Warm, friendly relations facilitate imitative learning while cold, hostile, or authoritarian relations impede it. There is a great deal of evidence, for example, that child-rearing practices affect the learning process. Children in "nurturant" (i.e., warm, friendly) environments seem to imitate more readily than children in non-

---

[59] Albert Bandura, Dorothea Ross, and Sheila R. Ross, "Vicarious Reinforcement and Imitative Learning," *Journal of Abnormal and Social Psychology*, Vol. 6 (1963), pp. 601–7.

[60] See Miller and Dollard, *Social Learning and Imitation*, chap. 15. Also see Chapter 8 of this volume.

nurturant (i.e., cold, unfriendly) conditions.[61] Furthermore, the characteristics of the model, his status or prestige, for example, affect the extent to which it is imitated.

Conclusion: The Limits of Learning Theory

Before concluding, we should mention some criticisms of social learning theory. Critics feel that the theory is too simple, too mechanical, and too deterministic to explain all of human behavior. It places too much emphasis on reinforcement, not enough on cognitive development. By stressing stimulus-response mechanisms, it understates the role of choice and intellectual growth in learning.

In addition, there are numerous alternative explanations of socialization which are supported by considerable data. Perhaps the most widely known of these approaches are the developmental or stage theories, as typified by the work of the famous Swiss psychologist, Jean Piaget. These theories assume that social development occurs in a sequence of stages which are more or less discontinuous. Occurring in fixed order and at specific ages, these stages are not changeable in any fundamental way by training. Developmentalists, in other words, believe a child must pass through each stage in a given sequence, and his intellectual and moral growth is only marginally affected by reinforcement and imitation.[62] Whereas social learning theory emphasizes reinforcement schedules which may be affected by socioeconomic variables, stage theories assert that all children must pass through one stage before they progress to another.

An example from one of Piaget's works, *The Moral Judgment of the Child,* illustrates stage theory. A group of children are read two stories:

I.   A little boy who is called John is in his room. He is called to dinner. He goes into the dining room. But behind the door there was a chair, and on the chair there was a tray with 15 cups on it.

---

[61] Albert Bandura and Aletha C. Huston, "Identification as a Process of Incidental Learning," *Journal of Abnormal and Social Psychology,* Vol. 63 (1961), pp. 311–18. Also see Robert Lane, "Fathers and Sons: Foundations of Political Belief," *American Sociology Review,* Vol. 24 (1959), pp. 502–11 for a discussion of how the quality of family life affects socialization.

[62] See, for example, Jean Piaget, *The Moral Judgment of the Child,* trans. Marjorie Gabain (New York: The Free Press, 1965).

John couldn't have known that there was all this behind the door. He goes in, the door knocks against the tray, bang go the 15 cups and they all get broken.

II.   Once there was a little boy whose name was Henry. One day when his mother was out he tried to get some jam out of the cupboard. He climbed up on to a chair and stretched out his arm. But the jam was too high up and he couldn't reach it and have any. But while he was trying to get it he knocked over a cup. The cup fell down and broke.[63]

After hearing these stories the children were asked if John and Henry were equally guilty or which one was naughtiest. The seven- and eight-year-olds considered John guiltiest because he broke 15 cups. For these youngsters the intention behind the act did not matter as much as the amount of damage. John broke 15 cups to Henry's one so John is the naughtiest. Piaget terms this stage "objective responsibility" because an act is judged by the magnitude of the damage, not the willfulness of the act. At nine years and above children take intention into account. The older children believe Henry is more guilty since he was doing something he was not supposed to be doing. This stage in Piaget's terminology is "subjective responsibility."[64]

According to this particular theory, children pass from the objective to the subjective stage. They do not skip a stage, nor do they go from subjective to objective. Presumably, the cause of the change is maturation which alters a child's relationships to other people and hence his ability to see their point of view. More important though, he does not progress from one to the other stage as a result of training involving reinforcement and imitation. Thus, stage theories at least partly contradict learning theory.[65]

Apart from these types of substantive challenges, learning theory has been attacked for its normative implications. More precisely, many scholars abhor proposals for applying learning theory to mass behavior control. B. F. Skinner, for instance, contends that social

---

[63] Ibid., p. 122.

[64] Ibid., chap. 2.

[65] For example, using principles of imitation and learning theory, Albert Bandura and Frederick McDonald ("Influence of Social Reinforcement and the Behavior of Models in Shaping Children's Moral Judgments," *Journal of Abnormal and Social Psychology,* Vol. 67 [1963], pp. 274–81) have challenged Piaget's findings that moral development occurs in stages.

scientists know enough about conditioning to modify or eliminate all of man's worst behavioral traits.[66] He suggests establishing behavioral goals and developing reinforcement contingencies which will help attain these goals. Such behavioral modification programs are regularly practiced in society as in "child care, schools and the management of retardates and institutional psychotics."[67] Applying similar behavior-control technology to society as a whole can lead to an entirely new culture in which people live together peacefully and harmoniously, in which everyone's material needs are reasonably satisfied and in which each person can obtain maximum self-fulfillment.[68]

These are lofty goals. But will their attainment come at the expense of personal freedom and responsibility? Many think they will.[69] There is considerable reluctance to accept Skinnerian proposals for fear they will lead to the sort of societies described in Aldous Huxley's *Brave New World* and George Orwell's *1984*.

This leaves us with the eternal dilemma of knowledge. It gives the power to do both great good and evil. Learning theory, however, in all of its ramifications *is* sound social science. It helps us understand how people develop as they do. It can, for instance, tell us something as simple and yet as important as why children learn nationalism. But as with any body of knowledge it has to be pursued and applied within an ethical framework. It cannot by itself replace these values.

---

[66] B. F. Skinner, *Beyond Freedom and Dignity* (New York: Alfred A. Knopf, Inc., 1971). Also see his *Walden Two*, paperback ed. (New York: The Macmillan Co., 1962).

[67] Skinner, *Beyond Freedom and Dignity*, p. 142.

[68] Ibid., pp. 204–5.

[69] See, for example, the Review Symposium in the *American Journal of Sociology*, Vol. 78 (1972), especially the papers by Guy E. Swanson (pp. 702–5) and Bennett Berger (pp. 705–8).

4

The Effects of the Mass Media on
Political Attitudes and Behavior

Everyone knows that the mass media are a dominant force in modern society. Still, statistics about present-day communications systems are staggering. In the United States in the mid-1960s, for example, there were more than 70 million television sets (more than 3 sets for every 10 people) and more than 250 million radios (more than one receiver for every person in the country). Daily newspaper circulation exceeded 60 million. The proliferation of modern communications has also been experienced by other nations, as is indicated in Table 4.1.

The impact of television alone on society is incalculable. Its effects on the common man—how he lives and what he thinks—rival that of any technical advance of the last 100 years. According to a recent government report, the average television set in America is turned on for more than six hours a day. Many adults report watching television for at least two hours a day.[1] Their use of other forms

---

[1] *Television and Growing Up: The Impact of Televised Violence*, Report to the Surgeon General, U.S. Public Health Service (Washington, D.C.: U.S. Government Printing Office, 1972), p. 2.

of communications—newspapers, radio, magazines, books, and movies—is also extraordinarily high. We live in an era of truly mass communications.

Table 4.1
THE USE OF THE MASS MEDIA IN SIX DEMOCRACIES

	Newspapers per 1,000 Population	Radios per 1,000 Population	Television Sets per 1,000 Population
United States	310	1,234	317
Canada	218	519	270
United Kingdom ...	479	297	248
France	246	313	131
West Germany	326	440	193
Australia	373	222	172

Source: Charles L. Taylor and Michael C. Hudson, *World Handbook of Political and Social Indicators II*. (See Appendix.)

Nor has the widespread dependence on the media been confined to the developed countries. Radio and television are central to the social, political, economic, and cultural life of most nations. The development of modern communications, like the emergence of industrialization or the discovery of nuclear energy, has profoundly transformed the world.

It is also common knowledge that the media have an enormous impact on politics. They can, of course, directly affect a government —as the press did with its revelations about the Watergate affair. More interesting, however, is the relationship of the media to public opinion and political behavior. It is easy to see the extent of this linkage by looking at the magnitude of political advertising.

In 1968, campaign spending by both parties at all levels exceeded $300 million. The lion's share of this amount was spent on advertising. Broadcast expenditures, for example, totaled more than $58 million, not including millions more for production costs.[2] Newspaper and magazine ads cost another $20 million, and more than $50 million was spent on novelties such as buttons, stickers, and posters.[3] The two major presidential candidates, Nixon and Humphrey,

---

[2] Herbert E. Alexander, *Money in Politics* (Washington, D.C.: Public Affairs Press, 1972), p. 32.

[3] Ibid., pp. 31–32.

alone spent over $16 million on broadcasting.[4] But the media costs of congressional and state and local campaigns are also enormous. Robert Kennedy's presidential primary efforts cost about $2 million;[5] Nelson Rockefeller, Governer of New York, reportedly spent over $6 million in his 1970 reelection campaign, while John Lindsay's mayoralty campaign exceeded $3 million.[6] Most of this money went directly or indirectly for the use of the mass media. Although at first glance prices may seem prohibitive—a single two-page ad in a national magazine may cost over $100,000—campaigners seem ready, even eager to pay them.

Yet these amounts represent only part of the effort to influence political attitudes and behavior. Most governmental agencies maintain public relations staffs and spend millions of dollars to publicize and justify their programs. Likewise, hundreds of private interest groups conduct expensive publicity campaigns trying to create support for or against various public policies.

Resorting to mass communications for political goals is not limited to democracies. In totalitarian regimes the media are controlled in an effort to instill obedience and conformity in the populace. Governments in developing nations employ radio and television both as a means of spreading education and technical innovations and as a way of creating a sense of national identity and common purpose.

The existence of vast and sophisticated communications networks and their utilization for political ends immediately raises the question of their effects on individual attitudes and behavior. How and to what extent are people influenced by the media? Can propagandists create and manipulate public opinion? Can public relations firms package and sell candidates the same as they package and sell toothpaste and deodorant? Are radio and television ready-made tools for ruthless despots bent on controlling men's minds? What are the long-range consequences of the mass media on social and political behavior?

These are the types of questions we address in this chapter. Although we cannot answer them completely, we have enough data

---

[4] Ibid.

[5] Herbert E. Alexander, *Financing the 1968 Election* (Lexington, Mass.: Heath Lexington Books, 1971), p. 94.

[6] Alexander, *Money in Politics,* pp. 30–31.

to supply some tentative answers. At the least, we can dispel some popular misconceptions about the mass media and put their effects in proper perspective. As we shall see, the media probably do not have the power commonly attributed to them, but nevertheless they have some ominous consequences.

MODELS OF MEDIA INFLUENCE

Direct Effects Model

Given the pervasiveness of the media and the prodigious amount of money, time, and effort invested in them by political leaders, one would suppose that mass communication would be extremely powerful in forming and shaping attitudes and behavior. Indeed, many observers share the feeling that anyone with enough resources and ingenuity can easily manipulate public opinion on almost any issue. This is an especially prevalent view of political campaigning. According to conventional wisdom big money spenders and electronic image-makers win elections just about every time. The same concern —a fear that people are easily manipulated—lies behind claims that the mass media are biased or that the government is managing the news. George Orwell's *1984* expresses, perhaps, the most extreme statement of these apprehensions.

Assertions regarding the omnipotence of mass communications rest on several assumptions about human nature. Many analysts see the individual as essentially a pawn, a hapless fellow who can be led hither and yon at the whims of the public relations men. Instead of relying on his own intellect, he is dominated by Madison Avenue images. To sell something, all that one needs is to package the product—whether it be a candidate, an issue position, or a can of beer—and it can be foisted off on the defenseless public. Many authors such as Vance Packard[7] have popularized the idea, but Leonard Hall, former Republican national chairman, summarized it most succinctly: "You sell your candidates and your programs the way a business sells its products."[8]

---

[7] Vance Packard, *The Hidden Persuaders* (New York: David McKay Co., Inc., 1955).

[8] Quoted in Joe McGinniss, *The Selling of the President 1968* (New York: Trident Press, 1969), p. 27. A similar expression of this view is "I think of a man

For a time social scientists supported this popular view, although they did so in more formal and scientific terms. Borrowing from early psychological concepts, they explained the relationship between individuals and the media in the language of *stimulus-response* theory. The mass media, it was believed, emitted stimuli (e.g., political commercials) which were uniformly received by the public and which produced a more or less common and predictable response. These theorists, in other words, believed that people had similar psychological dispositions and would respond in roughly the same way to a message. Consequently, they feared that the public could be swayed by those in control of the media.[9]

Figure 4.1 depicts this theory, called the Direct Effects of Mass Communications model, since the media are shown to act directly

Figure 4.1
DIRECT EFFECTS MODEL OF MASS COMMUNICATIONS

on the individual. As should be apparent, this thinking is implicit in many popularized discussions and studies of the mass media mentioned above.

A Filter Model of the Mass Media

In the 1940s, however, the theory of direct effects was called into question by several researchers who found that not all people respond to communications in the same manner. Paul Lazarsfeld and his associates uncovered some of the most interesting evidence. Their study, *The People's Choice*—now considered a classic in

---

in a voting booth who hesitates between two levers as if he were passing between competing tubes of toothpaste in a drugstore. The brand that has made the highest penetration in his brain will win his choice." Rossen Reeves as quoted in Jules Abels, *The Degeneration of Our Presidential Election* (New York: The Macmillan Co., 1968), p. 57.

[9] Melvin L. DeFleur, *Theories of Mass Communications* 2d ed. (David McKay Co., Inc., 1970), p. 16.

survey research—had, among others, two objectives: the first was to find out how voters made up their minds about candidates during an election period, and the second was to assess how much influence campaigning (particularly mass advertising) had on their decisions.[10] What their study turned up was startling.

In the first place, voters had well-defined party and candidate preferences and tended to decide long before the campaigns ever started how they were going to vote. Moreover, once they decided, very few of them could be persuaded to switch their positions.[11] Even more significant, it appeared to the authors that *interpersonal* communications exerted more power in shaping and changing opinions than did the mass media.[12] As a matter of fact, relatively few changes could be traced to the media themselves. Finally, *The People's Choice* concluded that the direction of a person's choice could more accurately be predicted from knowledge of his socioeconomic characteristics than from the short-term effects of the election campaign.[13]

As we will see, these findings have been echoed—with some modifications—in a wide variety of books and articles. Consequently, social scientists have gradually come to discard the Direct Effects model. In its place, they have substituted one which while appearing only slightly more complicated puts the effects of the mass media in an entirely new light. The basic concept of the new theory is that messages flowing along communications channels do not directly and uniformly impinge on all members of society but are rather *filtered* or *mediated* by a series of personal and group processes. The processes shield or screen the individual from direct exposure to the media.

Logically enough, this theory is called the Filter Model of Mass Communications, and its essential features appear in Figure 4.2.

The filter consists of several related components. An individual's personality itself partly determines how he will respond to commu-

---

[10] Paul F. Lazarsfeld, Bernard Berelson, and Hazel Gaudet, *The People's Choice* (3d ed.; New York: Columbia University Press, 1968), chap. i.

[11] Ibid., chap. x. A good discussion of *The People's Choice* is Peter Rossi's, "Four Landmarks in Voting Research," *American Voting Behavior,* ed. Eugene Burdick and Arthur J. Brodbeck (Glencoe, Ill.: The Free Press, 1959), pp. 5–54.

[12] Lazarsfeld et al., *The People's Choice,* chaps. xv and xvi.

[13] Ibid., pp. 25–27.

Figure 4.2
FILTER MODEL OF MASS COMMUNICATIONS

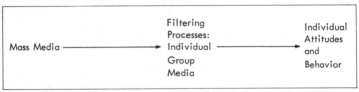

nications. To the extent that there is variation in personalities, the responses to the media will vary. Since people differ among themselves in terms of their interests, needs, drives, and other psychological traits, it is essential to take individual characteristics into account in assessing the effects of mass communications. No less important are group characteristics. Man is a social animal and his social environment influences how he responds to stimuli. In order to gauge the effects of the media one must understand group processes. Finally, the mass media themselves have properties which affect people's responses to them. Each of these components—individual, group, and media characteristics—will be considered in turn.

This approach, which is based on an extremely large amount of research, implies that the mediating factors act in much the same way a filter works on a camera: they screen out some messages, emphasize others, and distort still others. Naturally, the filters have a bearing on how and to what extent mass media affect personal attitudes and behavior.

THE FILTERING PROCESSES

Consider a typical English voter:

> Imagine a hypothetical elector, Mrs. Appleyard. She has voted before and she knows which party she intends to support at the General Election, which is announced for a month hence. There is a television set at home. The old radio set, which is now set up in the kitchen so that Mrs. Appleyard can occasionally switch on to some music while she works, is usually heard by the whole family round about breakfast time. During the election campaign, Mrs. Appleyard hears members of her family talking about the candidates, and there is an occasional argument between her husband and their eldest son as to whether they are "having it good" or not.

They all saw the first two Party election broadcasts and two or three others, though they did not make any special plans to do so. The set was switched on and there was nothing else to see. They also heard news of what the big speakers were saying, on the radio and in the television news. Election addresses came through the letterbox. Mrs. Appleyard glanced over the front pages and left them on the mantlepiece for her husband to read. He, too, glanced over them, but they were swept away with the unwanted newspapers at the end of the week. One day, Mrs. Appleyard heard a loudspeaker van in the street. She stopped to hear a few sentences but was in too much of a hurry to wait for long. The morning newspaper was full of politics. Sometimes she would pick it up between jobs and read a few paragraphs. "They all talk too much," was her usual comment, or "full of promises when they want your vote." Canvassers called one evening, when she was getting tea ready, and the youngest boy was watching a television serial. She would not stop to say much to them, though she did say she thought the old age pensioners, like her father, should get a bit more money. Two of their closest neighbours had posters up at their windows but the Appleyards had never been asked and they would not have put one up even if they had been asked. The children were having a mock election at school and her daughter asked her what the liberals stood for that the other parties did not. She told her to ask her older brother who had been to a political meeting the night before. When Polling Day came along, Mrs. Appleyard went on with her daily round of duties, much as she had always done. She voted, with her husband, as she had intended, and as far as she was concerned the business was over for a few more years.[14]

From the sound of it, Mrs. Appleyard behaves much like the typical voter in the United States, or, indeed, in any democracy. She seems to have a modest interest in politics and on polling day she fulfills her civic duty by voting. What interests us at the moment, however, is her reaction to the campaign. Quite obviously Mrs. Appleyard was not under the thumb of the media. Indeed, she appeared impervious to most of the persuasive appeals being made to her. How can we account for this reaction and what does it tell us about the effects of mass communications? Let us start by de-

---

[14] Joseph Trenaman and Denis McQuail, *Television and the Political Image* (London: Methuen & Co., Ltd., 1961), pp. 182–83.

scribing some individual characteristics which filter the flow of information from the media.

Individual Characteristics

Selective Exposure.   In the first place, Mrs. Appleyard did not receive all of the messages directed toward her. She paid cursory attention to a few and disregarded the rest. While we cannot be sure, it is likely that she especially tended to ignore propaganda emanating from the party she did not favor. This proclivity illustrates the principle of selective exposure: people are selective in what they read, see, and hear, and they are particularly disposed to screen out or avoid messages which contradict their own attitudes. It is, as it were, a defense mechanism.

In many cases the selective exposure is motivated by a lack of interest; in others it is produced by a conscious or unconscious desire to maintain the integrity of one's own views in the face of hostile information. Hence, Republicans do not usually attend Democratic rallies while Democrats normally avoid listening to Republican candidates.

The principle of selective exposure, widely accepted by political scientists, seems to operate in most political settings.[15] Furthermore, this principle is compatible with the consistency theories discussed in Chapter 2 which suggest that people try to avoid threatening or unpleasant information. Yet selective exposure is not absolute.

In the first place, one cannot always avoid contradictory ideas or opinions. And, as William McGuire points out, it is not practical to do so, for how can humans learn and advance unless they are willing to face new and challenging beliefs?[16] There is also abundant evidence that people intentionally or unintentionally expose themselves to contradictory messages.[17] It is easier, for example, to be

---

[15] Joseph T. Klapper, *The Effects of Mass Communication* (Glencoe, Ill.: The Free Press, 1960), pp. 19–21; and Bernard R. Berelson, Paul F. Lazarsfeld, and William N. McPhee, *Voting* (Phoenix ed.; Chicago: University of Chicago Press, 1966) pp. 240–51.

[16] William J. McGuire, "The Nature of Attitudes and Attitude Change," *The Handbook of Social Psychology*, Vol. 3, ed. Gardner Lindzey and Elliot Aronson, 2d ed. (Reading, Mass.: Addison-Wesley Publishing Co., 1969), pp. 218–21.

[17] Ibid., p. 221; and Walter Weiss, "Effects of the Mass Media of Communi-

selective with printed material than with radio, television, or outdoor advertising. Tuning out a 30-second spot commercial in the middle of one's favorite television comedy is harder than ignoring an ad in a newspaper. Thus, although selective exposure acts as a filtering mechanism, it does not totally explain a person's reactions to mass communications.

Selective Perception and Retention. It may not be evident from Mrs. Appleyard's reactions, but individuals frequently read their own meanings into what they see and hear. People have, in short, a tendency to selectively perceive and remember in a way which is congruent with their existing attitudes.

Studies of rumor transmission dramatically illustrate this principle. In a laboratory study conducted by Gordon Allport and Leo Passman, one of several subjects was shown a picture of a white man holding a razor and having an argument with a black man.[18] The subject was asked to describe what he saw to another subject who had not seen the picture. The latter individual was in turn requested to describe the picture to still another subject and the process was continued until the picture had been described to all of the subjects. In more than half the cases there was a tendency to reverse the roles of the attacker and victim. That is, at some point in the interpersonal transmission of information an individual distorts what he has been told to fit his preconceptions: in this case, that blacks, not whites, carry razors.[19] Social scientists use this type of experiment as evidence that men and women often consciously or unconsciously adjust their memory and perceptions to be congruent with their wishes, motives, stereotypes, and attitudes.

The upshot is that even the most cleverly designed and executed advertising campaign, because of misconstrued messages, may fail to convince and convert hostile opinions. In other words, ". . . individuals use propaganda for their own purpose, not for the propagandist's."[20] This psychological tendency blunts the effects of

cation," *The Handbook of Social Psychology,* Vol. 5, ed. Gardner Lindzey and Elliot Aronson, 2d ed. (Reading, Mass.: Addison-Wesley Publishing Co., 1969), pp. 87–89.

[18] Quoted from Ralph K. White, *Nobody Wanted War: Misperception in Vietnam and Other Wars* (Anchor Books ed.; Garden City, N.Y.: Doubleday & Co., Inc., 1970), pp. 262–64.

[19] Ibid., p. 263.

[20] Trenaman and McQuail, *Television and the Political Image,* pp. 152–53.

persuasive communications because the messages are simply distorted or ignored and hence fail to persuade. In short, people see
what they want to see.

Intellectual Ability.   In general, someone's susceptibility to persuasion depends on several conditions, among them his attention,
comprehension, and retention of the message's arguments.[21] Obviously, a person's intelligence affects these conditions and hence
how malleable his opinions and behavior are. Although it is difficult
to generalize because other personality variables influence the relationship (see the following section), intelligence both hinders *and*
facilitates persuasion. An intelligent person may be hard to convince
since he can detect *non sequiturs,* unfounded generalizations, and
emotionalism; he is better equipped to judge the adequacy of a
message's arguments. On the other hand, someone with lower intelligence may miss the point of a persuasive communication.[22] A
political advertisement appealing to the intellectual community
may be beyond the comprehension of other groups. So intelligence
is certainly related to susceptibility, but the relationship is quite
complex.

What implications can be drawn from these remarks? Obviously
what "works" on Mrs. Appleyard may not do as well when applied
to a person of higher or lower intelligence. So it is often difficult to
develop general-purpose appeals which, instead, must be geared to
specific audiences. In this sense (and in this sense only) it may be
misleading to berate demagogues who "oversimplify" issues and
inflame emotions. Doing so probably makes them more effective
speakers, given the education of the groups they face. Of course, this
is not to assert that the level of the political discourse cannot be
elevated. The point is simply that communications must be adapted
to particular audiences. Another implication then is that from the
standpoint of converting people, politicians may tend to intellec-
tualize issues too much when speaking to people with low levels of
formal education.

Personality Factors.   The description of Mrs. Appleyard reveals a
noticeable attribute: she seems to be hard to convince. Some psy-

---

[21] McGuire, "Nature of Attitudes and Attitude Changes," p. 243.

[22] Carl I. Hovland, Irving L. Janis, and Harold H. Kelly, *Communication
and Persuasion* (New Haven, Conn.: Yale University Press, 1953), p. 183.

chologists believe that for one reason or another some people are more readily persuaded than others—regardless of the type of communication source or its message. "Influenceability," they believe, is a general personality trait. On the basis of one study, Carl Hovland and his associates find that those who are easily influenced tend to have feelings of personal inadequacy. Lacking self-confidence and needing social approval, these people yield to persuasive arguments in order to gain acceptance.[23] Among the factors producing susceptibility to persuasive appeals are low self-esteem, shyness, and passivity. Apparently, individuals who lack confidence and a sense of personal adequacy are not as sure of their opinions and are not as willing to stand up for them as those with more self-confidence. Or they may be more afraid of disapproval from friends and neighbors.

Conversely, one can find other variables related to low persuasiveness. Generally, certain personality attributes and social situations interfere with or inhibit the learning of a message, thereby making them less acceptable. A person manifesting high overt aggression toward others, for instance, simply does not receive and evaluate communications in the same way as someone with less aggressive tendencies.[24]

It is not possible in this book to develop a general theory of the relationship between personality and persuasion. The linkages are too numerous and complex.

In any event, the lesson to be learned is simply that individuals are not blank slates upon which any belief or idea can be written. On the contrary, people are motivated by complicated psychological drives. To the degree that the motives vary there will be variable responses to external stimuli. Personality then acts as a filter or screen, making it difficult to achieve a common response from a single media campaign.

Group Characteristics

Men exist as part of social groups and these groups exert pressures on their opinions and behavior. A person's homogeneous face-to-face contacts—his family, peer groups, co-workers, and neigh-

---

[23] Ibid., pp. 184–92.
[24] Ibid., pp. 192–95.

bors—tend to induce conformity to commonly held values. To see the extent of the group pressure to conform and how it works, consider the following experiment.

Solomon Asch requested the members of a small group to match the length of a given line with one of three unequal lines.[25] In every trial there was, objectively speaking, a correct answer. Each person publicly stated his judgment as to which of the three lines matched the given line. All of the members of the group except one were accomplices of the experimenter who had asked them to give incorrect answers. Thus, the one naïve subject, who was a "minority of one," found himself in a dilemma: His choice of the correct line was consistently and unanimously challenged by the majority. In this situation, the subject could either stick to his judgment or abandon it in favor of the majority's incorrect answer.

Although most subjects in these experiments gave correct answers in spite of the majority, surprisingly one third of them made errors "identical with or in the same direction of the distorted estimates of the majority."[26] Experiments such as Asch's show that small groups exert pressure on an individual to conform to the group's standards and opinions.

It is worth pausing to explore the conditions which facilitate or maximize a group's influence. One of the most important factors is the salience or importance of the group to the individual. For most people, the family is the most significant social unit and its impact on attitudes is quite large. Whatever a man reads in the evening newspaper is not likely to sway his opinions if the message is at odds with his family's values and preferences. Similarly, to the extent that a group is small and cohesive, that its members share the same goals, that its norms are clear, that the individuals feel a need to belong, and that it can punish deviance, the group will be effective in producing conformity to its standards.[27]

---

[25] Solomon E. Asch, "Effects of Group Pressure upon the Modification and Distortion of Judgments," *Group Dynamics,* ed. Dorwin Cartwright and Alvin Zander, 2d ed. (New York: Harper & Row, Publishers, 1960), p. 191.

[26] Ibid., p. 191.

[27] Dorwin Cartwright and Alvin Zander, "Group Pressures and Group Standards: Introduction," *Group Dynamics,* ed. Dorwin Cartwright and Alvin Zander, 2d ed. (New York: Harper & Row, Publishers, 1960), pp. 174–76; Robert E. Lane and David O. Sears, *Public Opinion* (Englewood Cliffs, N.J.: Prentice-Hall, Inc., 1964), pp. 35–39.

Also important is the certainty of the individual's opinions. In many instances, a person can test the validity of his beliefs by reference to an external criterion such as a physical scale. Political and social judgments, however, are often hard to validate empirically or objectively. A person may therefore have to rely on others opinions to reinforce his own, which means that his perception of social or political reality depends on what his family, friends or neighbors think. In this manner, he comes under their influence.[28] Therefore, how confident one is in his beliefs partly determines his susceptibility to group pressures to conform.

These ideas suggest the advantages and limitations of the mass media. It is important to remember that such communications work in conjunction with rather than in spite of one's group memberships. If persuasive appeals which come from the media are formulated in a way that makes them seem consistent with or supportive of group norms which the individual accepts, then the messages will tend to be seen as acceptable and convincing, and the group may in fact reinforce the appeals. On the other hand, if the messages appear to counter group values and expectations, the individual is less likely to accept them.

We can see the importance of group attachments by examining the interplay of interpersonal and formal communications in underdeveloped nations. One formidable task facing political leaders in new nations is to break down tribal or parochial allegiances and to instill in the citizens a sense of national loyalty and common purpose. An obvious method for accomplishing this goal is to use the mass media to transmit cues (e.g., political symbols and slogans) which will encourage people to identify with the nation as a whole. Consequently, the mass media in many underdeveloped countries are dominated in one way or another by patriotic and nationalistic themes. The difficulty, however, comes in reaching the individual in "the bush" who may have very close and abiding ties with tribal or kinship groups. Very often his group's norms require him to give allegiance to local chiefs rather than to the capitol. Since group standards are normally quite strong, the messages coming from the central government fall on deaf ears, meaning the individual still

---

[28] Leon Festinger, "Informal Social Communication," *Group Dynamics,* ed. Dorwin Cartwright and Alvin Zander, 2d ed. (New York: Harper & Row, Publishers, 1960), pp. 287–89.

retains his childhood loyalties even in the face of massive nation-building campaigns. This situation explains in part why creating political consensus and stability in underdeveloped areas is a long and arduous process. It also underscores the general point that the group bonds act as a mediating force.

The Two-Step Flow of Communications Hypothesis. Until now the media and the group have been described as contenders for the attention of the individual. Actually, the connections are more complicated. Not only are a person's group loyalties a source of potential conflict with the media, but, paradoxically, mass communications also *operate primarily through interpersonal contact.* This interpretation, originally proposed by Lazarsfeld and his colleagues, is called the two-step flow of communications hypothesis.[29]

The two-step flow idea is simple: Information flowing from the media is not received directly by the individual himself but is instead relayed to him by various opinion leaders or opinion influentials. Both terms, leaders and influentials, may be misnomers since most of them merely act as conduits for information and are often not "influential" in the usual sense of the word. (This idea will become clearer in a moment.) Opinion leaders are simply people who happen to pay slightly more attention to the media than their friends do. The hypothesis asserts that we tend to learn about the content of the media from personal sources rather than from the media themselves.

One good way to see this is to note how people first learn of important events and issues. In many cases they hear about them from personal contacts. Paul Sheatsley and Jacob Feldman give a good example of this phenomenon. President Kennedy was shot about 12:30 P.M. By the time he died 30 minutes later, two thirds of all adult Americans had heard of the assassination and within two hours 92 percent of the public was aware of what had happened. How did the news travel so rapidly? About half of the people heard of it directly from the media, but the other half received the news indirectly via interpersonal contacts.[30]

---

[29] Lazarsfeld et al., *The People's Choice,* pp. 151–52.

[30] Paul B. Sheatsley and Jacob J. Feldman, "The Assassination of President Kennedy: A Preliminary Report on Public Reactions and Behavior," *Readings in Collective Behavior,* ed. Robert R. Evans (Chicago: Rand McNally & Co., 1969), pp. 261–62.

This example dramatically illustrates the principle that much of what we receive from the media comes not from the media themselves, but from someone's interpretation of it. In passing information along, opinion leaders certainly modify it to some extent. How much distortion occurs depends on innumerable factors, but it is unlikely we ever receive a totally "unbiased" account. This in turn means that the effectiveness of persuasive messages coming from the media is, potentially at least, limited at the outset. In view of the role of opinion leaders as filters in the communications process, it is difficult for anyone to manipulate opinions and behavior solely by relying on mass media.

The two-step flow principle which has received wide support, is diagrammed in Figure 4.3[31]

Figure 4.3
THE TWO-STEP FLOW OF COMMUNICATIONS PRINCIPLE

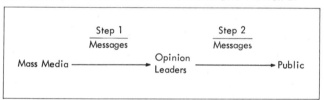

In order to understand fully the two-step flow idea, let us clarify the characteristics and role of the opinion leaders. These individuals should not be confused with "opinion elites" (e.g., journalists, editors, public officials). Opinion leaders come from all walks of life and are found in all social strata. They have the same attributes as the people they influence; that is, they are usually of the same age, occupation, race, and social class, although they may be slightly more educated and informed. What distinguishes opinion leaders is their interest in the subject matter. They tend to be somewhat more attuned to the media, at least in matters of interest to them.

The last sentence raises another point. Although there is some

[31] Lazarsfeld et al., *The People's Choice,* chap. xvi; Elihu Katz and Paul F. Lazarsfeld, *Personal Influence* (Glencoe, Ill.: The Free Press, 1955); Elihu Katz "The Two-Step Flow of Communication: An Up-to-Date Report on an Hypothesis," *Public Opinion Quarterly,* Vol. 21 (1957), pp. 61–78; and Berelson et al., *Voting,* chap. vi.

debate on the question, it appears that personal influence does not "generalize." For instance, a person who acts as an opinion leader on one topic is probably a follower in other areas. The example of Mrs. Appleyard is instructive. She probably takes the lead in household affairs but on political questions she defers to others, even to her sons. In the Appleyard home the husband or perhaps the eldest son serves as the opinion leader, if there is one. This observation calls attention to the fact that at any given time there are thousands and thousands of opinion leaders, the number depending on the specific topic. Finally, it is not always clear whether the leaders actively seek to transmit information. Some of them are sought out by others for their news and advice, while others take the initiative themselves in supplying information.[32]

In summary, we have seen how an individual's group memberships and personal contacts function to filter or mediate communications coming from the mass media. One's social attachments do not necessarily preclude the media from having a pronounced effect on his behavior and attitudes. What should be evident, though, is that these elements—the individual, the group, and the media—are linked by extremely complicated bonds.

Media Characteristics

So far mass communications have been described almost as if they were an undifferentiated, monolithic force. Obviously this conclusion is hardly warranted because the media and the uses made of them vary considerably. Consequently, in order to understand their effects we have to pay attention to how and under what conditions messages are formed and transmitted.

Characteristics of the Message.   Most of the research in the area of media characteristics deals with persuasive communications, or appeals designed specifically to alter someone's opinions or behavior. The goal of this research has been to determine what factors in the message produce changes in attitudes. Inasmuch as there has been an incredible amount of work done on the topic we can only scratch the surface by listing some of the major variables and results. Also, it is hard to make generalizations because these studies have produced a bewildering number of perplexing and contradictory find-

---

[32] Weiss, "Effects of the Mass Media," pp. 145–46.

ings. Still, the following propositions and variables may give an insight into what constitutes effective communications and propaganda.

Fear-Arousing Communications. On a priori grounds one might predict that "among the various types of assertions that are likely to have a motivating effect on an audience are those which predict, explicitly or implicitly, that by adopting the communicator's recommendations one can avoid social disapproval or avert some form of physical danger or deprivation."[33] In other words, if one first arouses anxiety in the audience and then assuages it by offering some recommendations (the persuasive message), then one might expect the communication to be acceptable and convincing.

Yet several investigators find that fear-arousing appeals are not as effective as other types and sometimes create the opposite effect.[34] In an effort to persuade people of the dangers of smoking and to convince them to obtain a chest X ray, Harold Leventhal and Jean Watts used films containing different levels of fear-arousing appeals.[35] One movie, the low fear stimulus, consisted mainly of charts and statistics showing the connection between smoking and lung cancer. Another film, designed to produce a higher level of fear, depicted an actual lung cancer operation including explicit scenes of the diseased lung and the open chest cavity.[36] Surprisingly, those subjects seeing the high fear-arousing movie were no more likely and in some cases even less likely to get a chest X-ray or to try to quit smoking. Fear arousal, then, can under certain conditions have a boomerang effect. Apparently creating tension in individuals causes them to avoid the message by ignoring or minimizing the threat. Politicians frequently resort to the technique of predicting dire consequences if they or their policies are not accepted. In view of the research cited above, this practice may be counterproductive.

---

[33] Hovland et al., *Communication and Persuasion,* p. 60.

[34] Ibid., chap. iii; Irving L. Janis and S. Feshbach, "Effects of Fear-Arousing Communication," *Journal of Abnormal and Social Psychology,* Vol. 48 (1953), pp. 78–92; and Irving L. Janis and R. Terwilliger, "An Experimental Study of Psychological Resistance to Fear-Arousing Communications," *Journal of Abnormal and Social Psychology,* Vol. 65 (1962), pp. 403–10.

[35] Harold Leventhal and Jean Watts, "Sources of Resistance to Fear-Arousing Communications on Smoking and Lung Cancer," *Journal of Personality,* Vol. 34 (1966), pp. 155–75.

[36] Ibid., pp. 159–60.

The Amount of Change Advocated.   In general, the more unlike or distant a communication is from one's own position the more likely he will perceive it as "less fair, less informed, less logical, less grammatical, less interesting" and so forth.[37] This generalization in turn implies that the more discrepant the message is the less likely it will be believed and accepted. So in order to be persuasive, communications cannot advocate too much change. Trying to convince a dyed-in-the-wool conservative Republican to vote for George Mc-Govern would in most instances be futile. On the other hand, if a message is to have any effect it should not be too similar to the receiver's attitude, unless the goal is simply to reinforce that attitude. The most effective communication advocates an intermediate amount of change.[38]

This line of reasoning also shows why a political party is usually unsuccessful when it attempts to canvass in the opposition's areas of greatest strength. The amount of attitudinal change is too large for it to succeed.

Stating the Conclusion.   Some attitude research deals with the question of whether a message should explicitly state a conclusion or leave it for each person to draw. Probably if an individual arrives at the conclusion on his own he will be more likely to be persuaded. After all, it is something he has done for himself. The snag is that in most natural settings the point of the communication may be lost unless it is explicitly stated because the receiver may be insufficiently motivated or intelligent to arrive at the intended inference. So in sum, it seems preferable to state the conclusion,[39] although this idea is often ignored in many political ads which are so subtle and sophisticated that their meaning may be beyond the comprehension of the disinterested observer.

One-Sided or Two-Sided Communications.   There is some debate about the effectiveness of mentioning the opponent's arguments in a persuasive communication. Intuition suggests the dangers of including the opposition's ideas. Although doing so might establish the communicator's credibility, it also alerts the receiver to the con-

---

[37] McGuire, "Nature of Attitudes and Attitude Changes," p. 221.

[38] Carolyn W. Sherif, Muzafer Sherif, and Roger E. Nebergall, *Attitude and Attitude Change* (Philadelphia: W. B. Saunders Co., 1965), chap. ii.

[39] McGuire, "Nature of Attitudes and Attitude Changes," pp. 208–9.

troversial nature of the issue.[40] It may also inadvertently call attention to strongpoints in the opponent's position.

These notions are often reflected in practice. An incumbent or a widely known candidate usually avoids even mentioning the other candidate's name for fear of unintentionally giving him exposure. President Nixon's 1972 presidential campaign was partly organized around this principle.

Attitude research indicates, however, that in many practical situations mentioning or ignoring contradictory arguments are about equally effective in producing attitude change. The most successful approach depends on numerous situational variables.[41]

Order of Presentation. Finally, considerable effort has been spent investigating the comparative benefits of "primacy effects" (that is, having the first say) versus "recency effects" (that is, getting the last word in).[42] Since first impressions seem compelling it seems plausible that the first argument a person hears will weigh more heavily on his judgment than will subsequent arguments. This is true because the first argument does not have to compete with other points of view. As with the previous considerations, though, the actual situation is not so simple. It appears that at times primacy effects are operative while at other times recency effects are more important. For example, if familiarity with a topic is low a recency effect is likely because the last information presented to a person will be fresh in his mind. But if he is already familiar with the subject, the first argument mention rather than the second will have the most impact on his attitudes.[43]

As with the previous generalizations, it is impossible to state a simple proposition regarding primacy versus recency effects. The point of discussing message characteristics is to demonstrate the difficulty of manipulating the media. The difficulty arises from the

---

[40] Ibid., p. 211.

[41] Ibid., p. 210.

[42] The most extended treatment of this topic is Carl I. Hovland et al., *The Order of Presentation in Persuasion* (New Haven, Conn.: Yale University Press, 1957). Also see William J. McGuire, "Attitudes and Opinions," *Annual Review of Psychology*, Vol. 17 (1966), pp. 475–514.

[43] Robert Lana, "Three Theoretical Interpretations of Order Effects in Persuasive Communications," *Psychological Bulletin*, Vol. 61 (1964), pp. 314–20. This conclusion, like the others, depends on numerous conditions and is thus difficult to generalize.

fact that what is effective in one situation will not necessarily be so in another. An individual's response to a particular message rests on dozens of factors and is therefore very difficult to predict. For example, it might be advisable for a candidate to begin his campaign before his opponent does in order to achieve a primacy effect. But this approach could backfire under certain conditions. And furthermore, his gains are apt to be marginal. Developing effective propaganda is not an easy matter, and one is never sure if it will be successful. Selling a candidate as if he were a tube of toothpaste is more a dream than a reality.

This is not to say advertising and propaganda do not have an impact on attitudes and behavior but only that the short-term and intended consequences are easily exaggerated. The long-range and unintended effects may indeed be profound, as we will see shortly.

The Nature of the Communicator. The most important factors affecting a communicator's effectiveness are his credibility and attractiveness.[44] (The term "communicator," of course, refers to both individuals and organizations such as a newspaper or television network.) We would logically anticipate that the higher the communicator's credibility with his (its) audience, the larger will be the changes in opinions and behavior. With some exceptions this expectation seems to hold water.[45] Credibility is established among other things by having expertise, stature, popularity, objectivity, and known reliability.

Although it may seem unnecessary to turn to laboratory experiments to prove the point—after all, everyone knows that a white tenant farmer in Mississippi is not going to put much credence in what the *New York Times* says about school integration—source credibility has been found to be an extremely important and complex variable in the study of persuasive communications and enormous energy has gone into studying its nuances.

Similarly, the communicator's attractiveness to the receiver enhances his persuasiveness. Part of this attraction is similarity of attitudes and outlooks. McGuire writes, for example, "There is a considerable body of evidence that a person is influenced by a persuasive message to the extent that he perceives it as coming from

---

[44] McGuire, "Nature of Attitudes and Attitude Changes," pp. 178–94.
[45] Hovland et al., *Communication and Persuasion,* chap. ii.

a source similar to himself."[46] A newspaper reflecting a community's style and values is more believable and presumably more effective than, say, a nationally known magazine. In this vein it is obvious that the greater the familiarity with and liking of the source, the more persuasive it is.

The Nature of Media. At this point we should interject a word regarding differences in the media themselves. As one might expect, some channels of communication are more popular than others. In the United States and Britain, at least, most people claim television as their primary source of political information, with newspapers, radio, and magazines trailing behind. (See Table 4.2.) David Butler and Donald Stokes show that television is the preferred medium in Britain: 65 percent of their sample reported that they used television more than newspapers and only 28 percent relied more on newspapers.[47] The popularity of television as a news source is especially pronounced among low-income families.[48]

This fact is significant because television is necessarily more non-partisan than are the printed media. In fact, many observers feel that television is too limited and bland to be of much use to the public in trying to understand politics. This is true even of newscasts and news specials which in their attempts to be neutral and objective

Table 4.2
TELEVISION, NEWSPAPERS, RADIO, AND MAGAZINES AS SOURCES OF INFORMATION ABOUT THE 1972 ELECTION CAMPAIGNS

Did Respondent Follow the Campaign in a Particular Medium?	*Television*	*Newspapers*	*Radio*	*Magazines*
Yes	88%	57%	43%	33%
No	12	43	57	67
	100%	100%	100%	100%
	(1,116)	(1,115)	(1,116)	(1,117)

Note: Figures in parentheses refer to the number of cases.
Source: *CPS 1972 American National Election Study.* (See Appendix.)

---

[46] McGuire, "Nature of Attitudes and Attitude Changes," p. 187.

[47] David Butler and Donald Stokes, *Political Change in Britain* (New York: St. Martin's Press, 1969), p. 219. Also see V. O. Key, Jr., *Public Opinion and American Democracy* (New York: Alfred A. Knopf, 1964), pp. 345–51.

[48] Bradley Greenberg and Brenda Dervin, "Mass Communication among the Urban Poor," *Public Opinion Quarterly*, Vol. 34 (1970), p. 233.

can sometimes create more ambiguity than clarity. Part of the problem is that news stories must be short and entertaining. Directors try to focus on the dramatic elements of a story and understate those aspects which cannot be presented visually. They also try to create interest by using music and careful editing. All of these efforts to provide entertainment come, according to some critics, at the expense of clarifying substantive problems for the audience. Coverage of a protest rally, for example, often focuses on what has happened, not on why it has happened.[49]

On the other hand, even if the press is biased, it can be more informative because its job is to supply news and because it can be more controversial. Also, the printed media can go into more detail. Yet, newspapers and magazines have gross biases of their own.

David Paletz and Robert Dunn illustrate how a typical American newspaper, even in a sincere effort to be objective, can inadvertently provide only half-truths. They extensively studied the *Winston-Salem (North Carolina) Journal*'s coverage of a minor racial disorder in Winston-Salem in 1967.[50] One of the *Journal*'s goals in covering the riot was to calm tensions and dispel rumors. As a result, the paper presented the story from a law and order point of view and featured interviews with law enforcement officials and prominent blacks, all of whom condemned the violence. This perspective had the intended consequence of creating an impression "that the majority of the Afro-American community was against the violence," a conclusion the authors call "debatable," and possibly erroneous.[51] The upshot was the reader of the *Journal* did not get a complete picture of causes behind the disturbance. They were instead left with the notion that it was simply a case of "normal criminal activity writ large."[52]

The Media Environment.   When studying the mass media one should keep in mind the kind of society in which they operate, for in

---

[49] For an excellent analysis of network news broadcasting in these terms, see Edward Jay Epstein, "Onward and Upward with the Arts: The Selection of Reality," *The New Yorker,* March 3, 1973, pp. 41–77.

[50] David L. Paletz and Robert Dunn, "Press Coverage of Civil Disorders: A Case Study of Winston-Salem, 1967," *Public Opinion Quarterly,* Vol. 33 (1959), pp. 328–45.

[51] Ibid., p. 339.

[52] Ibid., p. 340.

large measure, social and political conditions determine what relationship citizens will have with formal communications systems. More precisely, we should be alert to the presence or absence of competing messages. In other words, we should ask: What is the nature of the information flow? Is it dominated by a central government as in a totalitarian system and do the messages reinforce each other? Or, are there independent and autonomous sources of information producing a cacophony of disharmonious and conflicting ideas and appeals? These are vital questions in understanding mass media.

To the extent that there is variety and competition among media sources, it will clearly be difficult for any one of the sources to be effective in influencing opinions and behavior. Exposure to multitudinous and competing messages interferes with their being learned, remembered, or believed. If there is only one message there will be few standards for judging its validity and it may be accepted by default. For example, in the Soviet Union it is hard to check the adequacy of the "party line" simply because no other independent information is available.

It is useful here to consider for a moment the role formal communications plays in a democracy. Measured by one scale, the mass media in the United States supply a stream of heterogeneous information and points of view. We like to think that because of our traditions of a free society and a free press we receive (or can receive) all sides of every issue. Yet before congratulating ourselves we should put our view of freedom into proper perspective by considering two qualifications.

First, a relatively small elite dominates most (but not all) of the communications networks in our country. National television news, to take one instance, is dominated by the three major networks and by a few news agencies. These organizations are only in a very loose sense responsible to the people. The media elite consists of big business (through advertising), the major broadcast networks and publishing houses, and high public officials. Even though there are serious and far-reaching conflicts within the elite as in the case of the federal government's dispute with the *New York Times* over publication of the "Pentagon Papers," the group is more or less homogeneous in its acceptance of fundamental political and social values and norms. Among those beliefs are a general acceptance of existing governmental institutions and practices, basic agreement on capitalism, and a common understanding of legality. Furthermore, some voices speak more loudly than others. For example, can the man on the street compete equally in the "free marketplace of ideas" with the General Motors Corporation which has billions of dollars at its disposal? Consequently, although we all enjoy freedom of expression, some ideas and values receive more attention than others.

These thoughts lead to the second point. In spite of their freedom, what the media do transmit is really only a small part of the ideas and values that are theoretically available. As one illustration, the acceptance, even glorification of capitalism permeates advertisements, television and radio programs, editorials, magazine stories, and so forth. There is really very little serious and objective consideration of the merits of, say, socialism which is at least an alternative to capitalism. This is not to berate the American system but only to point out that the media themselves are selective and that, in a very real sense, not all sides of fundamental social and economic questions are fairly and accurately presented to the public. This selectivity partly determines, as will be seen later, what people consider to be the range of viable alternatives to their present condition.

In summary, we have seen that mass communications and political campaigns do not directly affect individuals but are mediated by three filtering processes: (1) individual characteristics, (2) group characteristics, and (3) media characteristics. Now let us tackle the more difficult and interesting problem of assessing the actual effects of the mass media.

THE EFFECTS OF MASS COMMUNICATIONS

Unfortunately and surprisingly, social scientists know relatively little about the consequences of mass communications and political campaigns on opinions and behavior. Even though we can confidently reject the Direct Effects model, it is still difficult to specify precisely the nature and extent of media effects. Since most research has concentrated on the short-term impact on attitudes, we will begin with these, after which we will consider the relationship of the media to generalized political orientations and behavior. We will conclude with a brief discussion of their long-range implications.

Short-Term Effects on Attitudes

Reinforcement. Most investigators agree that, in the short run at least, the main effect of persuasive communications is to reinforce existing opinions rather than to change them. If a person holds an attitude with any degree of intensity he is not apt to be shaken from his position by what he sees on television or reads in the newspapers. Data for this conclusion come from numerous surveys and experiments but we can perhaps best observe the phenomena by examining the results of political campaigns.

Most individuals make up their minds about who they will vote for even before the campaigns start. Table 4.3 shows the times when

Table 4.3
THE TIMES WHEN VOTERS MADE UP THEIR MINDS DURING
THE 1972 PRESIDENTIAL CAMPAIGN

*Time of Decision**	
Respondent knew all along how he would vote	34%
Before the conventions	11
At the time of the conventions	18
During the campaign	23
Within two weeks of the campaign	8
On election day	6
	100%
	(1,464)

* How long before the election did you decide that you were going to vote the way you did?
Note: Figures in parentheses refer to the number of cases.
Source: *CPS 1972 American National Election Study.* (See Appendix.)

voters decided their presidential preferences. The vast majority (63 percent) report having made up their minds before or during the national conventions. Only 14 percent decided in the latter part of the campaign. Thus it appears that only about a third of the electorate arrives at a decision during the campaign.

Table 4.4 confirms this statement by showing that very few people *changed* their preferences. These respondents were interviewed in September 1972 and again in November after the election.

Table 4.4
STABILITY OF VOTER PREFERENCES DURING THE
1972 PRESIDENTIAL CAMPAIGN

Respondents' Vote in November 1972	*Respondents'* Preferences Prior to October 1, 1972*		
	McGovern	*Undecided*	*Nixon*
McGovern	90%	41%	8%
Nixon	10	59	92
	100%	100%	100%
	(209)	(64)	(518)

* Among those respondents who actually voted.
Note: Figures in parentheses refer to the number of cases.
Source: *CPS 1972 American National Election Study.* (See Appendix.)

Ninety percent of the initial McGovern supporters stayed loyal to their man, as did most Nixon supporters. This finding suggests that political campaigns should be directed at the relatively small (but far from insignificant) number of undecided voters.

Buttressing the reinforcement proposition even further are data regarding the famous Nixon-Kennedy debates of 1960. The principal outcome of this widely publicized confrontation was the strengthening of one's commitment to his favorite party and candidate.[53] Even though some people conceded that their candidate's opponent performed better in the debates, most were not swayed by the arguments and remained loyal to their first choice. On the whole, the debates produced very few changes.

The reasons why the media serve primarily to reinforce opinions lie in the filtering processes. As we have noted, the mediating factors tend to screen out conflicting messages and cues and emphasize the familiar ones.

Activation. A second and extremely important consequence of the mass media is the activation, arousal, or creation of new opinions. There exist many potential attitude-objects toward which individuals either have not formed an opinion or have at most only a weak commitment. By bringing these to their attention in a particular way, the media may be instrumental as a socializing agent in forming new opinions. This is true because the mass communications are certainly a source of one's awareness of events—even if this

---

[53] Elihu Katz and Jacob J. Feldman, "The Kennedy-Nixon Debates: A Survey of Surveys," *Studies in Public Communications,* No. 4 (1962), pp 127–63.

awareness is channeled through opinion leaders. In the late 1950s, probably very few people had any opinion (or knowledge) of Malcolm X until he was "discovered," vilified and perhaps later popularized by the press. In other words, how individuals respond to personalities, events, and issues is often determined by the source of their first information about it.

Plausible as the activation principle is, it has been somewhat troublesome to document.[54] The problem is to find people who have not had a previous opinion and who can be shown to be influenced by the media. Nevertheless, there are a variety of suggestive studies such as Berelson, Lazarsfeld, and McPhee's study of the 1948 election.[55] They found that the campaign tended to mobilize "potential" Democrats (i.e., individuals who, on the basis of their past voting records or socioeconomic characteristics, might have been expected to vote Democratic but by the time the campaign had begun they had not made up their minds). The mobilization of these potential Democrats helped Truman win the election.

Conversion. Although the conventional wisdom expounded in best sellers such as *The Selling of the President 1968* might suggest otherwise, the least common short-term effect of a propaganda campaign is the conversion of attitudes.[56] People are simply not easily persuaded. The authors of *The People's Choice* found, for instance, that "changes in vote intention during the campaign were much fewer than changes in vote intention during the preceding three-and-a-half years."[57] Table 4.4 implies that this conclusion still holds.

In a laboratory environment an experimenter can very often produce attitude changes by means of persuasive communications. Yet the changes usually last for only a short period of time and are seldom accompanied by modifications in behavior. (See Chapter 2.) For example, one might get a heavy smoker to change his verbal opinions regarding the danger of smoking but it is much more difficult to convince him to stop smoking.

Hence, some attitudes and behaviors are harder to change than

---

[54] Klapper, *The Effects of Mass Communication,* chap iii.
[55] Berelson et al., *Voting,* chap. xi.
[56] McGinniss, *The Selling of the President 1968.*
[57] Lazarsfeld et al., *The People's Choice,* p. 102.

others. For example, most people are reluctant to change their party identification but would probably have no trouble changing their opinions of the government of Mali. Thus, conversion seems to be the least common effect of information campaigns waged through the mass media.

Summary. Efforts to change attitudes such as political commercials, advertising campaigns and propaganda are often successful in producing minor alterations in opinions, but seldom bring about major or lasting changes. Muzafer Sherif and Carl Hovland developed the notion of "latitudes of acceptance and rejection" to explain this phenomenon.[58] A latitude or area of acceptance is an issue position a person finds acceptable, plus other positions he can tolerate. A woman may favor a particular tax plan but she can live with other similar schemes. These positions constitute her latitude of acceptance on the issue. Similarly, the latitude of rejection is the most objectionable position, plus other objectionable positions.

Attitude research suggests that one can create changes of opinion *within* a latitude of acceptance. It is extremely difficult, however, to move an opinion into a latitude of rejection.[59] To do so requires an attack on an individual's total attitude system. For instance, the functional theory of attitudes holds that an opinion will not change unless its motivational basis is altered. If an attitude is serving an ego-defense function, then only by changing the underlying need can the attitude be expected to shift substantially. (See Chapter 2.) In addition to changing the motivational basis we can list some other conditions facilitating fundamental changes in opinions. Changes are likely when:

—the filtering processes do not operate or operate imperfectly;
—the individual experiences group "cross-pressures;"
—social or geographical mobility creates a readiness to adopt opinions which are congruent with the new group;
—it may be politically or socially expedient to be convinced by the media—as in a totalitarian country;
—the media and the other filtering mechanisms work together instead of at cross-purposes.

---

[58] Muzafer Sherif and Carl Hovland, *Social Judgment: Assimilation and Contrast Effects in Communication and Attitude Change* (New Haven, Conn.: Yale University Press, 1961).

[59] McGuire, "Nature of Attitudes and Attitude Changes," p. 169.

In concluding this section, a caveat is necessary. Even though the media and campaigns may cause only small changes when measured in terms of percentages, they can still have momentous consequences in politics. Think, for example, of how many election outcomes would be reversed by a switch of the part of five to ten percent of the voters. (Not many important elections are decided by more than ten percent.) So it makes sense for parties and candidates to invest time and money in the media. Besides reinforcing their supporter's beliefs and activating potential new voters, the media may make victory possible by winning away a few percent of the opponent's followers.

At any rate, the short-term effects of mass communications are (in order of magnitude) reinforcement, activation, and conversion.

The Effects on Political Behavior

Surprisingly, much less is known and agreed upon in regard to the effects of communications on behavior in general, so we can be selective and brief in handling this topic.

Since media exposure is associated with both interest in and knowledge of politics, they affect, in part, the rate of political participation, although perhaps not as much as is commonly believed. It is well known, for example, that the excitement and tension of presidential campaigns activate large numbers of normally apathetic and quiescent voters. Turnout is much heavier in presidential elections than in off-year congressional or state and local contests, suggesting that the mass media may stimulate participation. Some research, however, finds that mass communications are less important in increasing turnout than are grass root, face-to-face campaigns. Studies show, for example, that door-to-door canvassing increases voting participation more than media campaigns do.[60]

Going beyond electoral politics, however, the mass media do have implications for broader types of political behavior, behavior related to the stability and integration of the political system as a

---

[60] Gerald H. Kramer, "The Effects of Precinct-Level Canvassing on Voter Behavior," *Public Opinion Quarterly*, Vol. 34 (1970–71), pp. 560–72; William A. Glaser, "Television and Voting Turnout," *Public Opinion Quarterly*, Vol. 29 (1965), pp. 71–86; and H. Simon and F. Stern, "The Effect of Television upon Voting Behavior in Iowa in the 1952 Presidential Election," *American Political Science Review*, Vol. 49 (1955), pp. 470–77.

whole. In the underdeveloped areas of the world, modern communications networks are one means of fostering a sense of community. People who may be physically isolated from one another are brought closer together through their identification with symbols disseminated by the media.

In other words, as previously noted, the media can be useful in instilling a sense of national identity and togetherness. They help create what Daniel Lerner calls "empathy," or "the capacity to see oneself in the other fellow's situation."[61] The ability to empathize, Lerner maintains, is essential for the economic and political modernization of rural, preindustrial people. Mass communications provide one means for acquiring this skill. So indispensable is the role of the mass media in changing traditional outlooks and behavior that many political scientists regard the emergence of a modern communications system as a prerequisite for other aspects of political and social development.

The Mass Media and Violence.   Though we cannot delve into the subject deeply, it is worth pausing to mention the connection between mass communications and violence. It is both popular and intuitively appealing to attribute part of the recent increases in political disorders to the perverting influence of the media, many of which seem to delight in portraying violence and sadism. Consider, for example, a typical night's television programming which usually contains shootings, knifings, beatings, horse tramplings, automobile and airplane crashes, wild animal attacks, and so forth. It seems logical to suppose that prolonged exposure to such mayhem would eventually warp even the soundest mind. Indeed, many fear that the media, especially television, are glorifying violence to the point where it is becoming a grave political problem.

A good example of the public's concern about the deleterious effects of televised violence is an incident which took place in Boston. One Sunday night ABC presented *Fuzz*, a movie which among other things showed young hoodlums setting fire to some derelicts. On the following Monday night six youths dragged a woman into an alley, forced her to pour gasoline on herself and then set her on fire. Echoing local sentiment, Boston's police commissioner blamed the televised movie and stated, "It's about time that the public

---

[61] Daniel Lerner, *The Passing of Traditional Society* (New York: The Free Press, 1958), p. 51.

demanded an end to violence such as this in our movies and on television."[62]

There is considerable debate about whether the media can fairly be censured for causing this kind of behavior. Television networks and some academicians argue that mass media are not responsible for aggressive behavior. No one has produced convincing evidence, they claim, proving that televised or filmed violence has a lasting or cumulative effect on social behavior. Such violence may admittedly stimulate an underlying aggressive tendency, but it does not by itself create the predisposition. And studies which purportedly show a connection between exposure to media violence and aggressive behavior are technically deficient on numerous grounds.[63] Defenders of the media, in short, believe that there is simply no evidence that seeing a movie like *Fuzz* causes people to become violent.

Other observers are more pessimistic, however. One can find innumerable studies showing the adverse effects of media-portrayed violence. A particularly detailed investigation is the Surgeon General's Report, "Television and Growing Up: The Impact of Televised Violence."[64] Typical of the Report is a study by Robert Liebert and Robert Baron. A group of five- to nine-year-old children were shown a three-minute scene from a television series, "The Untouchables." The episode contained "a chase, two fist-fighting scenes, two shootings, and a knifing."[65] A control group composed of children of similar ages and backgrounds saw a three-minute sequence of sports activity. Liebert and Baron report that the youngsters who saw the violence were afterwards more aggressive as measured by several methods than those who viewed the sports film. The interpretation of this experiment and countless others like it is that television and movie violence can have serious negative consequences on the behavior of both young people and adults. Of course, demonstrating that something "can" produce an effect

---

[62] *The Philadelphia Sunday Bulletin,* October 14, 1973, p. 5.

[63] Weiss, "Effects of the Mass Media of Communication," pp. 138–41; Klapper, *The Effects of Mass Communication,* chap. vi.

[64] See footnote 1.

[65] Robert M. Liebert and Robert A. Baron, "Short-Term Effects of Televised Aggression on Children's Aggressive Behavior," *Television and Social Behavior,* Report to the Surgeon General, Vol. II (Washington, D.C.: U.S. Government Printing Office, 1972), pp. 181–201.

is not the same as showing that it "does." Nevertheless, there are compelling theoretical and empirical reasons for thinking prolonged exposure to violence has undesirable consequences.

Quite possibly the media are an indirect cause. As we saw in the previous chapter and as we will see in a later chapter on political violence, people learn by imitation. Television, movies, magazines, books—all provide attractive models which in a given situation a person may be motivated to follow. Leonard Berkowitz and Jacqueline Macaulay find that criminal violence may be "contagious" partly because of the publicity given to acts of violence.[66] They detect, for example, increases in national homicide rates following widely publicized killings such as the assassination of President Kennedy or Richard Speck's murder of eight nurses in Chicago in 1966.[67] The widespread coverage of these events presumably provides a model, lowers inhibitions, and stimulates other unbalanced individuals. In an analogous fashion the same may be true of political violence. By transmitting news of political bombings or an assassination in one area, the media may inadvertently cause similar occurrences elsewhere.

Thus we have seen that the mass media have short-term influences on political attitudes and behavior. The discussion has been brief and sketchy, but it illustrates the state of knowledge. Now we turn to an area that is even more speculative, the long-range consequences of the mass media.

Conclusion: The Long-Range Effects of Mass Communications

The preceding discussion asserted that the mass media do not act directly on opinions and behavior but are instead mediated by a variety of factors. By this point one may have the impression that the effects of the media are almost nil. Indeed, this has been the picture conveyed either explicitly or implicitly by some social scientists engaged in communications research. In arriving at these conclusions, survey analysts and experimentalists alike have mostly studied such topics as formal political campaigns and persuasive messages, and they have looked for more or less immediate conse-

---

[66] Leonard Berkowitz and Jacqueline Macaulay, "The Contagion of Criminal Violence," *Sociometry,* Vol. 34 (1971), pp. 238–60.

[67] Ibid., p. 254.

quences. Since the short-term effects may be small or may be obscured by other variables, investigators have tended to discount the media as a force in political and social life.

Quite obviously this conclusion may distort the true situation. For mass communications, as agents of socialization, no doubt have a long-range or cumulative effect. Arguing that it is sometimes unproductive to concentrate on just the short run, some social scientists believe that the messages being distributed through various communications networks slowly accumulate to mold our basic attitudes and beliefs about the government and the world.

Instead of looking only at a one- or two-month campaign period, for example, one might more profitably study the effect of the media between elections. In this vein, Butler and Stokes offer some fascinating evidence. Looking at interelection periods, they examined the behavior of partisans who voted for one party and yet read newspapers favoring the opposition. They discovered a "tendency [for] the reader of a partisan newspaper to move towards, rather than away from, his paper's party."[68] Stated in other words, people who voted for the Labor party in 1959 and who read pro-Conservative newspapers, tended to vote for the Conservatives in 1963. The authors do not elaborate their analysis to check for a possibly spurious or false relationship, but their results are nonetheless thought-provoking. They show, in particular, that media effects may take years to become noticeable.

If this line of reasoning is correct, one implication is that political parties might invest more money and effort between campaigns in order to improve their images. After all, this is exactly what many private groups do. The railroad and oil industries regularly sponsor TV commercials proclaiming their supposedly positive contributions to America's well-being and growth. The outcome of this type of advertising is not clear but seeing these messages year after year may well lead to the establishment of favorable attitudes and beliefs toward these industries.

The long-term consequences of the mass communications go deeper than this, however. Both the broadcast and printed media are sources of what we know, believe, and feel about the world. There are numerous areas where the media have a lasting impact

---

[68] Butler and Stokes, *Political Change in Britain,* p. 240.

on attitudes. We have already noted that Americans' ideas about foreign ideologies and economic systems are affected by what they see and read. In the same way basic opinions about government are shaped by the media. David Paletz and his associates offer an interesting case study of how a newspaper's reporting about a city council influences beliefs about local government.[69]

The paper, the *Durham (N.C.) Morning Herald,* routinely reports city council meetings. Although the reporters try to record objectively what happens, their reports tend to distort the sessions. In particular, the coverage is stereotyped because it overstates the rationality, orderliness, professionalism, and fairness of the proceedings. For example, the stories generally concentrate on specific ordinances. Viewed in isolation from the context of their passage, the ordinances appear to represent careful and judicious deliberation. They have an air of legitimacy about them. But city ordinances, like any laws, are the product of bickering, bargaining, compromise, and expediency. By considering only the finished product, the newspaper describes local government as civics books would, not as it is.[70]

The result, according to the investigators, is to reinforce the authority of local government. People are led to believe that such bodies behave rationally and act representatively and fairly. Whatever shortcomings local governments have are thereby obscured. This is not to claim that newspapers do not periodically uncover corruption or ineptness. Yet the long-range effect of this sort of coverage is to reaffirm beliefs in the responsiveness and expertise of government.

The media undoubtedly have similar effects in countless other areas of social, economic, cultural, and political life. By presenting certain themes and ignoring others, day-in, day-out, year-after-year mass communications (along with other agents of socialization) make us what we are. One wonders, for example, what the long-range impact of integrated television programs and commercials will be on attitudes toward minority groups. If blacks are portrayed

---

[69] David L. Paletz, Peggy Reichert, and Barbara McIntyre, "How the Media Support Local Governmental Authority, *Public Opinion Quarterly,* Vol. 35 (1971), pp. 80–94.

[70] Paletz et al., "How the Media Support Local Governmental Authority," pp. 91–93.

in professional or high-status roles it is quite possible that fundamental stereotypes may change. On the other hand, if they are presented in subservient or follower roles, existing beliefs and values may simply be reinforced.

The point is that mass communications have great potential for both good and evil. The danger is not that people can be manipulated in the short run by Orwellian propagandists. It is that the media partly affect our understanding of the world. If this understanding is consistently distorted we cannot intelligently face and solve problems. What remains in the future is to consider carefully the values being propagated by the media and how these values relate to our social and political goals.

5

Conventional Political Participation

Harold Lasswell entitled a short book *Politics: Who Gets What, When, How.*[1] At the heart of politics, according to this definition, is the distribution of values. A political system allocates rewards and punishment among the people of a society. The allocation of these values, however, does not depend solely on need or justice or equality. Some individuals get more than others, not because they are more deserving but because they have more power. What, then, determines who has political power? In a democracy, part of the answer can be found by looking for people who take an active part in political processes. A rule of thumb is that how much an individual or group gets out of politics depends largely on how much they participate in it.

Applying these ideas to the United States, it is not unfair to say that government benefits some groups—for example, businessmen —more than others—for example, migrant farm workers. Besides

---

[1] Harold Lasswell, *Politics: Who Gets What, When, How* (Cleveland, Ohio: The World Publishing Co., 1958).

direct rewards such as tax loopholes, subsidies, tariff protection, and the like, the business community profits from political institutions and practices designed to protect and promote capitalism. No doubt some benefits trickle down to migrant farm workers. But as they are now structured, the distributive processes really favor business interests. In fact, the system rewards the corporate world so much that cynics are fond of saying we have "welfare for the rich and private enterprise for the poor."

That rewards are distributed unevenly does not mean the government in Washington is run by an oligarchy—though some people think it is. It does suggest that some groups are more active than others. A businessman is likely to follow politics closely, to attend political rallies and donate money to campaigns, to vote, to write public officials, and to join organizations which represent his interests on Capitol Hill and in the bureaucracy. In short, a businessman takes part in politics on a day-to-day basis. Other people become involved only periodically and in limited ways, as when they vote for President once every four years. Still others, like migrant farm workers, participate hardly at all. Is it any wonder that businessmen are more influential?

We can better see this variation in political participation by looking at the number of people who are involved in different activities.[2] When we do this it becomes clear that mass political participation, both in this country and elsewhere, is relatively low.

About 39 million eligible voters did not vote in the 1960 presidential election. The number of nonvoters for 1964 and 1968 were 43 million and 47 million, respectively. (The last figure represents about a third of the eligible electorate.) Turnout in off-year congressional elections and in state and local contests is even smaller, often being more than 25 percent lower than in presidential elections.[3] Voting in primaries is so scanty that some people wonder how they can be considered representative. Even presidential primaries, for example, sometimes attract no more than 10 to 15 percent of the

---

[2] This chapter treats only conventional or "legitimate" forms of participation, especially those related to elections (e.g., registering and voting) and to influencing public officials (e.g., writing letters to congressmen). Later chapters will deal with nonconventional activities.

[3] Austin Ranney, "Turnout and Representation in Presidential Primary Elections," *American Political Science Review,* Vol. 66 (1972), pp. 21–37.

eligible electorate. These selected voters, it is feared, are not representative of either the public opinion or the socioeconomic characteristics of the constituency as a whole.[4]

Participation in other types of political activities is surprisingly low. The first row of Table 5.1 shows, for example, that Americans are not very active in political campaigns. Fewer than 10 percent do more than vote or talk about the election. The vast majority of people in this country have never written their congressman or even talked to local officials about solving some problem. Most citizens are, at most, occasional participants in the political process.

This generalization applies to other countries as well. Obviously, in some nations citizens cannot participate effectively because there is no provision for such participation or because appropriate institutions have not developed. But even in the industrialized democracies of Western Europe political apathy is widespread.[5] In France, for example, voting turnout is somewhat higher than in the United States—probably because it is easier to vote there—but overall interest and participation are lower than in America.[6] The data appearing in Table 5.1—drawn from a sample of British, Dutch, Canadian, as well as American citizens—further confirm the proposition that people in democracies are infrequent participants in politics. Their behavior is confined primarily to relatively passive activities such as voting and following political campaigns.

Thus, there is variation in political participation. If a group's profit from politics is commensurate with the energy it invests in it, then it is important to understand and explain why people do and do not become involved. Most people are legally free to be as active as they want. Yet the majority stay on the sidelines, leaving the field open to small minorities of activists. The businessman is a committed participant, the migrant farm worker is apathetic. Why? Answering this question will help us understand how political values are allocated for a society, and, in this way, will also help us under-

---

[4] Ibid., pp. 35–37.

[5] Giuseppe Di Palma, *Apathy and Participation* (New York: The Free Press, 1970), pp. 32–36.

[6] Georges Dupeux, "France," *International Social Science Journal*, Vol. 12 (1960), pp. 40–52; Philip E. Converse and Georges Dupeux, "Politicization of the Electorate in France and the United States," *Elections and the Political Order*, ed. Angus Campbell, Philip E. Converse, Warren E. Miller, and Donald E. Stokes (New York: John Wiley & Sons, Inc., 1966), pp. 269–91.

Table 5.1
POLITICAL PARTICIPATION IN FOUR DEMOCRACIES

				Percent Who:			
	Voted in a National Election	Voted in Local* Elections	Tried to Persuade Someone†	Attended a Political Meeting or Rally	Worked in a Campaign	Belong to a Political Group	Gave Money to a Candidate or Party
United States	73% (2,283)	54% (1,425)	27% (1,505)	9% (1,505)	7% (1,505)	5% (1,504)	–
Great Britain	89% (1,812)	56% (1,599)	–	8% (1,806)	3% (1,808)	–	13% (1,789)
Canada.........	86% (8,098)	84% (7,222)	23% (8,071)	15% (8,193)	5% (8,160)	4% (8,182)	1% (8,158)
Netherlands	74% (1,838)	–	12% (1,807)	15% (1,810)	6% (1,803)	–	–

* For the United States, "local" means voting in off-year congressional elections.
† Tried to persuade someone to vote for one of the candidates or parties.
Note: Dash signifies data not available. Figures in parentheses refer to the number of cases.
Sources: United States: CPS 1970 National Election Study, except for presidential voting which was based on the CPS 1972 National Election Study. (See Appendix.)
Great Britain: David Butler and Donald Stokes, Political Change in Britain 1963–1970. (See Appendix.)
Canada: John Meisel et al., 1965 Canadian Election Study. (See Appendix.)
Netherlands: Philip E. Stouthard et al., Dutch Election Study, 1970. (See Appendix.)

stand the strengths *and* limitations of modern democracies. By so doing we can see what needs to be done to make the distribution of political rewards fairer.

Several factors explain differences in political participation. The most important are:

Socioeconomic characteristics of individuals
Psychological characteristics of individuals
The expected costs of participation
The expected benefits of participation

After examining each of these interrelated variables, we will return to the question of how political participation affects the distribution of political values.

SOCIAL AND ECONOMIC EXPLANATIONS OF POLITICAL PARTICIPATION

The first set of factors, socioeconomic variables, are at the core of much theorizing about politics. Many social scientists believe that democracy must await social and economic development. Industrialization, urbanization, mass communications, the achievement of a decent standard of living—all are necessary to some extent before viable democratic institutions and practices can emerge in a society. The better off economically and socially a man is, the more likely he will have the skills, opportunities, and motivations necessary for an active political life.

To see why economic and social factors are linked to political participation, consider an extreme case. James Davies cites an experiment conducted on conscientious objectors.[7] The experiment, which took place during World War II, was designed to study the effects of severe deprivation on human behavior. Subjects were given a semi-starvation diet (about 1,400 calories a day) for 24 weeks. Describing the effects on one particular subject, Davies reports:

> By about the eighth week he reported having dreams about food. By the twelfth week not only his dreams but his conscious thoughts revolved around food and as steadily as the earth around

---

[7] James Davies, *Human Nature in Politics* (New York: John Wiley & Sons, Inc., 1963).

the sun. He got aches, pains, and cramps whether he exercised or not. He became restless, irritable, *and in one of the ominous and universal symptoms of starvation—increasingly apathetic.*[8]

Davies takes this study and ones similar to it dealing with the experiences of prisoners in concentration camps as evidence that human beings must achieve at least a minimal level of physical well-being and comfort before they will engage in social and political interactions. Unless physical needs are met, political activity does not occur. Davies writes, "The person who must concentrate all his energies merely on staying alive is in no position to concern himself actively or passively with policy decisions or their implementation."[9]

This line of thinking partly explains the low level of participation among people living in underdeveloped countries: "There must be relatively adequate food in a country before it can develop a general public, a broad group that is more than an unrelated agglomeration of people living within certain territorial boundaries."[10] In nations where starvation is widespread, political activism is characteristic mostly of those individuals who have satisfied their basic needs. This applies even to revolutions. Although a revolution may be born of hunger and poverty, it is usually led by relatively well-fed individuals such as intellectuals and military officers. The stultifying effects of abject poverty also produce political apathy among poor people in this country. As long as people are preoccupied with food and clothing and shelter, it is difficult to organize effective political action. This is why poor people in America have often been referred to as "faceless" or "invisible."

Social Status and Participation

In this sense, social and economic factors are fundamental to political participation. But even among the relatively affluent members of a society, socioeconomic variables account for differences in political activity. A proposition which explains these differences is:

---

[8] Ibid., p. 13. Italics added.

[9] Ibid., p. 26.

[10] Ibid., pp. 27–28.

The higher a person's social status, the more likely he will be an active participant in political life.

This proposition has received overwhelming confirmation and applies to all types of activities at national, state, and local levels.[11] People in the upper classes tend to be more interested and involved in public affairs—especially on a continuous basis—than middle- and lower class individuals. People in the lower classes, on the other hand, are apt to be apathetic. Of course, not all poor people are politically indifferent, nor are all the rich activists. Nevertheless, political participation of every type is strongly related to class.

To see why class and politics are related in this way, consider the components of a person's social class. Class position is determined by, among other factors, income, education, race, and place of residence. Analyzing these separately shows us how one's social class affects his political participation.

Income.   Most studies indicate that income determines the rate of political participation: the higher a person's income, the more likely he will be interested and involved in politics.[12] James Prothro and Donald Matthews find, for example, that income is the best single predictor of participation among Southern blacks.[13]

The relationship between income and political participation is illustrated in Table 5.2. For each activity (e.g., "Tried to persuade someone to vote for one of the candidates or parties") people with high incomes are more likely to have participated than those with low incomes. The highest income group is, in this sense, four times as active as the lowest income bracket.

The reasons why income is so significant are not hard to find. Having money usually gives one free time; it buys information in the form of books, magazines, and newspapers; it broadens one's experience through travel and participation in organizations; it accords status and prestige. With a high enough income one can afford to make campaign contributions and run for office. In short, income supplies the requisites for an active political life.

---

11 See Lester W. Milbrath, *Political Participation* (Chicago: Rand McNally & Co., 1965), chap. 5 for a long list of references on this topic.

12 Ibid., pp. 120–21.

13 Donald R. Matthews and James W. Prothro, *Negroes and the New Southern Politics* (New York: Harcourt, Brace & World, Inc., 1966), chap. iv.

Table 5.2
INCOME AND POLITICAL PARTICIPATION

	Percent Who:					
Respondent's Family Income	Voted in Last Presidential Election	Voted in Last Congressional Election	Tried to Persuade Someone*	Attended a Political Meeting or Rally	Worked in a Campaign	Belong to Political Group
Less than $1,999	55%	39%	11%	3%	2%	2%
$2,000–3,999	63%	50%	15%	4%	3%	2%
$4,000–7,499	64%	53%	19%	5%	6%	4%
$7,500–14,999	76%	65%	31%	10%	7%	6%
$15,000 and over	89%	77%	46%	22%	16%	11%

* Tried to persuade someone to vote for one of the candidates or parties.
Sources: *CPS 1970 National Election Study*, except for presidential voting which was based on the *CPS 1972 National Election Study*. (See Appendix.)

Robert Dahl says that wealth is not power.[14] Rather, money is a resource which must be put to work in order to produce political gains. So money is only potential power. Dahl's point is, of course, true, but it is similar to the aphorism that money cannot buy happiness. Wealth can provide essential political skills and opportunities; it buys the things that lead to power. In this sense, it gives the rich a head start on the poor. The head start is not insurmountable but it does explain partly why moderate and low-income groups participate less than the more affluent.

Education. Formal education is similarly related to participation. Educated people have politically relevant knowledge and skills; they are interested in politics and have opinions on issues and public officials. Perhaps more important, they have confidence in their ability to influence decision making and a sense that they ought to participate as much as they can, points we will explore later on. In general, then, high school graduates pay attention to current events, vote, participate in election campaigns, write their congressmen more than those without much formal schooling.

Some of these ideas are illustrated in Table 5.3, which shows the relationship between education and various kinds of political activities. Individuals with at least some college training are quite active compared to the other respondents. True, very few people

---

[14] Robert Dahl, *Who Governs* (New Haven, Conn.: Yale University Press, 1961).

take part in political campaigns or belong to a political organization, but those with the highest education are much more likely to be involved in these ways than those with little or no formal education.

Table 5.3
EDUCATION AND POLITICAL PARTICIPATION

	Percent Who:					
Respondent's Education	Voted in Last Presidential Election	Voted in Last Congressional Election	Tried to Persuade Someone*	Attended a Political Meeting or Rally	Worked in a Campaign	Belong to Political Group
0 to 7 grades	53%	43%	11%	4%	3%	2%
8 grades	63%	57%	12%	5%	2%	1%
9 to 11 grades ..	61%	45%	15%	3%	2%	3%
High school graduate	75%	59%	28%	7%	7%	4%
High school plus noncollege training	77%	64%	23%	8%	6%	4%
Some college ...	84%	71%	48%	18%	13%	10%
College	90%	83%	53%	28%	18%	16%

* Tried to persuade someone to vote for one of the candidates or parties.
Sources: CPS 1970 National Election Study, except for presidential voting which was based on the CPS 1972 National Election Study. (See Appendix.)

It is worth pausing to note, however, that formal education is not the same as "political education," though the two are closely related. Some people who have had little schooling are nevertheless quite knowledgeable about politics. Thus, the correlation between education and participation is only a tendency, not an absolute truth.

Occupation.   As everyone knows, a boy from the humblest origins can become President of the United States. What is usually forgotten, though, is that the road to the White House goes through occupational success. To be elected to the presidency—or, for that matter, to be elected to most public offices—requires time, money, skills, and access to politically influential people. Some occupations provide these resources; others do not. Donald Matthews' study of the Senate, for example, shows that the majority of senators were originally lawyers, a profession ideally suited to supply a man with the tools needed to run for public office.[15]

Attorneys have free time and can set their own schedules; they have political skills and, by the nature of their work, they have political contacts; they are usually wealthy, mobile, and experienced; they belong to numerous organizations. In short, lawyers have advantages not available to, say, skilled workers. Workers have fixed, eight-hour-a-day schedules, have limited education, income, and political experience, and spend most of their time meeting immediate family needs. Not surprisingly, then, lawyers are politically more active than factory workers.

These remarks illustrate a general principle applicable to all forms of political participation: people in higher status occupations are politically more active than people in lower status occupations. Table 5.4, for instance, shows unskilled, semiskilled and service workers to be less active than managers and professional people. For example, only about one third of the laborers (e.g., migrant farm workers) bother to vote. Given this fact, their lack of influence on decision making is more understandable. As with education and income, we should not think of occupation as strictly determining participation, but it is a well-established generalization.

Organizational Membership. Voluntary associations (such as the American Legion, the Elks, labor unions, and the American Civil Liberties Union) play a particularly important role in the political life of a democracy. One of their functions is to represent the interests of their members in the political arena. Since people have overlapping memberships, they also serve to dampen conflict and promote compromise and cooperation. Formal organizations have another purpose. They integrate the individual into community life, thereby encouraging him to become an active participant. As a result, people who belong to organizations—and identify with the groups' goals—tend to be more active than socially isolated individuals.

This proposition, like the others, has been well-documented. On the basis of a survey of the United States, Mexico, England, Germany, and Italy, Norman Nie and his colleagues conclude, "Within

---

[15] Donald R. Matthews, *U.S. Senators and Their World* (paperback ed.; New York: Random House, 1960), pp. 33–35.

Table 5.4
OCCUPATION AND POLITICAL PARTICIPATION

Respondent's Occupation	*Percent Who:*					
	Voted in Last Presidential Election	*Voted in Last Congressional Election*	*Tried to Persuade Someone**	*Attended a Political Meeting or Rally*	*Worked in a Campaign*	*Belong to Political Group*
Laborers and unskilled workers	52%	33%	15%	0%	2%	5%
Service and household workers	62%	60%	15%	5%	5%	2%
Operatives and semiskilled workers	68%	47%	14%	5%	3%	2%
Craftsmen and foremen	77%	63%	32%	11%	5%	7%
Farmers	88%	57%	22%	4%	4%	4%
Clerical and sales workers	78%	67%	32%	11%	10%	5%
Managers and officials	82%	71%	35%	10%	10%	6%
Professionals ...	87%	74%	45%	24%	16%	14%

* Tried to persuade someone to vote for one of the candidates or parties.

Sources: *CPS 1970 National Election Study,* except for presidential voting which was based on the *CPS 1972 National Election Study.* (See Appendix.)

each of the five nations the citizen who is an active member of social groups is more likely to be a political participant than the citizen with a few or no organizational involvements."[16]

Race. At first thought it seems obvious that blacks and other nonwhites do not participate as much as whites. For most of our history their exclusion has resulted from legal and extralegal barriers. But their lack of participation results from other causes as well. Nonwhites generally occupy lower social class positions; they have less education and money than whites. More important, many blacks believe that government, whether it be local, state, or na-

---

[16] Norman H. Nie, G. Bingham Powell, Jr. and Kenneth Prewitt, "Social Structure and Political Participation: Developmental Relationships, Part I," *American Political Science Review,* Vol. 63 (1969), p. 365.

tional, is unresponsive to their needs and interests and that it is therefore a waste of time to become involved. Confidence in one's ability to get things done is essential for political motivation. Without this confidence people tend to ignore politics.

It would not surprise us, then, if nonwhites were somewhat less interested in politics than whites, voted less often, belonged to fewer political organizations and held fewer party and public offices.[17] But interestingly, while it is true that whites do tend to participate more, the passivity of nonwhites can be overstated. Table 5.5 shows that both groups engage in most activities at almost the same rate.

Table 5.5
RACE AND POLITICAL PARTICIPATION

| | Percent Who: | | | | | |
Respondent's Race	Voted in Last Presidential Election	Voted in Last Congressional Election	Tried to Persuade Someone*	Attended a Political Meeting or Rally	Worked in a Campaign	Belong to Political Group
Nonwhite	65%	48%	20%	8%	7%	4%
White	74%	61%	27%	10%	7%	6%

* Tried to persuade someone to vote for one of the candidates or parties.
Sources: *CPS 1970 National Election Study,* except for presidential voting which was based on the *CPS 1972 National Election Study.* (See Appendix.)

Several other studies show that when socioeconomic characteristics are controlled, blacks participate at rates equal to or even higher than whites.[18] In Indianapolis, for instance, blacks registered and voted in the 1960 and 1964 presidential elections more frequently than did the whites.[19]

In summary, race is related to participation, but the relationship is mostly spurious, for many of the social characteristics which are associated with race, education, income, and occupation explain most of the differences.

Place of Residence. Historically, political participation has been higher in cities than in rural places. In fact, the urban setting with

---

[17] Milbrath, *Political Participation,* pp. 138–41.

[18] Marvin E. Olsen, "Social and Political Participation of Blacks," *American Sociological Review,* Vol. 35 (1970), pp. 682–97.

[19] Ibid., p. 692.

its communications networks was ideal to facilitate social and political interaction. Besides having less education, income, and free time and being more isolated, people in rural areas found it physically harder to become active participants. Consequently, most social scientists believed farmers were less likely to participate than urban dwellers.[20]

Recent evidence, however, casts doubt on this assertion. It indicates that urbanites are no more active than people living in rural areas.[21] Two forces may have produced the change. First, modern communications have opened up rural areas, making it easier for people to become involved in political life. Second, lower status individuals who are generally nonparticipants have been migrating to cities while upper class whites are leaving. The uneven migration patterns have hence reduced urban-rural differences.

Age.   Behind the 26th Amendment to the Constitution giving 18-year-olds the right to vote was the feeling that young people are now mature and active enough to deserve enfranchisement. Indeed, the political campaigns of Eugene McCarthy, Robert Kennedy, and George McGovern seemed to demonstrate an almost boundless eagerness to get involved. If the rallying cries of the fifties were panty raids and Fort Lauderdale, the cry of the late sixties was for commitment, commitment to change the system and make it better for minorities, for women, for the poor, for the powerless. Most seemed willing to work within the "rules of the game" by "playing the game."

It is too early to tell if and how long this apparent involvement will last. Nevertheless, we have some indications. In the past, people under 25 have been the least interested and least active age group. And, despite the impressions created by the mass media, the situation may not be altogether different from what it was in the fifties. In the 1972 election, fewer than half of the newly enfranchised young people bothered to vote. The 18-to-20-year-olds constituted only 6 percent of the vote.[22]

---

[20] Angus Campbell, "The Passive Citizen," *Acta Sociologica,* Vol. 6 (fasc. 1–2, 1962), pp. 9–21.

[21] See, for example, Nie, Powell, and Prewitt, "Social Structure and Political Participation," pp. 365–66; and Milbrath, *Political Participation,* pp. 42, 128–29.

[22] *New York Times,* January 4, 1973, p. 19.

As people grow older they become more involved in politics. Participation by people in the oldest age brackets, of course, declines somewhat because they are in poorer health and less able to get around. Young people are usually mobile and not settled into a definite life-style. Their preferences on issues and candidates tend to be weak and unstable. As was pointed out in Chapter 3, most people follow the political attitudes and loyalties of their parents. Yet it takes time for these feelings to crystallize enough to motivate behavior. Unmarried young citizens are especially likely to be apathetic.[23]

Saying that the young are politically less active than older people does not mean that the "youth vote" will not have a serious impact on the political system. For one thing, the population is becoming younger. The 18- to 30-year-olds outnumber practically every other age group. Even if a relatively small percent of them do vote, the absolute number will be very large. Also, the participation may occur in selected geographical areas. For example, some congressional districts have numerous colleges and universities in them. If the students in those districts vote—and if they have generally the same preferences—their votes could substantially alter the ideological character of the House of Representatives.

Finally, very small numbers of intense activists can create quite a hullabaloo. Some interesting data come from a study by Sidney Verba and Richard Brody, who find that very few people actively protested the war in Vietnam.[24] Nevertheless, a small percent of the population is large in absolute numbers: one-half of 1 percent of the U.S. adult population is almost three-quarters of a million people. Such a large number marching and protesting may be quite visible and give the appearance of even larger numbers.[25] Although there is no definite evidence on the point, there is some indication that protest demonstrations of the late 1960s affected America's Vietnam policies. These demonstrations also seemed to have affected the way in which the government explained the war. David Halberstam reports that both the Kennedy and Johnson

---

[23] Milbrath, *Political Participation*, pp. 134–35.

[24] Sidney Verba and Richard Brody, "Participation, Policy Preferences, and the War in Vietnam," *Public Opinion Quarterly*, Vol. 34 (1970), pp. 325–32.

[25] Ibid., p. 332.

administrations were quite sensitive to criticisms of their policies and insisted on optimistic reports from the battlefield.[26]

Sex. In the past, politics was a man's affair and men participated more than women. The Women's Liberation Movement may be changing sex roles, but for the present there are still marked differences between the political participation of men and women. As the educational level of women increases, these differences will no doubt vanish. Gabriel Almond and Sidney Verba find, for example, that the rate of participation among females depends partly on the economic and social modernization of the country in which they live. Women in Italy and Mexico are less active than women in the United States.[27]

These, then, are the most important social and economic variables in the determination of political participation. We have seen how they more or less directly encourage or discourage political activity. These factors are important in another way, however. In addition to affecting participation, social and economic variables also influence certain other attitudes, predispositions, and orientations which are in turn related to political involvement. In other words, a person's social and economic standing has both direct and indirect effects. Without taking into account the intermediate "psychological" variables we cannot hope to explain fully variations in political participation.

PSYCHOLOGICAL EXPLANATIONS OF POLITICAL PARTICIPATION
Political Information

Most civics textbooks assume that a well-informed citizenry is essential for democracy. In order to take part in politics a citizen needs some basic information: when and where elections are to be held, how to register, whom to contact at city hall, and where the protest rally is forming. He also needs to know something of the mechanics of government so he can assign responsibility for decisions he does not like. Finally, if he is to participate meaningfully he should be familiar with the candidates and the issues.

---

[26] David Halberstam, *The Best and the Brightest* (New York: Random House, Inc., 1972).

[27] Gabriel A. Almond and Sidney Verba, *The Civic Culture* (Princeton, N.J.: Princeton University Press, 1963), pp. 177–78.

Participation is strongly linked with information about politics and government.[28] The most active individuals are also most aware and knowledgeable. Although the level of political information increases with formal education, it is related to participation itself. Matthews and Prothro find that the long exclusion of blacks from political life in the South contributed to their lack of political information.[29] As their level of participation increases they acquire more knowledge and skills. Thus there is an interaction between participation and information: as one increases, so does the other.

Given the importance of information as a determinant of participation, what the masses know about government and politics is not altogether encouraging. Norval Glenn writes:

> . . . in 1967, when possible federal legislation on open housing was being widely discussed in the media, 42 per cent of the respondents to a Gallup poll did not know the meaning of the term "open housing." In the same year, only 28 per cent of the respondents to another Gallup poll knew who would represent their district in the State Senate the following year, and only 24 per cent could name their representative in the State Legislature or Assembly. In 1966, only 19 per cent of a national sample said they knew what their Congressman thought about Vietnam; 19 per cent said they knew what he thought about civil rights, and only 14 per cent said they knew his stand on strikes and labor problems. In 1970, only 21 per cent of a Gallup sample knew how their Congressman had voted on any major bills during the year. More than a third of these respondents admitted that they did not even know whether their Congressman was a Democrat or Republican.[30]

The authors of *The American Voter,* an important study of political behavior, discover that familiarity with important issues of the day is not impressive: in many cases about half the respondents to their questionnaire either did not have an opinion on the issue or did not know what the government was doing about the matter.[31]

---

[28] Milbrath, *Political Participation,* chap. iii.

[29] Matthews and Prothro, *Negroes and the New Southern Politics,* p. 274.

[30] Norval D. Glenn, "The Distribution of Political Knowledge in the United States," *Political Attitudes and Public Opinion,* ed. Dan D. Nimmo and Charles M. Bonjean (New York: David McKay Co., Inc., 1972), p. 273.

[31] Angus Campbell, Philip E. Converse, Warren E. Miller, and Donald E. Stokes, *The American Voter* (New York: John Wiley & Sons, Inc., 1960), pp. 171–76.

The relatively low level of information among the public has led some to conclude that people are not sufficiently knowledgeable to make intelligent choices. The voter, it is argued, is too concerned with superficial images and does not care about important issues.

Although we will pursue this point in later chapters, we can conclude this section by observing that politicians and parties often obscure their positions on policy questions. In fact, some political advisors and candidates say candidates should never reveal their true attitudes, but should instead stay in the middle of the road where most of the votes are. This may be good advice. Yet, it then seems unfair to blame the average citizen for his lack of knowledge of his representatives.

Furthermore, the mass media are not always helpful in this respect. Robert McClure and Thomas Patterson supply some interesting data which shows that during the 1972 presidential campaign the network television news programs did a "poor job" of informing viewers of the candidates' positions on issues.[32] For example, George McGovern made corruption in government a major issue. Yet his stand on the matter was virtually ignored by the three networks.[33] Not surprisingly, then, voters know less about politics than might be desirable.

Political Involvement

From what has already been said, we should not be surprised to find that interest in politics varies. Some people are extremely interested in what is going on in Washington or the State Capitol. Others pay attention only intermittently, as during elections, while still others could not care less about politics. We call this concern with politics *political involvement*. Though the term has several specific meanings, it is usually measured by asking people how interested they are in politics, how closely they follow campaigns and how much they care about the outcomes of elections. Using answers to such questions, political scientists try to determine how important politics is to an individual.

---

[32] Robert D. McClure and Thomas E. Patterson, "Television News and Voter Behavior in the 1972 Presidential Election," unpublished paper presented at the 1973 annual meeting of the American Political Science Association, New Orleans, September 4–8, p. 7.

[33] Ibid., p. 10.

Involvement is strongly related to participation. The authors of *The American Voter* find, for example, that 96 percent of the most highly involved respondents voted in 1956, whereas only 22 percent of the least involved bothered to go to the polls.[34] The highly involved are also more likely to take part in activities beyond voting.

Why are some people more involved than others? Involvement is itself related to social status, with well-educated people being more involved than others. Men are more involved than women, whites more so than blacks, the over 30 more than the under 30. As can be expected, involvement is correlated with the other psychological factors we are discussing such as information and partisanship.

Partisanship

We now come to one of the most important concepts in the study of political behavior, partisanship. Partisanship refers to how closely a person identifies with one of the major political parties. Some individuals consider themselves strong Democrats; others think of themselves as strong Republicans. Many feel close to neither party, preferring instead to call themselves Independents.

According to conventional wisdom, Independents stay above party politics; they diligently and carefully study the issues and then vote for "the man, not the party." Actually, survey data contradict this myth. Independents do not have concern or information about politics and they tend to vote only when a campaign has been particularly exciting. Partisans, on the other hand, are very active. Besides being involved and informed, they are more likely to register and vote, to talk about politics, to try to influence their friends, to engage in campaign activities, and the like. In fact, it is the partisans who more nearly fit civics textbook definitions of the ideal citizen. We, of course, hear a great deal these days about increasing numbers of independent voters. But the increase may reflect growing disenchantment with politics rather than an improvement in the quality of the citizenry.

The relationship between partisanship and political participation is clearly seen in Table 5.6. Strong partisans—that is, those who strongly identify with a political party, are much more likely to vote

---

[34] Campbell et al., *The American Voter*, p. 107.

Table 5.6
PARTISANSHIP AND POLITICAL PARTICIPATION

	Percent Who:					
Level of Partisanship*	*Voted in Last Presidential Election*	*Voted in Last Congressional Election*	*Tried to Persuade Someone†*	*Attended a Political Meeting or Rally*	*Worked in a Campaign*	*Belong to Political Group*
Strong partisans.	83%	72%	36%	15%	14%	12%
Weak partisans .	74%	57%	24%	8%	5%	3%
Independents ..	53%	46%	19%	6%	3%	1%

* Strong partisans are those respondents who say they identify "strongly" with one of the two parties; weak partisans identify, but not strongly, with one of the parties or lean to one of the parties; independents do not identify with or lean toward any party.
† Tried to persuade someone to vote for one of the candidates or parties.
Sources: *CPS 1970 National Election Study*, except for presidential voting which was based on the *CPS 1972 National Election Study*. (See Appendix.)

and to take part in campaign activities than Independents. Independents, in fact, seemed to be very weakly motivated.

Political Efficacy

Politics is awesome. In large industrial democracies where so many conflicts are waged in the political arena, it is not easy to comprehend all that goes on. It is difficult to know who is doing what and with what effect. Nor is it easy to know for sure if one's own behavior matters, matters in the sense of producing results or bringing about change. After all, how much impact can one man have?

In this connection, Morris Rosenberg believes that one obstacle to participation is the feeling that such involvement is futile.[35] According to Rosenberg, many people have a sense of personal inadequacy, and with good reason: "It is rather easy to see why, in a mass society characterized by broad disparities in power, an individual may tend to develop a sense of personal insignificance and weakness."[36] Some people feel powerless, unimportant, and ignorant; others think government is unmanageable and political power resides in the hands of invisible forces. Many feel they have a voice

[35] Morris Rosenberg, "Some Determinants of Political Apathy," *Public Opinion Quarterly*, Vol. 18 (1954–55), pp. 349–66.
[36] Ibid., p. 355.

only during elections, and even then it is not a loud one. The important thing is that there is a measure of truth to these feelings. Rosenberg, along with many other social scientists, feels that in modern "mass" society, political power *is* remote from the individual. It is difficult for one person to wield much influence in a political system as vast and bureaucratized as ours is.

An example based on the experiences of the citizens of a small town in Illinois illustrates this point. A large motel chain wants to build a $40-million amusement park in Gurnee, Illinois. The corporation has asked the town to annex and rezone 600 unincorporated acres. Most residents of the town fear that the park will destroy the rural atmosphere of their community. Yet they feel powerless to fight the corporation. A woman explains why:

> They come in here with their millions and their big lawyers and their studies and graphs and all those officials who are good public speakers . . . and they say a park wouldn't hurt Gurnee.
> And we get off work at 4:30 and we're tired and we go to the meeting when we should fix up the house and we say "You're going to ruin our town" and they say "Prove it." It's so hard.[37]

Obviously, given the uneven distribution of political resources many residents believe it is simply futile to fight. Unfortunately, such reactions are quite common in a democracy.

Still, some people have more confidence in their power to influence decision making than others have. These feelings of being able to affect government go under various names, but we will use the term political *efficacy*, as it is more common and descriptive. It means ". . . the feeling that individual political action does have, or can have, an impact on the political process, i.e., that it is worthwhile to perform one's civic duties."[38]

Many citizens do not have much political self-confidence. Reporting on a study of the 1960 gubernatorial primary in Massachusetts, for example, Murray Levin and Murray Eden find that:

> Forty-eight percent of the respondents "agreed" with the statement, "Public officials in Massachusetts don't care what people like me think." Forty-seven percent of the respondents disagreed

---

[37] *New York Times*, November 15, 1973, p. 43.

[38] Angus Campbell, Gerald Gurin, and Warren E. Miller, *The Voter Decides* (Westport, Conn.: Greenwald Press, 1971), p. 187.

with the statement, "The way people vote in Massachusetts is the main thing that decides how things are run in this state. . . ." Forty-three percent of the respondents agreed with the statement, "People like me don't have any say about what the state government does," while sixty-six percent agreed that "Politics and government in Massachusetts seem so complicated that people like me can't understand it."[39]

These figures, which are indicative of the nation as a whole, show that the lack of self-confidence is widespread.

There is abundant evidence that political efficacy and participation go together. In a study already cited, *The American Voter,* about half of those people who scored "low" on a measure of self-confidence did not bother to vote; 91 percent of the "highs" did vote.[40] Almond and Verba's five-nation survey finds that these feelings are related to partisan activities, awareness and interest in politics, adherence to democratic values and satisfaction with the political system.[41]

As we would expect, political efficacy is related to social class, with those in the upper classes being most confident. Confidence also seems to be related to an individual's experience in politics. If his past participation has not been fruitful it is not likely that he will have much hope for his future efforts. The experience of black Americans is a case in point: until recently state and national governments have not paid much attention to their troubles, even in spite of years of vigorous protest. Not surprisingly, their level of efficacy is lower than that of whites. Table 5.7 compares white and nonwhite responses to a series of questions dealing with confidence. The differences are striking. No doubt some of them can be explained by differences in socioeconomic status. Yet it seems probable that the long disenfranchisement and powerlessness of blacks has contributed to these feelings. In short, doubts about one's abilities to affect political events may indeed be a realistic assessment of the situation.

To the extent that a person can overcome these feelings of political inadequacy he will be an active participant. Achieving

---

[39] Murray B. Levin and Murray Eden, "Political Strategy for the Alienated Voter," *Public Opinion Quarterly,* Vol. 26 (1962), p. 48.

[40] Campbell et al., *The American Voter,* p. 105.

[41] Almond and Verba, *The Civic Culture,* chap. ix.

Table 5.7
RELATIONSHIPS BETWEEN POLITICAL EFFICACY
AND RACE

	Whites	*Nonwhites*
People like me don't have a say in what the government does	34% *	50%
Voting is the only way to influence the government	59%	79%
Politicians don't care what the common man thinks	46%	70%
Congress loses touch with the people after an election	60%	78%
Political parties only want your vote	53%	74%

* Figures are percents agreeing with each statement.
Source: *CPS 1970 American National Election Study.* (See Appendix.)

self-confidence is easier for some people than for others. Middle-class whites, because of their social positions and experiences, generally find it easier than do blacks. One of the unsolved problems of democracy is to build confidence in the citizenry. Part of the solution, however, requires that political institutions be made more relevant and sensitive to the needs of lower status individuals.

THE COSTS OF POLITICAL PARTICIPATION

People must allocate their time and energy among various activities. Whether or not a person will find it profitable to do something requires him to weigh the expected benefits against the anticipated costs of the action. Participating in a protest march, for example, takes time and energy. In some instances, the individual risks arrest or physical injury. Moreover, marching means he cannot be doing something else, so he forgoes rewards from alternative activities. When we take the *costs* of political participation into account we further our understanding of why people do and do not become involved in politics.

For some individuals the cost of an activity may be too high; for others, it may be acceptable. Many poor people, migrant farm workers, for instance, avoid protest marches because they cannot afford the time and energy required. College students generally have an abundance of both, and for that reason, they are better able to take part.

Naturally, laws and regulations partly determine how costly an activity will be. Voting turnout in European countries exceeds that of the United States because eligibility requirements are less strenuous. Here, in order to vote a person must register and re-register. Although amendments to the Constitution have eased registration requirements, it is still necessary to wait in line, to establish residency, to pledge allegiance, and so forth. For many these costs are too burdensome. Communities vary in the restrictiveness of their registration requirements, and the severity of these requirements affects turnout at the polls. Areas with liberal regulations have higher voting rates than those with tighter rules.[42] As another example, Allen Shinn reports that the average registration level of Texas counties increased by 7.5 percent immediately after the poll tax was declared unconstitutional. This sudden increase compares with previous increases of only 0.33 percent.[43]

Laws affect the costs of participation in less obvious ways. Many communities have "nonpartisan" elections. A product of the reform movement, nonpartisan elections require candidates to run without an identifying party label on the ballot. By stripping candidates of party labels, the reformers thought, the influence of political machines would be reduced and voters would be encouraged to vote for the man, not the party. The rate of participation in nonpartisan elections is surprising, however, for far fewer people vote in them than in partisan contests.[44] Nonpartisan elections increase the costs of participating because people use party labels as "cues" to guide their behavior. (Recall the data in Table 5.6 showing the relationship between partisanship and participation.) These cues cut the cost of acquiring information about candidates and make choosing that much easier. Thus, the political structure of a com-

---

[42] Stanley Kelley, Jr., Richard E. Ayres, and William G. Bowen, "Registration and Voting: Putting First Things First," *American Political Science Review*, Vol. 61 (1967), pp. 359–79. Also see Campbell et al., *The American Voter*, chap. xi, for similar conclusions.

[43] Allen M. Shinn, Jr., "A Note on Voter Registration and Turnout in Texas 1960–1970," *Journal of Politics*, Vol. 33 (1971), pp. 1120–29.

[44] Robert R. Alford and Eugene C. Lee, "Voting Turnout in American Cities," *American Political Science Review*, Vol. 62 (1968), pp. 796–813.

munity, like its election laws, partly determines the cost of participation.

As another example, consider provisions for straight ticket voting. Many communities prohibit the voter from pulling just one
lever to cast a ballot for a party's entire slate of candidates. They
require instead that the individual vote for each office separately.
Yet most elections involve numerous contests, from president to
dog catcher. Wading through lengthy ballots, item by item, taxes
even the most dedicated citizens. Long, complicated ballots and
ones which prevent straight ticket voting discourage electoral participation, especially in state and local affairs.[45]

Other factors affect costs. Unwritten norms and customs can de-
crease participation, as in the South where—even after the abolition
of legal restrictions—informal pressures keep nonwhites from voting. The availability of information is still another variable. There
are no hard data on this point, but it seems reasonable to expect that
readily available information will increase participation. In a particularly close and bitterly contested election, everyone seems to
know about the candidates and the major issues. They are discussed
on radio and television, in the newspapers, and by word of mouth.
It is possible for people to stumble onto information. Most elections do not generate much excitement—and hence little information as well. Parties frequently obscure their differences, making it
difficult for the voter to obtain relevant information. Not knowing
where the parties and candidates stand no doubt creates apathy
among many citizens.

Finally, political participation may be costly in terms of interpersonal relations. Political activity, Rosenberg points out, may
disturb business and personal relationships.[46] Let us say a man
decides to take part in a peace rally. The issue is surely going to
be controversial. So if his friends and business associates discover
his involvement he risks incurring their displeasure; he may lose
customers; his neighbors may shun him. He may have to justify
himself in front of others. Many people are not willing to pay these
costs. They would rather be apathetic but more secure in their
interpersonal relationships.

In summary, political participation is more or less expensive.

---

[45] Campbell et al., *The American Voter,* chap. xi.
[46] Rosenberg, "Some Determinants of Political Apathy," pp. 349–53.

Whether or not a person will pay the price depends partly on how many resources he has. But it also depends on what benefits he expects his participation will bring, a topic to which we now turn.

THE PERCEIVED BENEFITS OF POLITICAL PARTICIPATION

Political participation is a matter of motivation: nonvoters abstain because the value of voting is, in these people's minds, simply not large enough.[47] People engage in activities which satisfy their needs or offer rewards. Or, stated in the words of Chapter 3, responses which are reinforced occur more frequently than those which are not reinforced. Widespread apathy in a democracy means many citizens find politics unrewarding. Since, as we have already seen, rewards are related to participation, this attitude may seem strange. After all, if people want something, they have to work for it. The common man, however, has good reasons for thinking political activity in inherently unrewarding.

Rosenberg suggests that many people lack inducements or "spurs" to action.[48] The great issues of the day are, when all is said and done, quite far removed from one's personal needs and interests. (How important is foreign aid to one's immediate problems?) "The individual's incentive to political activity," Rosenberg writes, "is often dulled by the absence of direct and immediate satisfactions to be derived from the activity itself."[49] In the language of psychology, there are few instrumental gratifications to be obtained from politics. (See Chapter 3.) Earning a living or solving family problems call for nonpolitical activity. Politics is, generally speaking, irrelevant to a man or woman's daily life.

The expected payoff from political participation is, of course, influenced by other factors. Are the outcomes of an election worth worrying about? Many local elections probably do not seem very important to the average voter. The offices lack power and prestige and the issues are trivial. If the stakes in an election are not large, neither will be the involvement.

Perceived alternatives also affect the level of interest and participation. Conventional wisdom holds that when faced with a choice

---

[47] Campbell, "The Passive Citizen," p. 9.
[48] Rosenberg, "Some Determinants of Political Apathy," pp. 353–55.
[49] Ibid., p. 362.

between "tweedledee and tweedledum," an individual will vote for neither. And why should he? Since he sees little difference between them, it makes little difference to him which is elected.

At the risk of exaggeration, it appears that the American political system produces more than its share of "nonchoices." One can find many reasons for this state of affairs, but they boil down to one generalization: most candidates try to follow a middle-of-the-road path, appealing to as many voters as possible while at the same time antagonizing no one. The best way to stay in the middle is to be noncommittal and to espouse only those policies on which there is consensus. But since other candidates are doing the same, the choices available to the voters are limited. Hence, many of them show little or no interest in what is going on.

Arguing in this same vein, E. E. Schattschneider attributes mass apathy—there were 40 million eligible nonvoters in 1960—to the unresponsiveness and irrelevance of the American political system.[50] He believes the nonparticipants do not find many issues relevant to their needs or interests. For these people to become active would require changing the "agenda" of politics. Millions of people, in other words, do not see the relevance of politics to their lives. Political battles are waged over matters of little concern to them. The migrant farm worker, for example, is not likely to see the national debt, oil depletion allowances, nuclear testing, the latest crisis in Berlin, or even social security as having any great significance for him personally. Others may see the importance but feel any activity on their part is not going to affect the outcome on these issues one way or another.

These comments are not meant to apply only to the United States. Governments vary in their responsiveness to the demands of citizens. If people feel public policy is remote and unrelated to their needs they will tend to be apathetic. This principle applies to other democracies.[51] It also applies to underdeveloped nations in which mass apathy is especially prevalent. Governments in these areas are simply not able to meet the demands placed upon them.

---

[50] E. E. Schattschneider, *The Semi-Sovereign People* (New York: Holt, Rinehart & Winston Co., Inc., 1960), p. 107.

[51] Di Palma (*Apathy and Participation,* p. 84) notes: "Whatever their socioeconomic development, some polities are remote and unresponsive, and because of this they elicit disaffection regardless of citizen status."

Sometimes instability or even revolution result; more often citizens become apathetic.

In conclusion, four classes of variables affect political participation: socioeconomic status, attitudes toward politics, expected costs, and expected rewards. These factors are all interrelated. A highly educated businessman earning a good income is apt to be interested and involved in politics; the costs of his participation are probably not too high for him to pay; and he no doubt finds his experiences in politics rewarding even if he does not always get his way. Hence, his participation reinforces his confidence and expectations which in turn motivate further activity. A migrant farm worker, on the other hand, who has almost no education and a minimal (if not subsistence) income has little time for public affairs. Not having the skills and resources of the businessman he will probably not be as active. If he does participate it will more than likely be a momentary affair as when he stops to listen to a political commercial on the radio. He will no doubt vote in a presidential election only once or twice in his life. Since the farm worker is not an activist and since he is estranged from political life, he is not likely to have much confidence in his political prowess nor expect to gain much from the political system. So, as in the case of the businessman, political participation is a cumulative experience: since he has not been involved he is likely to stay inactive and his passivity will continue to influence his attitudes and expectations.

HOW MUCH PARTICIPATION IS DESIRABLE?

We have sought to explain why people do and do not take an active role in politics. Certain groups—the poor, blacks, and the young, for example—do not participate as much as others. We have also seen that the political system distributes rewards, both tangible and intangible, unevenly and partly on the basis of participation.

Knowing these things, we might advocate that these groups become more involved. And, furthermore, we can offer some clues as to how to increase their participation because we now understand what motivates them. But before recommending this course we might ask whether increased involvement is really in the best interests of democracy.

According to civics textbooks, the good citizen pays attention to local and national affairs, informs himself about the issues, votes, complains to the appropriate officials when he feels wronged, and works for change within the "system." Some political scientists, though, say there can be too much of a good thing.

In *The Civic Culture,* Almond and Verba argue that democratic political systems contain a contradiction: on the one hand, ruling elites have to be controlled and made responsible to the people. To do so requires an attentive, active citizenry. On the other hand, elites must have some leeway to rule. Large industrial societies cannot be run like town meetings. If the masses question and criticize every decision, every law, every regulation, public officials will have no room for maneuver.[52]

Moreover, mass participation would mean every issue could be the basis of divisive polarization. If everyone actively sought to get his way, conflicts over what are now relatively trivial matters would become unbearably intense. Political institutions would be unstable and would lose legitimacy. Compromises would be difficult to arrange. Policy makers would be paralyzed for fear of alienating large blocks of citizens.

Bernard Berelson wonders: "How could a mass democracy work if all the people were deeply involved in politics? Lack of interest by some people is not without its benefits, too."[53]

There are other dangers in mass participation. Numerous studies indicate that nonparticipants are more likely than participants to be intolerant of minority groups and dissent; to be more authoritarian and xenophobic; to be more resistant to change; to be more uninformed about the Constitution and the Bill of Rights. The nonparticipant, some observers fear, would not make a welcome addition to the electorate since his attitudes are inconsistent with the principles of democracy.

The ideal democracy to Almond and Verba, then, is one composed of a mixture of activism and passivism, involvement and indifference, questioning and deference to authority. "The citizen," Almond and Verba maintain, "is called on to pursue contra-

---

[52] Almond and Verba, *The Civic Culture,* chap. xv.

[53] Bernard R. Berelson, Paul F. Lazarsfeld, and William N. McPhee, *Voting* (paperback ed., Chicago: The University of Chicago Press, 1966), p. 314.

dictory goals: he must be active, yet passive; involved, yet not too involved; influential, yet deferential."[54]

Yet many regard this line of thinking as conservative, even reactionary. After all, how are injustices to be rectified if not by the affected individuals themselves? Robert Lane argues that if political stability is achieved through the apathy of low-status groups it will be at the "cost of fair representation and a just distribution of governmental goods and services."[55] More important, perhaps, is the assumption that increases in mass participation cannot be achieved without conflict. It is not clear that this is so. And even if instability occurs, some groups may thereby achieve their legitimate aspirations. The alleviation of poverty and racial injustice seem at least as desirable as social harmony. Writing during the Depression, Reinhold Niebuhr, the theologian, said in this regard:

> Think of all the kind souls who stand in horror of a social conflict who are at this moment benefitting from, and living comfortable lives at the expense of, a social system which condemns 13 million men to misery and semi-starvation. Failure to recognize this covert brutality of the social struggle is probably the greatest weakness of middle-class liberals, and it lends a note of hypocrisy and self-deception to every moral pretension which seeks to eliminate violence in the social struggle.[56]

Human advancement by political means and social and political stability may not be antithetical but they coexist precariously. In concluding, we can at this point do no more than take note of this dilemma.

---

[54] Almond and Verba, *The Civic Culture,* p. 479.

[55] Robert E. Lane, *Political Life* (New York: The Free Press, 1959), p. 346.

[56] Reinhold Niebuhr, "After Capitalism—What?" *The World Tomorrow,* vol. xvi (1933), quoted from *New Deal Thought,* ed. Howard Zinn (Indianapolis: The Bobbs-Merrill Co., Inc., 1966), p. 21.

6

Voting Behavior: How the Common Man Chooses His Leaders

David Charles and Gene Guzzo have a problem, one shared by many Americans every four years, who to vote for as President. In 1972 the choice was between Richard Nixon, the incumbent, and George McGovern.

It is particularly interesting and important to know how men like these make up their minds. For in theory at least, free and open elections are the mainspring of democracy. They are the source of power which allows a democratic society to progress and adapt to change. According to conventional wisdom, elections have several purposes. By allowing people to choose their leaders and to vote on public policies, they express the "general will." They mandate public officials to carry out certain policies. And since political leaders serve at the pleasure of the people, elections also provide the means for rewarding good conduct and punishing bad. Perhaps more important, the electoral system makes peaceful change possible. Once citizens have agreed on "the rules of the game," they can engage in nonviolent political competition. In short, the ballot is the quintessential symbol of democracy.

149

Although elections do not always fit these ideals, they are nevertheless the most important form of mass political participation in a democracy. Voting is as far as the average person goes in politics and many citizens feel it is their only way to influence government.

Because elections are perceived to be so important in the functioning of democracy and because so many people vote in them, the motives of the voter is one of the most prodigiously studied subjects in social sciences. Bookstores are full of books purporting to explain how the voters make up their minds. Scholars, politicians, journalists, and laymen all have their favorite theories. Within political science probably no single topic receives more attention. Each year thousands of dollars are spent trying to figure out why individuals vote for one man over another.

Unfortunately, in spite of the seemingly endless research we know relatively little. Peter Natchez summarizes the divergence of thinking:

> There is no scarcity of popular wisdom devoted to explaining why the American people vote as they do. They vote their interests (Truman), their fears (Nixon), and their aspirations (Kennedy). They vote *for* candidates (Eisenhower) and *against* candidates (Goldwater). They learn quickly (L.B.J.), they forget slowly (F.D.R.). They know what they want (The New Deal, peace, prosperity) but they do not want very much (a persistent 35 percent do not vote at all). Party allegiances are stable (Humphrey almost won) but not determinant (Nixon did win). In short, we know a great deal after each election, but over the long run, all electoral explanations seem to cancel each other out.[1]

The goal of this chapter is to sort out some of the information on voting and to put it into a perspective which makes the voting act a bit more comprehensible. It is not possible to present a complete and verified theory, for none exists, but we can identify and describe a few of the main forces acting on people as they make up their minds about who to vote for.

To facilitate our task, let us meet the hypothetical Mr. Charles and Mr. Guzzo as they approached the election of 1972. David Charles is 45 years old, Protestant, married, a father of three girls,

---

[1] Peter Natchez, "Images of Voting: The Social Psychologists," *Public Policy*, Vol. 18 (1970), p. 553. Italics his.

and a suburbanite. After graduating from college with a major in engineering and serving two years in the Army during World War II, he started his own business, a construction firm, which is now quite successful. Active in several community organizations, Charles feels he is a good citizen, carefully follows current events, votes regularly and has even run for local office. Like his father he considers himself a conservative Republican.

If David Charles epitomizes an upper middle-class American, Gene Guzzo represents the blue-collar workers. Since his father died while he was still in high school, Guzzo did not receive a diploma but instead worked at odd jobs to help support his mother and five brothers and sisters. After several years he found employment on the assembly line of an appliance factory where he is now a foreman. He belongs to a union but is not very active in it. Right now he lives near the center of a large city; he hopes to move out to the suburbs as soon as he and his wife, who also works, have saved enough money for a down payment on a house. Gene Guzzo, a Catholic, considers himself a Democrat. Unlike Mr. Charles, however, he is not particularly interested in politics although he usually votes in presidential elections. He does not know too much about what is going on in Washington except that "taxes are too damned high."

Faced with a choice between Nixon and McGovern, how would these two men vote? Some observers say people vote on the basis of their group memberships, memberships ranging from the family to a social class. Others think the voter is motivated by psychological forces such as his perceptions of candidates and loyalties toward a particular party. Both of these views—or "schools of thought"—stress the nonpurposive nature of voting: when a person selects one candidate over another he is reacting to various stimuli, and is not voting to attain some ultimate goal. There is another group of social scientists who feel people do act with a purpose. When a man votes, he *is* trying to achieve some goal. This second group, the instrumentalists, can be further divided. Some of them, decision-making theorists, argue that voters vote in a way to maximize rewards and voting is seen as a means to various ends. The last group claims voting is determined largely by voters' preferences on public policy.

These four approaches, the group membership, the psychological, the decision making and the public policy, are illustrated in

Figure 6.1 which also shows the main concepts of each. Each of them will be explored in turn. The distinctions are a bit simplistic

Figure 6.1
EXPLANATIONS OF VOTING

Approach	*Explanatory Principles*
Noninstrumental Approaches:	
Group	Attitudes and values of family, friends, neighbors, the community and larger groups influence the individual's vote.
Psychological	Party identification and partisan attitude influence the individual's vote.
Instrumental Approaches:	
Decision making	Individuals try to maximize utilities.
Public policy	Voters respond to their attitudes on public policy issues.

and artificial due to the overlap among the categorizations, but by dividing the material this way we may learn of the wide variety of influences acting on Mr. Charles and Mr. Guzzo.

THE EFFECTS OF SOCIAL GROUPS ON VOTING BEHAVIOR

An individual's group memberships—his family, friends, co-workers, neighbors, community, and social class—shape his political and social characteristics. Not surprisingly, then, many scholars turn to the group as an explanation of voting behavior. Their belief is that a person's social attachments determine his preferences among candidates.

In taking this approach, they question the rationality of the average voter. Instead of giving careful consideration to the issues and qualifications of the candidates, the voter supposedly responds rather mechanically to social pressures; he substitutes group loyalties for political judgment; he does not think for himself but is guided by the standards of his friends, his fellow workers, and his class.

Perhaps the best example of this school of voting behavior is contained in Bernard Berelson, Paul Lazarsfeld, and William Mc-

Phee's seminal work, *Voting*, first published in 1954.[2] Their analysis hinges on a refutation of the civics book image of the "rational" voter. In most civics textbooks, the ideal voter carefully examines each candidate's qualifications and position on issues and votes for the "best" man. This traditional approach, of course, assumes the availability of clear-cut alternatives. It also assumes that voters weigh the relevance of issues to their own needs and then act in ways best serving these needs. According to the authors of *Voting*, however, voters usually do not behave in this "rational" manner.[3]

If people are not rational, if they do not weigh alternatives, what does explain their behavior? The authors say politics is ambiguous and confusing. It is often hard for the man in the street to know what side to take in a controversy or which candidate to vote for. Consequently, he tends to respond in two ways. First, he can rely on previously acquired loyalties and experiences. These loyalties and values are usually formed by an individual's association with various groups. Not knowing what to make of either Nixon or McGovern, Gene Guzzo can choose by falling back on what he learned in his family, in his neighborhood, and at the factory. All of these groups are by and large Democratic so he might vote not for McGovern, the man who promises to end the war in Vietnam, but for McGovern, the Democrat.

Second, and more important, the individual can follow the lead of those people around him whom he likes, trusts, and respects. By taking cues from others, he is relieved of making the choice by himself. Furthermore, most individuals are susceptible to some extent to social pressures. This susceptibility is heightened when a person faces an ambiguous, confusing situation.[4]

In other words, what better way is there to solve a problem than to ask someone's advice? Perhaps Mr. Guzzo does not have much information about McGovern, but he knows the union leader, Alex, and his neighbor, Sid, are for McGovern. So why shouldn't he vote for McGovern as well? Many people follow (consciously or not) the lead of the groups to which they belong. In this way, social memberships, whether they are face-to-face groups as in the family,

---

[2] Bernard Berelson, Paul F. Lazarsfeld, and William McPhee, *Voting* (paperback ed.; Chicago: The University of Chicago Press, 1966).

[3] Ibid., pp. 114–15.

[4] Ibid., p. 115.

or larger groupings as a union or community, provide cues or guides to behavior. As such, they offer a shortcut to decision making.

Group Effects on Voting

There is abundant evidence showing the connection between group memberships and individual attitudes and behavior. Table 6.1 presents some data indicating that a man votes in the same way his friends and co-workers do. In particular, among those respondents reporting that all of their friends voted for Humphrey in 1968, 91 percent also voted for Humphrey; in only about 1 out of 10 cases did an individual "defect" from a homogeneous group. Notice also that there is overwhelming agreement among spouses: husbands and wives usually vote for the same candidate, suggesting that one partner is providing cues to the other. (Although it is not clear from the data, this function is most likely performed by the husband.) Finally, there is homogeneity of preference within fam-

Table 6.1
RELATIONSHIPS BETWEEN GROUP MEMBERSHIPS AND VOTING

(a)

Respondent Voted for	Number of Respondent's Friends Who Voted for Humphrey				
	All	*Most*	*Some*	*A Few*	*None*
Humphrey	92%	87%	42%	21%	7%
Nixon or Wallace	8	13	58	79	93
	100%	100%	100%	100%	100%
	(279)	(1,080)	(1,685)	(1,120)	(477)

(b)

Respondent Voted for	Number of Respondent's Co-Workers Who Voted for Humphrey				
	All	*Most*	*Some*	*A Few*	*None*
Humphrey	85%	76%	43%	23%	17%
Nixon or Wallace	15	24	57	77	83
	100%	100%	100%	100%	100%
	(78)	(423)	(747)	(374)	(194)

Table 6.1 (continued)

(c)

Respondent	Respondent's Spouse Voted for:		
Voted for	Nixon	Humphrey	Wallace
Nixon	92%	7%	11%
Humphrey	6	92	9
Wallace	2	1	80
	100%	100%	100%
	(1,724)	(1,674)	(449)

(d)

	Respondent's Family Voted for:*			
Respondent Voted for	Mostly for Nixon	Mostly for Humphrey	Mostly for Wallace	About Even
Nixon	88%	7%	11%	42%
Humphrey	8	91	8	43
Wallace	4	2	81	15
	100%	100%	100%	100%
	(303)	(365)	(74)	(43)

* Includes only single respondents.
Note: Figures in parentheses refer to the number of cases.
Source: David Kovenock, et al., *Comparative State Election Project.* (See Appendix.)

ilies. In those few cases where the family itself was divided (the last column of Table 6.1d), the respondents split about evenly between Nixon and Humphrey. All in all, these data show that a person's political preferences are closely related to the preferences of his family, friends, and co-workers.

Other findings suggest that social class (another indicator of group membership) is also related to voting. Lazarsfeld, for example, constructed an *Index of Political Predisposition* using religion, place of residence (urban-rural), and socioeconomic status. They found their index to be a good predictor of how a person will vote and conclude, rather boldly, ". . . . a person thinks, politically, as he is, socially. Social characteristics determine political preference."[5]

This view of social determinism has been repeated in numerous studies. But as we will see in a moment, the strength and meaning of the relationship can be overstated.

---

[5] Paul Lazarsfeld, Bernard Berelson, and Hazel Gaudet, *The People's Choice* (New York: Columbia University Press, 1944), p. 26.

Cross-Pressure

Before looking at the contrary evidence, however, let us consider what happens when a person's group environment is not homogeneous. What happens to Gene Guzzo when he moves to a Republican suburb but continues to belong to a heavily Democratic union? In his new situation he is under *cross-pressure*. Some of his friends and co-workers will push him in one direction while others push him in another. How does he respond?

In a pluralist society it is difficult to avoid at least some cross-pressures. The authors of *Voting* estimate that as much as a third of the electorate may be subjected to conflicting pressures of one sort or another. Studies show that people react to the conflict by either abstaining from voting or delaying their vote decision until the last minute. Not surprisingly, the cross-pressured citizen has unstable preferences and often changes his mind. A common reaction is to become apathetic and lose interest in politics.[6]

How Valid Is the Group Approach?

However important concepts like group memberships and cross-pressures are in explaining voting, they obviously do not tell the whole story. For example, Angus Campbell and his colleagues note that between 1948 and 1952 thousands of people who voted for Truman, a Democrat, voted four years later for Eisenhower, a Republican. This enormous switch in sentiment could not be accounted for by changes in group and class characteristics, which usually shift rather slowly.[7] Other researchers find that while socioeconomic factors are strongly related to a person's vote, there are even more important variables, such as attitudes on issues.[8]

Group attachments, it now appears, are antecedent conditions

---

[6] Berelson et al., *Voting*, pp. 128–42; and Robert Melson, "Ideology and Inconsistency: The 'Cross-Pressured' Nigerian Worker," *American Political Science Review*, Vol. 65 (1971), pp. 161–71.

[7] Angus Campbell, Philip E. Converse, Warren E. Miller, and Donald E. Stokes, *The American Voter* (New York: John Wiley & Sons, 1960), pp. 65–66.

[8] See, for example, David M. Kovenock, Philip L. Beardsley, and James W. Prothro, "Status, Party, Ideology, Issues, and Candidate Choice: A Preliminary Theory Relevant Analysis of the 1968 American Presidential Election," paper presented at the Eighth World Congress of the International Political Science Association, Munich, Germany, August 31–September 5, 1970.

which point an individual in a given direction (e.g., make him liberal or conservative, Democratic or Republican) but do not completely determine which specific path he will follow in making up his mind about a candidate. Thus, Mr. Guzzo's upbringing and work and neighborhood environment predispose him to vote for the Democratic candidate, McGovern, and over the long run we might expect him to vote for more Democrats than Republicans. But at the very moment he votes, Gene Guzzo is also subjected to a variety of other attitudes and motives. In order to understand fully his decision, we need to consider his thoughts at the moment he makes up his mind. Thus, we now turn our attention to the analysis of psychological forces acting on the voter.

THE PSYCHOLOGICAL APPROACH TO VOTING

According to the psychological school, voting for a particular candidate, like making any choice, results from psychological processes. Instead of looking at a person's life history, we should attempt to reconstruct the attitudes and motives immediately preceding the decision. The authors of *The American Voter,* the major inspiration for the psychological approach, write: ". . . voting is in the end an act of individuals, and the motives for this act must be sought in psychological forces acting on individual human beings."[9] Hence, voters are not motivated in an immediate sense by social group pressures, but rather by their own psychological makeup, including attitudes and perceptions about candidates, parties, and issues.

Though there is some disagreement and confusion, the adherents of this school agree that the psychological field acting on the individual consists mainly of two factors, a partisan attitude and party identification. Taken singly or together, these two variables are excellent predictors of how a person will vote, at least in a presidential election.

The Six Dimensions of Partisan Attitude

People have attitudes toward political objects such as parties, candidates, and issues. These attitudes often implicitly favor one

---

[9] Campbell et al., *The American Voter,* p. 64.

party over another. David Charles feels the Republicans do a better job of running the federal government than do the Democrats. Republicans, he thinks, are more honest, efficient, businesslike. Looking at the parties as "managers" of government, Mr. Charles' attitudes are pro-Republican. If we look at objects like the parties as managers of government and combine a person's attitudes toward these objects into a single measure, we get what the authors of *The American Voter* call a partisan attitude.

A simple technique is used to measure a person's partisan attitude. He is given a series of questions asking about his likes and dislikes of the candidates and parties. (For example, "Is there anything in particular about Eisenhower that might make you want to vote for him?") Answers to these questions are analyzed in two ways. The investigators first look for substantive matters. What does the respondent like and dislike? He may like Ike's ideas on foreign policy but feel a military man is not qualified to be president. For reasons which are not entirely clear, the investigators classified the substantive responses into six categories or "dimensions": "The personal attributes of Stevenson; the personal attributes of Eisenhower; the groups involved in politics and the questions of group interest affecting them; the issues of domestic policy; the issues of foreign policy; and the comparative record of the two parties in managing the affairs of government."[10]

The second way in which the answers were analyzed was to see if they were pro-Republican or pro-Democratic. Should a person mention something favorable about Eisenhower's abilities he would be given a score of plus one. If the person says he likes Eisenhower because Ike helps the working man, then he would be assigned a score of plus one on the group dimension. If he says something unfavorable about Eisenhower he is given a score of minus one on the appropriate dimension. All of the person's answers are coded and scored in this way with the score on each dimension being simply the sum of the plus ones and minus ones. Of course, not every person in the study had a score in each dimension—some people said they did not like or dislike anything about either party or either candidate. Enough people answered, however, so that the authors could estimate the overall importance of these attitudes.

The partisan attitude measures how a person feels about the

---

[10] Ibid., p. 67.

major parties and candidates. The authors feel their measure is an excellent tool for explaining and predicting an individual's vote. Using the measure of partisan attitude they claim to predict correctly the vote for more than 85 percent of the sample.[11] That is, a person who was, say, a Republican partisan on the scale would in all probability vote for the Republican candidate. So good was their measure when applied to the 1956 election that it actually did a better job of predicting the respondents' votes than the respondents themselves could do.[12] This is because before the election many people said they were unsure of whom to vote for, even though they had a well-defined partisan attitude.

Despite its effectiveness in predicting voting, the measure of partisan attitude raises two points. First, by inquiring into the likes and dislikes of the major candidates the approach seems to overstate the importance of the candidates' personalities and qualifications. If we are asked what we like about a man, we are probably going to mention his personal attributes. This does not mean that we do not know or care about his stand on issues. The wording of the question simply turns our attention to the candidate's personal qualities.[13] This is an important bias because the partisan attitude has been used as evidence that people are primarily motivated by images of candidates and not by the candidates' positions on substantive issues. So by themselves, data on the partisan attitude do not tell us if voters act rationally or not.

The second point deals with how much information we really obtain from knowing a person's score on the partisan attitude. Asking a person what he likes and dislikes about candidates and then finding out who he voted for leaves a number of questions unanswered. In particular, we want to know why a person arrived at a given attitude in the first place. Why does he say "I like Ike because he favors the common man?" What factors affect his perceptions of the candidates and parties? Are his opinions based on information or ignorance? The measure of partisan attitude may, in other words, tell us that a person will vote for a candidate he likes but it does not tell us how he came to like the candidate in the first place.

---

[11] Ibid., p. 74.

[12] Ibid.

[13] John H. Kessel, "Comment: The Issues in Issue Voting," *American Political Science Review*, Vol. 66 (1972), pp. 459–65.

Party Identification

Party identification or partisanship refers to the "closeness" a person feels toward a political party. It is a useful variable for explaining many behaviors—the rate of political participation, interest and concern with politics, knowledge of issues and candidates, ideology, and political preferences. Most political scientists consider partisanship essential in the study of voting and they have accumulated a vast store of information about it.

Party identification is measured directly by asking individuals if they think of themselves as belonging to one of the two major parties and, if so, how closely they identify with it. (For example, "Do you think of yourself as a Democrat, a Republican, or an Independent?" Should someone say "Independent," he is asked if he "leans" toward one of the parties.) Usually about 70 percent of a sample can be classified as at least a weak partisan. Direct and simple, this measurement procedure consistently yields theoretically interesting and practical results: knowing a person's party affiliation tells us a great deal about his political behavior.

Of course, we hear a lot these days about the declining importance of political parties. Most people, it is claimed, vote for the man, not the party. The number of Independents is increasing rapidly. The day of the city machine and the party boss is gone. Finally, some assert that issues, not party labels, are foremost on the minds of the voters, especially those who are young and educated.

Without completely refuting these assertions, the data in Table 6.2 puts them in better perspective. Although the proportion of Independents has increased slightly over the years, they are still outnumbered by identifiers almost two to one. Note also the stability of the preferences; Democrats have been the dominant party throughout the period. Other research shows that party identification is an enduring allegiance acquired during adolescence. (See Chapter 3.) People generally keep their party identification for life, changing it mostly in times of social and political upheaval—as during the Depression of the 1930s—or when they are socially mobile.

Parties are roughly related to social classes. The typical Republican, like Mr. Charles, is white, Protestant, well-educated, a professional or white-collar worker, at least moderately affluent and a resident of a suburb, small town, or farm. Democrats, like Mr.

Table 6.2
PARTY IDENTIFICATION FROM 1952 TO 1970

	1952	1954	1956	1958	1960	1962	1964	1966	1968	1970	1972
Democrats	47%	47%	44%	46%	46%	47%	51%	45%	45%	43%	40%
Independents	22	22	24	19	23	23	22	28	29	31	35
Republicans	27	27	29	29	27	27	24	25	24	25	23
Nothing, don't know ..	4	4	3	5	4	3	2	2	2	1	2
Total	100%	100%	100%	100%	100%	100%	100%	100%	100%	100%	100%
	(1,614)	(1,139)	(1,772)	(1,269)	(3,021)	(1,317)	(1,571)	(1,291)	(1,558)	(1,507)	(2,705)

Note: Figures in parentheses refer to the number of cases.
Sources: William H. Flanigan, *Political Behavior of the American Electorate*, 2d ed., Copyright © 1972 by Allyn and Bacon, Inc., Boston, p. 33.
1970 data from *CPS 1970 American National Election Study*. (See Appendix.)
1972 data from *CPS 1972 American National Election Study*. (See Appendix.)

Guzzo, generally come from humbler social origins, they are typically blue-collar workers, Catholics, city dwellers, and have less income and education. There are exceptions to these patterns—so many, in fact, that it is difficult to generalize. Nevertheless, the Democratic party is largely a party of the lower classes and the Republican party represents the wealthier classes.

Parties and party identification are not simply phenomena of the American political system. In Norway and Britain, countries with strong party systems, partisanship is widespread and is strongly related to public opinion and political behavior.[14] In other democracies such as France and West Germany, party affiliations are less widespread but still play an important role in political life.[15] It appears, then, that political parties act as reference points for the ordinary citizen. The reasons why people, both here and abroad, identify with parties and feel some degree of loyalty to them will become clearer in a moment.

In addition to being associated with interest, involvement, and participation, partisanship is highly related to voting. *"Partisanship is the most important single influence on political opinions and voting behavior,"* says William Flanigan.[16] Party identification is especially important in state and local elections and in congressional races as the data in Table 6.3 indicate. More than 90 percent of the strong partisans vote for their party's candidate. People are more apt to cross party lines in presidential elections than in lesser contests, but even so partisans still generally support their party's nominee. Given the kinds of relationships shown in Table 6.3, the psychological school thus concludes that people really do not "vote for the man." Like those adhering to the group approach, these scholars doubt the rationality of the average voter. (Whether or not

---

[14] Angus Campbell and Henry Valen, "Party Identification in Norway and the United States," *Public Opinion Quarterly,* Vol. 25 (1961), pp. 505–25; David Butler and Donald Stokes, *Political Change in Britain* (New York: St. Martin's Press, 1969), chaps. x–xiv.

[15] Philip E. Converse and Georges Dupeux, "Politicization of the Electorate in France and the United States," *Elections and the Political Order,* ed. Angus Campbell, Philip E. Converse, Warren E. Miller, and Donald E. Stokes (New York: John Wiley & Sons, 1966), pp. 269–91; and Wolfgang Hartenstein and Klaus Liepelt, "Party Members and Party Voters in West Germany," *Acta Sociologica,* Vol. 6 (fasc. 1–2, 1961), pp. 43–52.

[16] William H. Flanigan, *Political Behavior of the American Electorate,* 2d ed. (Boston: Allyn & Bacon, Inc., 1972), p. 37. Italics his.

Table 6.3
RELATIONSHIP BETWEEN PARTY IDENTIFICATION AND VOTING IN CONGRESSIONAL, STATE, AND LOCAL ELECTIONS

(a)

*1970 U.S. Senatorial Elections**

Respondent Voted for	Strong Democrat	Democrat	Independent-Democrat	Independent	Independent-Republican	Republican	Strong Republican
Democratic candidate	98%	85%	84%	56%	42%	24%	9%
Republican candidate	2	15	16	44	58	76	92
Total	100% (114)	100% (110)	100% (55)	100% (52)	100% (36)	100% (87)	101% (59)

(b)

*1970 Election for Representative**

Respondent Voted for	Strong Democrat	Democrat	Independent-Democrat	Independent	Independent-Republican	Republican	Strong Republican
Democratic candidate	89%	77%	75%	52%	35%	18%	5%
Republican candidate	11	13	24	48	65	83	96
Total	100% (156)	100% (148)	99% (58)	100% (58)	100% (52)	101% (120)	101% (89)

(c)

*1970 State and Local Elections**

Respondent Voted for	Strong Democrat	Democrat	Independent-Democrat	Independent	Independent-Republican	Republican	Strong Republican
Mostly Democratic	96%	83%	74%	30%	27%	5%	0%
Even	4	12	20	46	22	18	1
Mostly Republican	1	5	6	25	52	77	99
Total	101% (171)	100% (171)	100% (66)	101% (74)	101% (64)	100% (182)	100% (105)

* Columns may not total 100 percent because of rounding.
Note: Figures in parentheses refer to number of cases.
Source: *CPS 1970 American National Election Study.* (See Appendix.)

it is rational to vote on the basis of party identification will be discussed shortly.) Instead, they argue, party loyalties are largely responsible for a person's political preferences and behavior.

Party identification and voting are related in other countries as well. Table 6.4, for example, shows this relationship among Canadians. There are four major parties in Canada and respondents have been classified according to the strength of their party identification. Strong party identifiers overwhelmingly support their party's candidate; weak identifiers are less likely to do so. Notice, finally, that the Independents distribute their votes more evenly among the four parties. These and similar data from other countries suggest that partisanship has a significant relationship with voting in democracies.

The Functions of Party Identification.   To see why partisanship and voting are so closely related, consider the functions of party identification. In the first place, party identification simplifies an individual's political world. We have already discussed the "costs" of obtaining information and making sense of it. Gene Guzzo puts in a hard day's work at the factory; much of his work is monotonous; it is physically and mentally tiring. When he gets home at night he usually wants a beer and some relaxation; he likes to spend his nights bowling or watching television. He does not have the time, energy, or inclination to study and evaluate all of the political claims and counterclaims that he hears. To help him understand the world, he can rely on his party identification. He sees the world in simple "Democratic-Republican" terms. Knowing a man like McGovern is a good Democrat may tell Guzzo that the senator is right on the issues. Mr. Guzzo may be wrong but the costs of finding out probably outweigh the benefits.

Party identification also supplies cues to the voter. As the authors of *The American Voter* note, public affairs are often complex and, to a large extent, remote from the individual. It is helpful to have simple guides to what is going on in the world.[17] By evaluating politics in terms of party labels one can achieve a simplified understanding of these otherwise mysterious matters. Most people have long-standing beliefs about the parties and what they stand for. These beliefs which have developed since childhood provide cues for interpreting and responding to political events.

---

[17] Campbell et al., *The American Voter,* p. 128.

Table 6.4
PARTY IDENTIFICATION AND VOTE IN CANADA

Respondent's Vote in 1965	Respondent's Direction and Strength of Party Identification													Indepen- dent
	Conservatives			Liberals			NDPs*			Social Credit				
	Strong	Moderate	Weak	Strong	Moderate	Weak	Strong	Moderate	Weak	Strong	Moderate	Weak	
Conservative ...	95%	85%	64%	1%	4%	11%	1%	5%	0%	11%	33%	0%	26%
Liberal ...	3	11	26	98	93	78	4	7	22	6	6	0	45
NDP	1	3	6	1	2	11	95	88	73	4	2	0	20
Social Credit ...	1	1	4	0	1	0	0	0	5	79	59	100	9
	100%	100%	100%	100%	100%	100%	100%	100%	100%	100%	100%	100%	100%
	(473)	(1,325)	(166)	(765)	(1,844)	(221)	(259)	(519)	(63)	(113)	(162)	(12)	(419)

* NDP stands for National Democratic Party.
Note: Figures in parentheses refer to the number of cases.
Source: John Meisel et al., *1965 Canadian Election Study*. (See Appendix.)

Rationality and Party Identification. Hence, partisanship which is learned early in one's life is an allegiance that one can fall back on when confronted with the ambiguity of politics. Yet we might wonder if this is a rational strategy for the average voter. Is Gene Guzzo smart to trust party labels?

Superficially, there is no necessary contradition between voting strictly according to party labels and being rational. If an individual's values and goals are the same as those of his party, then he can save himself considerable time and energy (i.e., costs) by simply voting for his favorite party's nominees. In fact, he would be foolish to do otherwise.[18]

This argument rests on two considerations, however. First, it depends on people's knowing—in at least a rough way—where the parties stand on important issues. For how else can the individual judge whether his interests and those of the party's are the same? Yet the evidence about people's awareness of party positions is contradictory. Some scholars, especially those in the psychological school, claim that most voters do not know where the parties stand. Nor do these citizens see the parties in ideological terms.[19] Other observers believe that voters not only see party differences but they relate these differences to their own needs as well.[20] This debate— whether or not individuals recognize party differences on issues—is still unresolved, but the most recent findings seem to be running against the psychological school.

The second and related consideration deals with the nature of the party system. In Britain political parties are centralized, disciplined, and tightly organized; the party presents a platform and sticks to it. It is easy to find out what the parties stand for. American

---

[18] See Anthony Downs, *An Economic Theory of Democracy* (New York: Harper & Row, 1957), pp. 233–34, for an explanation of why this is true.

[19] See Campbell et al., *The American Voter,* chaps. ix and x; and Philip E. Converse, "The Nature of Belief Systems in Mass Publics," *Ideology and Discontent,* ed. David E. Apter (New York: The Free Press, 1964), pp. 206–61.

[20] See V. O. Key, Jr., *The Responsible Electorate* (Cambridge, Mass.: Harvard University Press, 1966); Gerald M. Pomper, "Toward a More Responsible Two-Party System: What, Again?" *Journal of Politics,* Vol. 33 (1971), pp. 916–40; David E. RePass, "Issue Salience and Party Choice," *American Political Science Review,* Vol. 65 (1971), pp. 389–400; and Martin Fishbein and Fred S. Coombs, "Basis for Decision: An Attitudinal Approach toward an Understanding of Voting Behavior," paper presented at the Sixty-Seventh Annual Meeting of the American Political Science Association, September 7–11, 1971.

parties by contrast are extremely decentralized and heterogeneous. After all, the Democratic party houses George Wallace and George McGovern, James Eastland and Edward Kennedy, Richard Daley and John Lindsay. What is more, regional variations within a party often exceed those differences existing between parties. As a result, in a particular local election in a particular region, knowing only that a candidate is a Democrat or a Republican probably will not tell a voter much about how the candidate will behave if elected to office. In other words, even if a man is sure that a party as a whole shares his interests he cannot be sure that a given member has those views or will put them into action if he is elected. So in this country voting for a party is somewhat risky: it may or may not produce the desired effects.

Independent Voters.   Conventional wisdom claims that the Independent voter solves these problems by not committing himself to any one party. Instead, he carefully studies the candidates, their records, their positions on issues, their promises, and then weighing the alternatives, he votes for the best man. In short, the Independent voter, it is presumed, fits civics book versions of the ideal voter: interested, motivated, concerned.

Unfortunately, empirical data gathered from numerous surveys belie this image.[21] The self-styled Independent voter turns out to be generally less interested and concerned about politics than the average partisan. (See Chapter 5 for some evidence on this point.) He certainly does not have more information about candidates, he votes less regularly, he switches his choices more often, and seems to be more susceptible to short-term events than those holding stronger party identifications. The Independent voter, is, in a word, an occasional participant.

As a matter of fact, the Independent voter accounts for three rather curious phenomena in American electoral politics: (1) turnout in off-year congressional and state and local elections is lower than in presidential elections; (2) the party whose candidate is elected to the presidency loses seats in Congress two years later; and (3) even though Democratic party identifiers (and registrants) outnumber Republicans—in some states by two or three to one—

---

[21] Flanigan, *Political Behavior of the American Electorate,* chap. ii; Campbell et al., *The American Voter,* chap. v.

Democratic candidates do not always win. Two characteristics of the Independent, his low level of motivation and his susceptibility to transitory events, help explain these oddities.

The reason is that in presidential elections about 55 to 65 percent of the eligible voters go to the polls, but in midterm elections the turnout drops to about 45 percent. This difference is largely accounted for by Independents and weak partisans who stay home during congressional elections. According to many political scientists, these Independents, who have little interest in politics, tend to vote for the presidential candidate with the most charisma or with the most effective campaign.[22] At the same time, partisans, that is, strong Democrats and Republicans, vote for their parties' nominees. Also, both groups, partisans and Independents, tend to vote a straight ticket, meaning that one party has an advantage at both the presidential and congressional levels. (This tendency changed in the 1972 election with the result that President Nixon, despite his landslide victory, did not carry many Republicans with him into office.)

In off-year congressional elections, however, the Independents generally stay at home because they are not motivated by the excitement of a presidential campaign and because their interest in elections is low. In this way, the president's party loses many of the votes in the midterm elections that it had won in the presidential year. With the abstention of the Independents, congressional elections revert to the "normal" two-party division of the vote, and the opposition party usually gains a few seats.[23] This phenomenon has occurred most recently in 1966 and 1970: in 1966 Republicans made gains in the House while Democrats picked up seats in 1970.

The Independents and weak partisans constitute a fluid bloc of voters, swinging first one way and then another. If most of them vote together they add considerably to one party's totals. Since this large chunk of voters moves from one party to another, Democrats can never be certain of winning majorities.

The Independent voter is, as it were, a wild card, and at the very

---

[22] Lewis A. Froman, Jr., *Congressmen and Their Constituencies* (Chicago: Rand McNally & Co., 1963), pp. 62–64.

[23] Philip E. Converse, "The Concept of a Normal Vote," *Elections and the Political Order*, ed. Angus Campbell, Philip E. Converse, Warren E. Miller, and Donald E. Stokes (New York: John Wiley & Sons, Inc., 1966), pp. 9–39.

least he adds some excitement to the game of politics. Whether or not this type of behavior is beneficial to the electoral process is an open question, but it is clear the Independent is not a better, more rational citizen than the committed partisan.

Third Parties and Party Identification. Party identification also explains in part the difficulty third parties have in attracting and maintaining mass support. The United States is a diffuse, pluralistic society and it has often seemed that the two major parties are not able to serve the needs of various groups. Even today there is widespread dissatisfaction with the party system, as is evidenced by the success of George Wallace's American Independent party in 1968. Hence, one increasingly hears calls for the establishment of third and fourth parties based on, say, a coalition of blacks, poor people, workers, and students.

There are many reasons why third parties fail. Many of these reasons involve the constitutional arrangement of our government and need not concern us here. The persistence of party identification, however, is a formidable obstacle new parties must face. As we have already noted, a sense of identification with a party helps an individual understand and adjust to political realities. When voting in most elections, Mr. Guzzo, for example, has to wade through long, cumbersome ballots, sometimes containing as many as 50 to 100 choices. Party labels aid him in making these choices.

New parties are not able to take advantage of name familiarity. People who are not familiar with a party label cannot use that label as a cue in ambiguous situations. As a result, the head of the ticket on a third-party ballot may do well, but his coattails do not stretch very far. Less well-known third-party candidates cannot benefit from widespread identification with their party, for none exists. And when the party's leader retires or dies the party often falters because it lacks a loyal following.

It could also be argued that party identification promotes political stability. In France, which has a multiparty system, party identifications are weak and diffuse. Unlike the United States, many French citizens do not feel loyalty to any of the major parties. The absence of partisanship leads to a proliferation of "flash" parties, parties which rapidly come and go.[24] These parties, some observers

---

[24] Converse and Dupeux, "Politicization of the Electorate in France and the United States," p. 270.

argue, have contributed to the instability and turmoil of French politics. So here again we see that partisan loyalties may be rational from the point of view of the political system, if not from the point of view of the individual.

The Psychological School's Approach to Rationality and Voting

Returning now to our main topic, the explanation of voting behavior, recall that the psychological school asserts the primacy of partisan attitudes and partisanship. In making this assertion, the adherents insist that voters do not behave rationally, at least in a narrow sense. More specifically, they wonder if many voters are concerned with issues. Their reasoning is as follows.

Logically speaking, if a citizen votes on the basis of issues, then he should be familiar with at least some issues, care about them, and be able to detect differences between the candidates on these matters. A voter not satisfying these minimal conditions probably does not take issues into account.

How many citizens meet all three criteria? The data in Table 6.5 suggest an answer. In the first place, issue familiarity is not altogether high—in some cases as many as 25 percent do not have an

Table 6.5
OPINIONS ON ISSUES AND PERCEPTIONS
OF WHERE THE PARTIES STAND ON THESE ISSUES

	Five Public Policy Issues				
	Aid to Education	Foreign Aid	Job Guarantee	School Integration	Fair Employment
Percent having an opinion	81%	71%	81%	85%	84%
Percent who have an opinion and see a difference between the parties	44	31	48	48	49
Percent who have an opinion, see a difference, and think the Democrats are "liberal" on the issue	32	26	39	42	41

Source: *SRC 1968 American National Election Study.* (See Appendix.)

opinion. More disturbing, still fewer see any difference between the Republican and Democratic parties or know which party is most liberal on the matter. The table shows, for example, that only about 40 percent of the intended voters had an opinion on the question of school integration *and* thought there was a difference between the parties *and* knew the Democrats were more liberal. Percents on the other issues are even smaller.

Based on this type of evidence, one can conclude that many Americans do not have opinions on issues or connect their opinions to differences between the parties or candidates. These facts, coupled with widespread apathy among voters and their lack of a sophisticated political ideology, lead to the conclusion that the typical voter is not rational.

In defense of the average voter, we can say his inability to make "connections" between issues and parties may not be a fair test of his rationality. After all, it *is* difficult to know where the parties stand; sometimes even experts have trouble And, as we have seen before, the voter is not helped by the parties or candidates themselves, who often obscure their differences, or by the mass media which spend little time talking about the parties' ideological differences.

At any rate, the psychological school feels voters are motivated mainly by the party identification and their partisan attitudes, especially candidate images. Theirs is, in effect, a noninstrumental approach: the voter does not try to achieve consciously selected goals with his vote: In this respect, the psychological school, like the group theorists, differs from the decision-making and public policy approaches.

THE DECISION-MAKING APPROACH TO VOTING

Decision theorists study how people should and do make choices. They usually begin by defining a simple situation in which choice among several alternatives must be made. Next they derive rules for choosing among the alternatives, the rule being based on some standard of rationality. Finally, after setting out a model in this manner, they test it to see if people do, in fact, follow the prescribed rule.

Since most decision making is complicated, these analyses are based on simple settings. Moreover, the majority of the work has been done by psychologists and economists interested in explaining such things as risk taking, consumer behavior, coalition formation, and behavior in games of chance. Few have applied the principles, hypotheses, and findings of decision-making theory to political science.

In spite of the simplicity and limited applicability, however, this approach can tell us a great deal about voting. For one thing, it helps us clarify the meaning of rationality and provides an explicit set of criteria for judging the rationality of voters. For another, it calls our attention to aspects of voting which are frequently ignored by political scientists.

We will start with some simple concepts and then later see how they apply to electoral behavior.

Utility

Decision theory begins with the premise that people have preferences which they can rank according to desirability, and these preferences determine their behavior. Everything in life can be examined in terms of its pleasure- or pain-giving properties. These properties are the "utility" of the object. Utility is positive if the object gives pleasure, negative if it gives pain.[25]

On the surface, this appears to be an entirely reasonable description of human behavior. But these seemingly simple remarks contain some slippery concepts. Material objects, activities, psychological states-of-being have different values to different people. In many cases, people can rank the worth various objects have for them. David Charles may prefer Nixon to McGovern and McGovern to Wallace. Utility is how much something is worth to an individual.

But how is utility measured? We cannot use money as a yardstick because people do not or will not measure many objects in terms of dollars and cents. And besides, money itself has different utility to different people. So difficult is this problem that social scientists have been hard pressed to measure utility on a meaningful scale.

---

[25] Ward Edwards, "The Theory of Decision-Making," *Decision-Making*, ed. Ward Edwards and Amos Tversky (Baltimore: Penguin Books, 1967), p. 16.

In addition to the problem of creating a numerical scale (cardinal utility) decision theorists find instances of people not having consistent preferences, as perhaps in the case of Mr. Guzzo who prefers McGovern to Nixon and Nixon to Wallace but also Wallace to McGovern. Were his preferences "transitive" or consistent, we would expect him to prefer McGovern to Wallace. The lack of transivity of this sort often prevents us from measuring utility on even an ordinal (or ranked) scale.

These are formidable problems which prodigious amounts of research have still not completely solved. Nevertheless, utility is a helpful concept, and we will continue to make the inference that people have utility scales even though they may be hard to measure and even though the individuals themselves may not be consciously aware of them. To see how the concept of utility fits into decision-making theory we will consider a very simple situation.

Riskless Choice

An individual is faced with a limited number of alternatives. Each alternative leads to an outcome. If there is no doubt that each alternative will lead to the specific outcome, then we have the following rule for rational behavior: rank the outcomes from lowest to highest in terms of their utility and choose the alternative which leads to the highest utility. This is called riskless choice since each alternative is known to produce a particular outcome.

Suppose that McGovern pledges to end the war in Vietnam within 90 days of his inauguration while Nixon refuses to commit himself on this point and indeed hints at a continuation of the war. Further, assume for the moment that Gene Guzzo's vote will be decisive; that is, if he votes for McGovern, McGovern will be elected; if he votes for Nixon, then Nixon will be elected. In this case, Mr. Guzzo has a simple choice. If he prefers an end to the war in Vietnam he votes for McGovern; if not, he votes for Nixon.

Now you may think this analysis woefully unrealistic and simplistic. True, it is unreal and simple, and we will modify it in a moment. But it does illustrate a basic principle of decision-making theory: people should (and do) act in a way to *maximize their utility*.

We can add to the realism simply by expanding the number of

outcomes attached to each alternative. In addition to his statements on the war, McGovern has suggested that he will raise taxes. So voting for McGovern leads both to an end to the war *and* to higher taxes. Guzzo must now add the utilities of these two outcomes and compare them to what he gets if Nixon is elected. Additional outcomes are handled the same way by looking at their utilities and picking the alternative which produces the highest total utility. (See Figure 6.2 for an example.)

Figure 6.2
DECISION MAKING UNDER RISKLESS CHOICE
(two outcomes for each choice; choices are Nixon and McGovern)

Alternatives	*Outcomes*	*Utilities*
McGovern .... $\left\{\vphantom{\begin{array}{c}a\\b\end{array}}\right.$	End to war	U_{G_1}
	Higher taxes	U_{G_2}
		Total $= U_{G_1} + U_{G_2}$
Nixon .... $\left\{\vphantom{\begin{array}{c}a\\b\end{array}}\right.$	Continuation of war	U_{N_1}
	Same taxes	U_{N_2}
		Total $= U_{N_1} + U_{N_2}$

Note: U_{G_1}, U_{G_2}, U_{N_1}, U_{N_2} are the utilities of the various outcomes. U_{G_1}, for instance, is the utility or worth to an individual of McGovern's ending the war in Vietnam.

Decision Rule: If the sum of the utilities for McGovern exceeds the sum for Nixon—i.e., if $(U_{G_1} + U_{G_2}) > (U_{N_1} + U_{N_2})$ (">" means greater than), then vote for McGovern; if Nixon's total is higher, vote for him. If they are equal, abstain from voting or flip a coin.

Uncertainty and Decision Making

So far we have assumed that, if elected, McGovern would in fact end the war in Vietnam and raise taxes. We have treated these outcomes as certain results of his election. Yet we all know campaign promises are not always kept. Unexpected events and new developments cause plans to change. At best, then, we can only say if McGovern is elected he will *in all probability* end the war and raise taxes. In making this weaker statement we are introducing *uncertainty*.

According to some decision theorists, uncertainty is taken into account in the following way: first, the individual determines the probability that an alternative (e.g., vote for McGovern) will lead to an *expected utility*. The expected utility or expected value is what one expects to get by following a given course of action. It is not certain he will receive the utility because the occurrence of the outcome is only problematical. So the utility is discounted by the probability of its being attained.

Generally, a person will not know exactly what these probabilities are. Instead, he has to estimate them himself. Estimated probabilities are called subjective probabilities. These probabilities, multiplied by the utilities, give the subjectively expected utility (SEU).[26] In this situation, a decision rule for rational behavior is simply: *maximize subjectively expected utility* (SEU).

The data in Figure 6.3 illustrate this principle as it applies to a single voter. The utilities are measured on a hypothetical scale.

Figure 6.3
DECISION MAKING UNDER UNCERTAINTY

	Hypothetical Calculation for One Voter with a Choice between Nixon and McGovern						
Choice	*(Utility of Outcome 1, i.e., Ending the War)*	$\times$	*(Subjective Probability of Outcome 1)*	$+$	*(Utility of Outcome 2, i.e., Higher Taxes)*	$\times$	*(Subjective Probability of Outcome 2)*	$=$	*Subjectively Expected Utility (SEU)*
McGovern	(100	$\times$	0.8)	$+$	(−90	$\times$	0.5)	$=$	35
Nixon	(100	$\times$	0.2)	$+$	(−90	$\times$	0.1)	$=$	11

Decision Rule: Vote for alternative leading to highest expected subjective utility (SEU); for this voter, the choice is McGovern.

The probabilities show the individual's *own* assessment of what will happen if he selects a given alternative. (Remember, we are assuming this person's vote is decisive.) Hence, he believes that if he chooses Nixon there is a 20 percent chance the war will end and a 10 percent chance taxes will be raised. Since for this individual subjective expected utility is higher for McGovern than Nixon, he should vote for McGovern.

Once again, this model may seem totally unrealistic: people simply do not add up utilities and probabilities when deciding how to

---

[26] Ward Edwards, "Behavioral Decision Theory," *Decision-Making,* ed. Ward Edwards and Amos Tversky (Baltimore: Penguin Books, 1967), pp. 65–95.

vote. On the other hand, it may not be too far-fetched. A model is a simplified representation of reality. It does not (nor is it supposed to) describe all of the nuances of a complicated psychological process like decision making. Even so, it does suggest how people make up their minds. After all, most of us in one way or another weigh the pros and cons of a decision and we often take probability into account when doing so. Thus, even if we do not use terms like "utility" and "probability," we do say things like "I'll bet Nixon won't raise taxes" or "I'm not sure, but my guess is that McGovern can end the war faster than Nixon." These statements reflect the belief that a particular choice will *probably* lead to a certain outcome.

What is more, the model has received limited empirical verification. Studies involving simple gambling experiments show that people's utilities and subjective probabilities can be measured and that their decisions follow the maximizing principle.[27] Other approaches very similar to the SEU model have also been empirically confirmed.[28]

In spite of this encouraging support, however, problems remain. The main difficulty is information. Rationality, according to these standards, requires knowledge of the outcomes associated with each alternative. It also requires an estimate of the probabilities of the outcome's occurrence. Locating and evaluating this type of information, especially in a presidential race, probably exceeds many people's capacities.[29]

---

[27] F. A. Mosteller and P. Nogee, "An Experimental Measurement of Utility," *Journal of Political Economy,* Vol. 59 (1951), pp. 371–404; D. Davidson, P. Suppes, and Sidney Siegel, *Decision-Making: An Experimental Approach* (Stanford, Calif.: Stanford University Press, 1957); and Ward Edwards, "The Prediction of Decisions among Bets," *Journal of Experimental Psychology,* Vol. 51 (1955), pp. 201–14.

[28] N. T. Feather, "Subjective Probability and Decision under Uncertainty," *Psychological Review,* Vol. 66 (1959), pp. 150–64 and Icek Ajzen and Martin Fishbein, "The Prediction of Behavioral Intentions in a Choice Situation," *Journal of Experimental Social Psychology,* Vol. 5 (1969), pp. 400–16.

[29] As a partial solution to this problem, Herbert A. Simon ("A Behavioral Model of Rational Choice," *Quarterly Journal of Economics,* Vol. 69 [1955], quoted from Charles Lindblom, *The Policy-Making Process* [Englewood Cliffs, N.J.: Prentice-Hall, Inc., 1968], p. 24.) proposes an alternative strategy, satisficing. The *known* outcomes of an alternative are classified as satisfactory or unsatisfactory and then the first alternative leading to merely a satisfactory outcome is selected. The benefits do not have to be maximized since maximizing requires too much information.

Another problem with the SEU model is that the voter realizes his vote, only one of thousands or millions, will in all probability not be decisive. We have so far assumed that Mr. Guzzo's vote automatically leads to a set of outcomes. But this is an unrealistic assumption. The probability that one man's ballot will be decisive is exceedingly small, perhaps as small as one in several million. One theory of how the voter should and does take this probability into account is illustrated by Anthony Downs' work, *An Economic Theory of Democracy*, which is now a classic in the study of voting behavior.

Downs's Theory of Voting

Downs outlines a simple model of rational voting behavior. He adopts the following notation:

U—Utility or benefits received from the government during some period of time
A—The incumbent party
B—The opposition party
t —A time period
E—Expected value

The rational voter, according to Downs, compares the benefits he expects to receive from party A, $E(U^A_{t+1})$, with those he expects to get from party B, $E(U^B_{t+1})$.[30] This comparison is called the *expected party differential* (EPD):

$$\text{EPD} = E(U^A_{t+1}) - E(U^B_{t+1})$$

If the EPD is positive (i.e., if $E(U^A_{t+1})$ is greater than $E(U^B_{t+1})$), then he votes for party A's candidates; if it is negative, (i.e., $E(U^A_{t+1})$ is less than $E(U^B_{t+1})$), he votes for party B; and if it is zero he abstains from voting. In short, the voter simply picks the party which offers him the most.[31]

Note that the EPD must be estimated since it refers to a future time, $(t+1)$, and to expected values. In order to estimate its value, the voter can rely on a variety of tricks. The most important of

---

[30] Downs, *An Economic Theory of Democracy*, pp. 55–60. The symbol $E(U^A_{t+1})$ should be read as: The expected utility from party A when it is in office in the future.

[31] Ibid., pp. 37–39.

these is the *current party differential* (CPD). The CPD is a comparison of what the incumbent party is currently doing with what the opposition might have been expected to do had it been in power during this period.

The EPD is the key element in Downs's model of voting behavior but his work contains several other interesting implications.

The first of these implications, the costs of acquiring information, has already been discussed. In order to calculate either the EPD or the CPD the voter must know what the parties have done and can be expected to do. Besides studying the parties' platforms and past records, he must also make predictions about the future. All of this requires time and effort plus a certain amount of guesswork.

For this reason, the rational voter should (and does) try to shift these costs to others by relying on various organizations, such as interest groups, clubs, and the parties themselves. His desire to lower the costs of obtaining information can also explain the importance of party identification. If a person can assume his interests are about the same as those of a political party, then he can vote that party's line knowing his interests are thereby being served.[32] The rub, of course, is that in order to save on information costs in this way he has to trust the party's slate of candidates.

Another implication is the improbability that one's vote will be decisive. The expected party differential—the main calculation in deciding how to vote—must be discounted or reduced because the voter knows his ballot is not likely to influence the outcome of an election. Seen from another perspective, even if he mistakenly votes for the wrong party (the one giving him a lower EPD), his mistake will not make much difference to him or to the outcome. After all, one vote is "lost in a sea of other votes."[33] In short, an individual cannot affect the result of the election one way or the other.

Since the EPD must be discounted, the question then arises: does the cost of acquiring information not outweigh the expected benefits? Downs concludes, paradoxically, that it does: ". . . we believe

---

[32] Actually, for reasons which need not concern us, Downs asserts that the voter can never assume his interests and those of a party are the same. Ibid., pp. 233–34.

[33] Ibid., p. 246.

that it is rational for a great part of the electorate to minimize investment in political data. For them, rational behavior implies . . . a refusal to expend resources on political information *per se.* . . ."[34]

In other words, why should Mr. Guzzo take the time to study Nixon and McGovern's records and campaign promises? He knows he has just one vote out of millions. If he stays home or if he mistakenly casts his ballot for the wrong man, it probably is not going to affect the outcome one way or the other.

One may wonder if it is even rational to vote. If a man's ballot is lost in a sea of ballots, why bother to cast it in the first place? Why not stay home? Downs gives a somewhat tortuous answer. Men, he says, have a long-run interest in maintaining democracy. To maintain democracy, however, requires that people participate in elections. Otherwise, democratic institutions would atrophy and oligarchy would prevail. Therefore, political participation has value of its own. Voting brings benefits apart from those supplied by the candidates and parties: it helps maintain the democratic system. Consequently, this additional reward, which Downs calls the "long run participation value" (LRPV), must be considered along with the EPD and costs.

Political scientists have plenty of evidence that Downs's LRPV exists, though it has not been called by the name. Several voting studies have included a scale of "citizen duty." This scale is measured by asking how important it is to vote even if one's favorite candidate has no chance of winning. Individuals scoring high on the scale vote more regularly than those scoring low.[35]

According to Downs's model, then, a voter takes into account four quantities, the expected party differential (EPD), costs (C), the probability that his vote will be decisive (P), and the long-run participation value (LRPV). If a voter sees a difference between the parties (i.e., if $|EPD| > 0$), then he discounts this difference by multiplying by P.[36] Next, he adds in the LRPV. If this total is greater

---

[34] Ibid., p. 245.

[35] Lester Milbrath, *Political Participation* (Chicago: Rand McNally & Co., 1965), pp. 61–62.

[36] If the EPD equaled zero, then the individual would see no difference between the parties. If it is greater than zero he believes one of the parties will give him a higher utility than the other.

than the costs of participating, he votes for the party of his choice; otherwise he abstains. (Figure 6.4 illustrates these rules.) The voter makes a similar calculation in the case of EPD = 0.

Figure 6.4
DOWNS'S MODEL OF RATIONAL VOTING

Case 1: The voter's *preliminary* guess or estimate is that the parties or candidates differ; that is, $|\text{EPD}| > 0$.
Decision Rule for Case 1:
    If $(P\,|\text{EPD}| + \text{LRPV}) > C$, then vote for party or candidate of choice.
    If $(P\,|\text{EPD}| + \text{LRPV}) \leq C$, then abstain.

Case 2: The voter's *preliminary* guess or estimate is that the parties or candidates do not differ; that is, $|\text{EPD}| = 0$.
Decision Rule for Case 2:
    If $\text{LRPV} > C$, then vote for a party or candidate at random.
    If $\text{LRPV} \leq C$, then abstain.

Key:
    EPD —Expected Party Differential
    P   —Probability that vote will be decisive (i.e., discount factor)
    C   —Cost of acquiring information and voting
    LRPC—Long-run participation value
    $\leq$ —Less than or equal to
    $>$ —Greater than
    | | —Absolute value

Source: Based on Anthony Downs, *An Economic Theory of Democracy* (New York: Harper & Row, 1957), pp. 271–72.

Suppose, for example, that Mr. Guzzo, on the basis of what he has heard around the factory, believes McGovern, the Democratic candidate, will do a better job than Nixon, the Republican nominee. Thus, according to his preliminary estimate, the EPD is greater than zero (Case 1 in Figure 6.4). But Guzzo instinctively feels that voting and keeping up with all the issues in the campaign is going to be hard or costly. Also, the election may not be close. So he has to decide if the expected benefits (EPD), times the probability of their occurring, (P), outweigh the costs of gathering information. As we saw in the last chapter, it takes time and energy to vote. On the other hand, as we saw in Chapter 3, children are taught to accept voting as a civic duty regardless of the outcome. Hence, Guzzo compares his discounted party differential plus the long-range value of voting with the costs of voting. If the benefits outweigh the costs he votes for his favorite candidate; if not, he abstains.

Remember, this is an abstract representation of how people vote. It is not meant to be a literal description. Downs says, in effect, voters juggle various quantities: how much they expect to get out of the elections, either directly or indirectly; how much effort and time they should spend learning about the issues and candidates; and how much the whole process will ultimately be worth to them. People obviously do not make these calculations consciously or formally and they certainly do not use Downs's vocabulary. But in making up their minds people probably do take many of these factors into account. In deciding whether or not to vote, and whom to vote for, voters must compare and calculate various potential gains and losses—whether they are aware of what they are doing or not. The decision-making approach, especially Downs's version of it, provides a simple picture of how this is done. It makes explicit what is implicit in human behavior. As such, its value to us stems not from the realism of its descriptions but the relevance and accuracy of its predictons.

Therefore, decision-making theory helps us understand voting. It suggests that we look at not only a person's goals, but also his perception of how and with what probability he can attain these goals; we need to look at not only the benefits of rationality, but also its costs; we need to look at not only his evaluation of parties and candidates, but also his evaluation of voting per se.

THE PUBLIC POLICY APPROACH TO VOTING

We conclude the discussion of voting with an analysis of the fourth school, the public policy approach. Like the decision theorists, adherents to this view believe that behavior is instrumental or purposive and that voters act rationally. But they define rationality somewhat more narrowly. According to the adherents of this approach, a rational vote is one based on public policy considerations: insofar as a person's candidate preference is consistent with his issue preferences he is behaving rationally.

The belief that voters are by and large rational in this sense runs counter to the group and psychological approaches, as V. O. Key, Jr. suggests:

The perverse and unorthodox argument . . . is that voters are not fools. To be sure, many individuals act in odd ways, yet in the large the electorate behaves about as rationally and responsibly as we should expect, given the clarity of the alternatives presented to it and the character of the information available. . . . In American presidential campaigns of recent decades the portrait of the American electorate that develops from the data is not one of an electorate straightjacketed by social determinants or moved by subconscious urges triggered by devilishly skilled propagandists. It is rather one of an electorate moved by concern about central and relevant questions of public policy, of governmental performance, and of executive personality.[37]

More specifically, Key and others believe that in general, (1) people are more knowledgeable about politics than previously thought; (2) they have definite beliefs about where the parties and candidates stand on issues; (3) they themselves have positions on many issues; and (4) they care enough to translate their preferences into a vote for the candidate coming closest to their own position.[38]

Data supporting these assertions are accumulating rapidly. Key, for example, notes the large proportion of "switchers" in the electorate. A switcher votes for the candidate of one party in one election and then in the next election votes for the opposition's candidate. If, for example, Mr. Charles voted for Lyndon Johnson, the Democrat, in 1964 and then for Richard Nixon, the Republican, in 1968, he would be classified a switcher.

The Democratic vote in 1960 was composed of about 19 million voters who voted Democratic in 1956 (standpatters), plus 10 million who switched from Republican in 1956 to Democratic in 1960 and about 5 million new voters. Similarly, the Republican candidate, Nixon, attracted about 3 million former Democrats. Oviously there is a great deal of movement in the electorate.[39]

---

[37] Key, *The Responsible Electorate,* pp. 7–8.

[38] See, for example, James L. Sundquist, *Politics and Policy* (Washington, D.C.: The Brookings Institution, 1968); Gerald M. Pomper, "Toward a More Responsible Two-Party System," and "From Confusion to Clarity: Issues and American Voters, 1956–1968," *American Political Science Review,* Vol. 66 (1972), pp. 415–28; Michael Shapiro, "Rational Political Man: A Synthesis of Economic and Social-Psychological Perspectives," *American Political Science Review,* Vol. 63 (1969), pp. 1106–19; RePass, "Issue Salience and Party Choice;" Kovenock et al., "Status, Party, Ideology, Issues, and Candidate Choice;" Fishbein and Coombs, "Basis for Decision."

[39] Key, *The Responsible Electorate,* chap. ii.

What is most interesting, Key says, are the policy preferences of these various groups of voters. The switchers, he finds, seem to seek out the party which is most compatible with their own policy preferences. For example, he discovers that Republican voters who favor social welfare legislation (e.g., increasing the minimum wage) tend to switch their votes to Democratic candidates. Standpatters appear to be comfortable with their party's issue positions. New voters generally support the party which is closest to their views. These are, of course, only trends, and numerous exceptions arise. But Key regards these data as evidence that issues are, indeed, on the mind of the average voter.[40]

The connection between issues and voting can be seen in another way. Along with their own opinions of public policy matters, voters have beliefs about where the candidates and parties stand on those issues. Both attitudes and beliefs should be taken into account in studying voting behavior. To see why, consider the data in Table 6.6a.

The top portion of the table shows a relationship between the respondents' attitudes toward school desegregation and their 1968 presidential vote. (Attitudes toward desegregation have been classified "Liberal" and "Conservative" for convenience.) Although liberals are slightly more likely to have voted for Humphrey (presumably the liberal candidate) than for Nixon or Wallace (presumably the conservative choices), there is no clear trend. The relationship between issue attitudes and voting is weak.

Yet, not everyone may have seen Humphrey as the "liberal" candidate or Nixon as the "conservative." In fact, some may have believed Humphrey to be more conservative than Nixon. What is needed, then, is an indication of the voters' beliefs about the candidates. Where do they think the candidates stand on this issue? One way of finding out is to ask each respondent which party is liberal on school desegregation. The results of this analysis are shown in the bottom portion of Table 6.6.

In particular, it indicates that of liberals who thought that the Democratic party was also liberal, over 75 percent voted for Humphrey. Among the liberals who believed that the Republicans (and not Democrats) were liberal, about 85 percent voted for Nixon. A similar pattern holds for the conservatives: those who thought the

---

[40] Key, *The Responsible Electorate,* p. 44.

Table 6.6
RELATIONSHIP BETWEEN ATTITUDES TOWARD SCHOOL DESEGREGATION,
PERCEPTIONS AND VOTE FOR PRESIDENT IN 1968

(a)

Respondent Voted for:	Respondent's Attitude on School Desegregation Is:*	
	Liberal	Conservative
Humphrey	49%	31%
Nixon	45	52
Wallace	6	17
	100%	100%
	(448)	(345)

(b)

	Liberals			Conservatives		
	Respondent Believes:†					
Respondent Voted for:	Democrats Are Liberal	No Differ- ence	Republicans Are Liberal	Democrats Are Conservative	No Differ- ence	Republicans Are Conservative
Humphrey .	76%	39%	15%	64%	31%	10%
Nixon	19	53	85	9	52	81
Wallace ...	5	8	0	27	17	9
	100%	100%	100%	100%	100%	100%
	(171)	(197)	(59)	(44)	(216)	(69)

    * "Do you think the government in Washington should: see to it that white and Negro children are allowed to go to the same schools or stay out of this area as it is not its business?" Answers favoring government intervention are considered liberal for convenience.
    † "Which party is more likely to do what you want on this issue—the Democrats, the Republicans, or wouldn't there be any difference between them?"
    Note: Figures in parentheses refer to the number of cases.
    Source: *CPS 1970 American National Election Study.* (See Appendix.)

Republicans were conservative voted overwhelmingly for Nixon while the conservatives who believed the Democrats shared their views tended to vote for Humphrey. Notice also that Wallace drew strength from among those who saw no difference between the parties.

The relationships are not perfect, but only one issue has been considered. If others had been included, the predictive capacity of this approach would doubtlessly be improved.

This line of reasoning also applies to congressional voting. Tables 6.7 and 6.8 show the relationships between attitudes and voting and attitudes combined with perceptions and voting. At each level, most voters behave consistently. Liberals vote for the party they believe is liberal; conservatives vote for the party they believe is conservative. For example, in Table 6.7b, among the conservatives who think the Democrats share their conservative views over 90 percent voted for the Democratic senatorial candidate.

Table 6.7
RELATIONSHIP BETWEEN ATTITUDES TOWARD SCHOOL DESEGREGATION, PERCEPTIONS AND VOTE FOR U.S. SENATOR IN 1970

(a)

Respondent Voted for:	Respondent's Attitude on School Desegregation Is:*	
	Liberal	Conservative
Democratic candidate	65%	54%
Republican candidate	35	46
	100%	100%
	(255)	(196)

(b)

Respondent Voted for:	Liberals			Conservatives		
	Respondent Believes:†					
	Democrats Are Liberal	No Differ- ence	Republicans Are Liberal	Democrats Are Conservative	No Differ- ence	Republicans Are Conservative
Democratic candidate.	87%	50%	36%	91%	57%	19%
Republican candidate.	13	50	64	10	43	81
	100%	100%	100%	100%	100%	100%
	(107)	(118)	(22)	(21)	(122)	(37)

* "Do you think the government in Washington should: see to it that white and Negro children are allowed to go to the same schools or stay out of this area as it is not its business?" Answers favoring government intervention are considered liberal for convenience.
† "Which party is more likely to do what you want on this issue—the Democrats, the Republicans, or wouldn't there be any difference between them?"
Note: Figures in parentheses refer to the number of cases.
Source: *CPS 1970 American National Election Study.* (See Appendix.)

One can, of course, find fault with this line of reasoning. For one thing, it does not tell whether or not the beliefs or perceptions are accurate. If a man thinks the Democratic party is liberal on some issue when it really is not, we might say that he is acting irrationally. On the other, truly objective information about politics is not easy to obtain and so we should not be too critical if voters are occasionally misled. Nor do the data tell us where the individual got his perceptions in the first place.

Another criticism is that voters may bring their perceptions of the candidates into line with the vote. In other words, if a person votes for Nixon he may later, after voting, claim Nixon stands for the things he does. After all, as indicated in Chapter 2,

Table 6.8
RELATIONSHIP BETWEEN ATTITUDES TOWARD SCHOOL DESEGREGATION, PERCEPTIONS AND VOTE FOR U.S. REPRESENTATIVE IN 1970

(a)

Respondent Voted for:	*Respondent's Attitude on School Desegregation Is:**	
	Liberal	*Conservative*
Democratic candidate	55%	51%
Republican candidate	45	49
	100%	100%
	(279)	(242)

(b)

	Liberals			*Conservatives*		
	Respondent Believes:†					
Respondent Voted for:	*Democrats Are Liberal*	*No Differ- ence*	*Republicans Are Liberal*	*Democrats Are Conservative*	*No Differ- ence*	*Republicans Are Conservative*
Democratic candidate.	74%	49%	23%	78%	51%	26%
Republican candidate.	26	51	77	22	49	74
	100%	100%	100%	100%	100%	100%
	(104)	(130)	(35)	(37)	(152)	(43)

    * "Do you think the government in Washington should: see to it that white and Negro children are allowed to go to the same schools or stay out of this area as it is not its business?" Answers favoring government intervention are considered liberal for convenience.
    † "Which party is more likely to do what you want on this issue—the Democrats, the Republicans, or wouldn't there be any difference between them?"
    Note: Figures in parentheses refer to the number of cases.
    Source: *CPS 1970 American National Election Study.* (See Appendix.)

people strive for cognitive consistency. So it could be argued that some of the voters in Table 6.6 to 6.8 were not acting rationally, but were simply rationalizing their vote. Still, at this point there is no evidence to say which interpretation, rationality or rationalization, is most valid.[41]

Therefore, we have some evidence from Key and others, [42] as well as in the tables presented above, that voters do act rationally by taking issue preferences into account when voting. Why do these findings seem to conflict with the psychological approach?

Several explanations are possible. First, the differences may be more apparent than real. The psychologists describe much political behavior in terms of partisanship. Yet partisanship is itself associated with issues. Traditionally, the Democratic party has stood for social welfare legislation and an expansion of the federal government's role in the economy on behalf of the "little man." Mr. Guzzo may sense this connection between the Democratic party and these policies. Since he favors many of these programs himself, his identification with the party is not inconsistent with his issue preferences. Indeed, if he votes Democratic he may *feel* that his policy preferences are being advanced. So even if we find partisanship is a strong predictor of voting we cannot automatically assume that issues are being disregarded. We need to remember that attitudes toward parties may be based on beliefs about the parties' issue positions. Mr. Guzzo may feel comfortable as a Democrat precisely because the Democratic party stands for many of the things he does.

There is, of course, conflicting evidence. The psychological school says people do not know where the parties stand. Others like David RePass, Gerald Pomper, and Michael Shapiro claim that the voter *is* aware of party differences.[43] Part of this debate can be resolved by looking at the methods of the two approaches.

The psychologists rely almost exclusively on the methods and data of *The American Voter*. As we noted, an integral part of the book's technique is the open-ended question in which individuals

---

[41] See Benjamin I. Page and Richard A. Brody, "Policy Voting and the Electoral Process: The Vietnam War Issue," *American Political Science Review*, Vol. 66 (1972), pp. 979–95, for a discussion of this point.

[42] See footnote 38 above.

[43] RePass, "Issue Salience and Party Choice;" Pomper, "Toward a More Responsible Two-Party System" and "From Confusion to Clarity;" and Shapiro, "Rational Political Man."

are asked about their likes and dislikes of the parties and candidates. These questions probably encourage the respondent to mention personality factors more than issues. Consequently, the answers seem to reflect a lack of concern with policy. Had the authors inquired specifically about issues, they might have emerged with a different picture of voting.

Also, the psychological school tends to work with a standard set of issues which the investigators feel are important. The problem is that the respondents may feel these issues are not important. Consequently, their opinions on this set of issues may not reflect their true views, and the role of issues may therefore seem unimportant.

The public policy group works from a different perspective. Let the voter describe what he *perceives* are the characteristics of the parties and candidates. These perceptions are his *beliefs*. Many of these beliefs involve issues. Mr. Charles, for example, thinks Democrats are reckless spenders. If you asked him only for his dislikes of Democrats he may not mention it but he nevertheless believes that they are. And since he does not approve of reckless spending, he dislikes Democrats. The point is that individuals have policy-related beliefs which are highly related to their attitudes. It is the task of the investigator to discover these beliefs.

The public policy group, on the other hand, often forgets or ignores the role of variables such as partisanship. We have already seen that voting one's party line is not necessarily irrational. Furthermore, as we noted above, issue positions are frequently correlated with candidate and party images, at least in a loose way. Also, some scholars feel the significance of issues on electoral decisions varies with time and place,[44] and issues may be more important in presidential than in state and local elections.

CONCLUSION

Much of the preceding description is perplexing. There is confusion and debate even among social scientists about how a voter makes up his mind. Unfortunately, the controversy still continues.

---

[44] Pomper, "Toward a More Responsible Two-Party System," pp. 916–40; and Richard W. Boyd, "Popular Control of Public Policy: A Normal Vote Analysis of the 1968 Election," *American Political Science Review*, Vol. 66 (1972), pp. 429–49.

Most of these positions have compelling evidence in back of them and it seems obvious that no single theory or model will explain everything. Voting, like many choice situations, is a complex process. All of these approaches contribute to the explanation of the process. We know intuitively that Mr. Charles and Mr. Guzzo are influenced by many factors, but at this time it is impossible to tell which of these is most important.

Research in this area will no doubt continue for years to come since voting is considered the most important form of mass political participation. But even as important as elections are in Western democracies, their significance should be kept in proper perspective.

On the one hand, we will see in the concluding chapter that the connection between public opinion as expressed in election and public policy is often tenuous. Some scholars feel elections have symbolic rather than substantive importance. Elections, they argue, do not control public policy, except in an indirect way. By and large, decision makers have the freedom to do what they want when they want, subject to broad constraints imposed by public opinion. Elections may set limits on what can be done but they do not determine the content of public policy. Instead, the main function of voting is to provide reassurance, to convince the electorate that it has some part in governing. And in so doing, the vote contributes to the legitimacy and hence stability of the political system.

On the other hand, there are other kinds of participation besides the conventional electoral activities. We consider two, extremism and violence, in the following chapters. These "nonconventional," sometimes illegitimate behaviors may occasionally be as widespread as voting. And often they, rather than elections, determine the course of political policy.

So although voting occupies a central place in the study of political behavior, its significance should not obscure other aspects of political life. Once we have expanded this inquiry, our understanding of politics will be greatly enhanced.

7

Political Discontent: The Case
of the Radical Right

Former President Dwight D. Eisenhower has been the subject of many biographies, some of them favorable, some of them critical. *The Politician* by Robert Welch is unique, however.[1] Although it, too, is a biography of Eisenhower, it sees him in a totally different light. Eisenhower, according to *The Politician,* was part of a Communist conspiracy to overthrow the U.S. government and enslave the world.

Welch has been ambivalent about Eisenhower's role in the conspiracy. In the original edition of the biography, Welch called Eisenhower a "dedicated, conscious agent of the Communist conspiracy."[2] In later versions, he toned down this accusation by stating two possible interpretations of Eisenhower's behavior. Either Eisenhower was an unwitting dupe, "a shell through which the Communist mix of action and propaganda is extruded" or he was at least

---

[1] Robert Welch, *The Politician* (Belmont, Mass.: Belmont Publishing Co., 1964).

[2] George Thayer, *The Farther Shores of Politics* (New York: Simon & Schuster, 1967), p. 185.

"sympathetic to ultimate Communist aims, realistically and even mercilessly willing to help them achieve their goals, knowingly receiving and abiding by Communist orders, and consciously serving the Communist conspiracy for all of his adult life."[3] Although he concedes both interpretations are possible, he makes it clear that he believes the latter.

To support his contention Welch cites incident after incident in Eisenhower's career which "prove" that he must have been acting on behalf of the Communists: the rise of Fidel Castro in Cuba, the U-2 affair in 1960, economic aid to Yugoslavia, the appointment of Earl Warren to the Supreme Court, proposals for sharing nuclear technology, and sending troops to Little Rock, Arkansas. These were not isolated happenings, but rather parts of a Communist plan to take over the world, a plan consciously aided by Eisenhower.

Welch did not rest with the publication of *The Politician*. He was so concerned with the dangers of Communism and with the inability of existing political institutions to meet this challenge that he founded the John Birch Society. The society's main purpose is to alert and educate the American people about the threat from Communism. The society, whose membership is unknown but probably exceeds several thousand, publishes magazines and books, operates bookstores, maintains speakers' bureaus, conducts letter writing and fund-raising campaigns and organizes for political action at both the local and national levels. Its avowed goal is to expose the Communist menace, but the society has become involved in numerous political issues ranging from school busing to fluoridation of water.

The John Birch Society is an example of political extremism. There are, of course, different points of view on most current events. When one uses adjectives such as "extreme" or "radical" to describe someone else's ideas he is usually casting a value judgment on those ideas. Yet in the present context, calling groups like the John Birch Society extreme or radical seems justified for several reasons. For one, these groups often go beyond mere criticism to impugn the motives, intelligence, honesty, and patriotism of their opponents. They also believe the dangers facing their country are massive and call for drastic remedies. Existing institutions (e.g.,

---

[3] Welch, *The Politician,* pp. 277–78.

political parties, legislative bodies), they think, are corrupt and ineffective. Many of these groups advocate sweeping changes in the political and social system. As may be apparent from *The Politician*, extremist organizations go beyond conventional politics in terms of their rhetoric, methods, style, and programs.

This chapter attempts to analyze political extremism. In particular we want to know what characteristics extremists share and what accounts for their attitudes and behavior. The discussion will be limited to extremism on the right, largely because there are more data on right-wing political movements than on left-wing movements. The social sciences seem to be biased in this respect because with some notable exceptions most systematic and empirical research deals with the radical right. This limitation is not too severe, however, since many of the principles and findings that are presented in this chapter are applicable to left as well as to the right.

THE RADICAL RIGHT AND AMERICAN POLITICS

The impact of the radical right on American politics is difficult to gauge. On one hand, literally hundreds of groups operate throughout the country. These organizations are concerned with different problems. Some are mainly political (Liberty Lobby, Southern States Industrial Council); some are anti-Communist (John Birch Society, American Security Council); some are racist (Ku Klux Klan, National Socialist White People's Party, White Citizens Councils); and some are fundamentalist (Christian Anti-Communism Crusade, Christian Crusade, Church League of America).

Rightist groups are quite active. Benjamin Epstein and Arnold Forster estimate that these organizations spend over $200 million a year on propaganda.[4] They sponsor hundreds of radio broadcasts, political schools, and rallies. Their magazines and newsletters reach thousands of people. They also produce books, newspapers, pamphlets, records, movies, and teaching kits by the score.[5]

---

[4] Benjamin R. Epstein and Arnold Forster, *The Radical Right* (New York: Random House, 1966), p. 3.

[5] For excellent descriptions of the activities of radical right organizations, see Thayer, *The Farther Shores of Politics;* Epstein and Forster, *The Radical Right;* and J. Allen Broyles, *The John Birch Society: Anatomy of a Protest* (Boston: Beacon Press, 1964).

On the other hand, popular support for these groups is generally not large. Occasionally a person on the right like Senator Joseph McCarthy or George Wallace will enjoy widespread sympathy, but many of the organizations operate in obscurity. The radical right, like the left, is not a cohesive, identifiable force with a mass following but is fragmented and has limited appeal.

That right-wing causes and leaders are not overwhelmingly popular in the United States is evident from Table 7.1. These data are

Table 7.1
ATTITUDES TOWARD EXTREMISTS AND CONSERVATIVES

		*Average Scale Scores**			
Extremists		*Conservatives*			
John Birch Society	*Wallace*	*Conservatives in General*	*Reagan*	*Agnew*	*Nixon*
23.4	31.3	52.9	51.8	45.9	58.5
(1,157)	(1,405)	(1,344)	(1,353)	(1,428)	(1,473)

* Figures in the table are average scale scores. Each respondent in the sample was asked to rate the individuals and groups on a scale running from zero to one hundred, with zero being the least favorable rating, one hundred most favorable.

Note: Figures in parentheses are the number of cases upon which the averages are based.

Source: *CPS 1970 American National Election Study.* (See Appendix.)

drawn from a poll conducted after the 1970 election. Respondents in the study were asked to rate different groups and individuals on a scale ranging from zero to one hundred with zero being least favorable, one hundred most favorable. The figures are the averages for the total sample. Though the data are only suggestive, they nonetheless show that support for extremism is not very high, especially in comparison with moderates: Nixon's support, for instance, is nearly twice Wallace's.

Yet these figures may be misleading because the power of the right is disproportionate to its membership. It seems most influential at the state and local level, particularly in certain regions such as the Southwest and Southern California. As Raymond Wolfinger and his colleagues point out, these groups are most effective in situations where numerical superiority is not as important as organization and persistence.[6] They pressure school boards and libraries to

---

[6] Raymond E. Wolfinger, Barbara Kaye Wolfinger, Kenneth Prewitt, and Sheilah Rosenhack, "America's Radical Right: Politics and Ideology," *Ideology and Discontent,* ed. David Apter (New York: The Free Press, 1964), p. 288.

keep subversive material from young people; they defend the community's morals by censuring movies and magazines; they organize campaigns in support of the police and against school busing to achieve integration. So although the radical right is ostensibly concerned with national and international policies it probably has its greatest effect on local issues.

Still, radicalism on the right has been a force on national affairs since the founding of the Republic. Know-Nothings, the American Protective Association, Coughlinites, the Ku Klux Klan, and others have periodically affected public policy.[7] They have been especially important in focusing attention on various issues, in injecting emotion into politics, and in limiting the options available to policy makers.

Joseph McCarthy, for example, profoundly affected domestic and foreign policy by raising the spectre of domestic Communism and subversion. Among other things, McCarthy was incensed about the ascendency of the Communist regime in China, an event which he blamed largely on bungling and treason in the State Department. His accusations and innuendoes forced the resignations of several career diplomats with considerable experience in Asia. Their departure had two consequences. One, the State Department lost much of its Far Eastern expertise and, two, it became hypersensitive to charges of being "soft on communism." According to some writers, the legacy of the McCarthy era was a predisposition to oppose Communism wherever it cropped up. As a result, when the Communist insurgency in South Vietnam began to make headway in the early 1960s, the Kennedy administration responded by making substantial military commitments. Many of the men who would have opposed this move had been driven from the government. In David Halberstam's words:

> The men who might have served at FE [the Bureau of Far Eastern Affairs in the State Department], John Davies, Jack Service, Edmund Clubb, had all been destroyed by the McCarthy investigations, and their successors had been men willing to serve in Asia under the terms dictated by Dulles, terms of the most rigid

---

[7] For a description of these groups, see Seymour Martin Lipset and Earl Raab, *The Politics of Unreason* (New York: Harper & Row, Publishers, 1970), chaps. ii–v.

anti-Communism, where viewpoint and rhetoric often had very little to do with the facts.[8]

Perhaps McCarthy did not have overwhelming popular support.[9] But he certainly had a traumatic effect on American diplomacy.

Similarly, George Wallace has raised issues but limited the scope of their discussion. His pronouncements on school busing, dissent, crime, and welfare spending doubtlessly contributed to a conservative approach to these issues. The late 1960s was a period of political unrest as many groups challenged the status quo. Wallace's style had the effect of both making these challenges more serious than they were and then offering simplistic ways to meet them. His strident opposition to school busing, for instance, did more to inflame the public than to produce constructive solutions to the real problems of racial segregation. The Wallace movement's impact on politics was all the more serious because, unlike McCarthyism, it had considerable popular support. After all, Wallace won more than 10 million popular votes and 56 electoral votes in his 1968 presidential campaign. Until he was wounded by an attempt on his life in May 1972, he was a major candidate for the Democratic presidential nomination.

The radical right makes its mark on American politics in other ways. Members of the John Birch Society have been elected to Congress and to important state and local offices. Various right-wing groups mount effective and occasionally successful information and lobbying campaigns.

Obviously extremism is not confined to the United States. Most nations have extremist groups. In some countries the membership is small and uninfluential; in others it may dominate politics, such as in Northern Ireland where militant Protestants and Catholics have been battling each other in open warfare for years. Sometimes

---

[8] David Halberstam, *The Best and the Brightest* (New York: Random House, Inc., 1972), p. 189.

[9] Nelson Polsby, for instance, believes that McCarthy did not have as much support among the populace as politicians and journalists once believed. His support, in other words, was more apparent than real. The senator's influence may have resulted partly from this common misperception of his strength. Nelson W. Polsby, "Toward an Explanation of McCarthyism," *Politics and Social Life,* ed. Nelson W. Polsby, Robert A. Dentler, and Paul A. Smith (Boston: Houghton Mifflin Co., 1963), pp. 812–14.

an extremist group may become the predominate force and take control of the government as in Germany and Italy in the 1930s.

DEFINING THE RADICAL RIGHT

It is misleading to define extremism solely in terms of personality traits. Although some social scientists disagree—we will consider a famous example shortly—the personality approach seems too simplistic. Complex social movements such as Nazism attract a variety of people, many of whom seem to have quite different temperaments. Also, we cannot distinguish extremists on the basis of their overt behavior. True, some of the most spectacular instances of extremism, like vigilantism or terrorism, frequently involve desperate and illegal acts. But the vast majority of active members or supporters of right-wing causes are normal, law-abiding citizens. They have families, attend church, go on picnics just like other people. If any behavioral attribute distinguishes them, it is the zealous pursuit of their goals through conventional political activity. Even groups like the Ku Klux Klan and American Nazis seem to spend most of their time organizing, raising money, publishing newspapers, and peacefully picketing their enemies.

What, then, does characterize the radical right? Two factors stand out: (1) their political and social beliefs, attitudes, and doctrines; and (2) their cognitive style.

The Ideology of the Right

The right can be defined in the first instance by its ideology. Naturally, there is heterogeneity of opinion. Rightists often disagree among themselves, sometimes vehemently so.[10] The right is not a monolithic ideological force. Instead, like most political movements it is a coalition of disparate groups with disparate ideas.

---

[10] George Wallace, a man who made his reputation as a segregationist, is probably considered by most observers to be in the far right. Yet the National Socialist White People's Party (i.e., the American Nazi Party) criticizes him for being "totally mum on the Jewish problem." (*White Power,* July 1972, p. 6) This example illustrates the fact that the right is a variegated territory inhabited by people with widely differing temperaments and points of view.

Nevertheless, there are some common thoughts running through right-wing literature and pronouncements.

Belief in Conspiracy.   Perhaps the most pervasive characteristic of right-wing thought is belief in conspiracy. For a member of the John Birch Society or of almost any right-wing group, events do not just happen. They are plotted and carried out by clever agents who work for foreign agents against the interests of the United States. In the minds of many, internal subversion, not foreign military threat, is the nation's number one enemy. Wolfinger et al., report that participants at an "Anti-Communism School" sponsored by the Christian Anti-Communism Crusade overwhelmingly believed that Communists have "a lot of influence" in the Democratic party and in colleges and universities.[11] The nearly universal cry of the right is "We have been betrayed"—betrayed by Communists, by intellectuals, by Jews, by blacks, by atheists, by misguided youth or by whatever minority happens to be in vogue.

According to Robert Welch, America's involvement in Vietnam is really the result of conspiracy, as he indicates in this interview:

Q.   These Chinese leaders may be unsavory characters, but there are advantages in talking with them.

A.   (Welch) There's nothing in it for us. Our country is being run for the benefit of the Communists. The Vietnam War was run for their benefit, too.

Q.   That's a new one on me. I thought we obliterated North Vietnam from the air.

A.   We obliterated them? Good Lord, what have you been reading? Why, we haven't even been allowed to attack North Vietnam. Yet in a single air raid we destroyed one-third of Saigon, the capitol of the country we were supposed to be protecting. That's what always happens when America is defending another country. All the damage is done to our allies—like South Korea . . . because our wars are designed to help the Communists.

Q.   But why did the North Vietnamese need us to win the war? They were winning it all by themselves in the mid-sixties before we stepped in.

A.   Are you being funny? Stop and think what you're saying. Of course, North Vietnam wanted to take over South Vietnam.

---

[11] Wolfinger et al., "America's Radical Right," p. 270.

But they couldn't just invade. The North needed some excuse. So we go in there pretending to aid the South while at the same time we were supplying the North with the actual equipment they needed to fight us with.[12]

In this tortuous explanation of the war in Vietnam, American participation results from a Communist conspiracy to weaken and ultimately destroy America and its free world allies.

One can easily find other examples of this kind of conspiratorial view of the world. The National Economic Council published a series of articles entitled "Patriots Die Untimely Deaths." The articles see a plot behind the deaths of an almost endless list of famous Americans including Abraham Lincoln, John Kennedy, Robert Taft, George Patton, Huey Long, William Borah, Calvin Coolidge, William Jennings Bryan, Joseph McCarthy, Robert LaFollette, and the men of the U.S.S. *Liberty*. Tying these deaths together, according to "Patriots Die Untimely Deaths," is the fact that each of "these persons was interfering or exposing the International Money Power which controls our banking system and the banking system of the world."[13] The concluding article warns the true patriot to be cautious for he, too, could be a victim of the conspiracy. Among other precautions it suggests:

Do not eat in public. When you must speak at a luncheon, eat at home. Do not frequent the same restaurants. There are many kinds of undetectable poisons, some of which can give you cancer or leukemia.

Do not smoke cigarettes given to you by anyone. Do not smoke cigarettes left unguarded at any time. A small thread of a certain plastic substance can cause you to be asphixiated.

Do not go into elevators unattended. A spray from a pressurized can containing a number of deadly substances can cause a "natural death" from heart failure, kidney poisoning or liver poisoning.[14]

---

12 Trenton, N.J., *Sunday Times Advertiser*, July 15, 1973, p. 17.

13 Economic Council Letter, March 1972, p. 3.

14 Ibid., pp. 3–4. This example may be atypical but it does reflect the right's preoccupation with conspiracy. As another example, Robert Welch originally limited the circulation of *The Politician* to his friends and "co-patriots." Yet, the preface is ominous:

But I shall not ask for it back in a hurry, because if anything happens to me I should like to have a goodly number of copies safely out in other hands. (Welch, *The Politician*, p. 1)

Scapegoats.   Closely related to the belief in conspiracy is the idea of scapegoats. Rightists frequently blame scapegoats for their personal problems or the woes of the country. If there are riots in the cities, radicals or anarchists planned them; if there is inflation, international Jewish bankers must want it; if schools must be integrated, Communist race-mixers have decreed it; if a foreign government becomes hostile to the United States, the State Department is to blame.

The main culprits in the eyes of the right are of course the Communist party and its fellow travelers. The radical right is most united in its anticommunism. Combating Communism is the *raison d'être* for groups such as the John Birch Society and the Christian Anti-Communism Crusade. Other organizations like the Ku Klux Klan have seized on anticommunism as a means advancing their programs. The second most popular group of scapegoats is Jews and Zionists, followed closely by blacks, intellectuals, hippies, bankers, members of the Council of Foreign Relations, and the liberal clergy. Rightists generally attribute most of America's problems to these groups.

Belief in conspiracy and scapegoats, many social scientists feel, serves psychological needs. Conspiracy and scapegoats provide particularly simple explanations of complex events, thus relieving the individual of the necessity to look for more detailed explanations.[15] For others, these beliefs are psychological defense mechanisms. Hans Toch, for example, suggests that "conspiracy beliefs respond to a real need *only* for persons who *cannot preserve their self-esteem unless they conceive of themselves as victims of a plot.*"[16] A man who spends his life struggling somewhat unsuccessfully to acquire the material goods and services he sees described in the mass media may find comfort and reassurance in blaming others for his failures. "After all," he says to himself, "it's not my fault the Niggers are getting all the good jobs."

A similar theme running through right-wing publications is the belief in the enormity of the enemy. Many rightists perceive of

---

[15] Ira S. Rohter, "Social and Psychological Determinants of Radical Rightism," *The American Right Wing,* ed. Robert A. Schoenberger (New York: Holt, Rinehart & Winston, Inc., 1969), p. 198.

[16] Hans Toch, *The Social Psychology of Social Movements* (Indianapolis: The Bobbs-Merrill Co., Inc., 1965), p. 69. Italics his.

themselves as underdogs whose time is running out in a last-ditch battle to save America and humanity. They typically see themselves as a tiny minority—a minority blessed with wisdom and insight—fighting desperately to awaken the masses to the dangers. "We still are 'very small potatoes,' " Welch says, "and we have a long way to go before we reach a realistic level of opposition against the Communist monster."[17] In response to a question in the same interview quoted above, Welch says of the size of the Communist conspiracy:

> We haven't been taken over? You don't think the Communists are running Washington? You don't believe what we do as a nation is in the control of the Conspiracy? For goodness sake, we've been saying so for years in print. Our scoreboard shows that the United States is 60 to 80 percent influenced by Communism.[18]

Loss of Freedom.   Acceptance of conspiracy, scapegoats and an enormous enemy are key elements of rightist thinking. Equally important is the belief in the loss of freedom. In a democracy everyone naturally worries about individual liberties. For many people freedom involves more than simply freedom to do what one wants; it also implies economic and social equality. In order to advance this concept of freedom, government, both at the national and local level, has grown considerably in the last decades. There is consensus that the expansion of the government's roles in society have created as well as solved problems. But rightists are persuaded that this expansion has been at the expense of personal liberty.[19] Consequently, they are invariably conservative on domestic social-welfare programs.

Most odious to the right are the income tax, deficit spending, the Federal Reserve System, and welfare programs. Generally, they fear that government has gotten too big, spends too much money, and regulates too many aspects of our lives. A pet project of many

---

[17] John Birch Society, *Bulletin*, January 1965, p. 14.

[18] Trenton, N.J., *Sunday Times Advertiser*, July 15, 1973, p. 17.

[19] Many liberals and radicals are similarly concerned about bigness in government. Their concerns differ from the radical right's, however. Where the radical right opposes government spending and regulation, the left believes the national government serves corporate interests against the masses. Unlike the right, they are also worried about the loss of freedom resulting from intimidation of the press, eavesdropping, mass accumulation of personal dossiers, repressive law and order legislation and intolerance of dissent. The left generally approves of social-welfare legislation.

right-wing organizations is the Liberty Amendment which would repeal the 16th Amendment legitimizing the income tax and would prohibit the federal government from engaging in any kind of business. The Liberty Amendment, already approved in several states, is designed to curtail government and promote competition, thereby restoring some of our lost liberties.

Although rightists disagree among themselves on many points, they generally oppose New Deal programs, foreign aid, school busing to achieve integration, "inflationary" spending, many Supreme Court decisions, and most kinds of taxes. Like many groups in society, they are suspicious of executive orders and feel the presidency has become too powerful. They are staunch defenders of the doctrine of states' rights.

Despite their opposition to bigness in government they usually endorse tough "law-and-order" laws: wiretapping, preventive detention, the death penalty, and no-knock arrests. They are less concerned with the rights of the accused than with the needs of the police. They have consistently blamed the Supreme Court's "leniency" with criminals for recent rises in crime, protest demonstrations, and urban riots.

It is interesting to note, however, that many elements of the radical right distrust and dislike the national government as much for its aid to large corporations as for its welfare programs. There is a pervasive dislike and distrust of interlocking banks and corporations, multinational conglomerates, and tax-exempt foundations. Many rightist groups portray themselves as defenders of the small businessman and farmer against the power and cupidity of big government and big business. *The Fiery Cross,* the official newspaper of the Ku Klux Klan, complained recently that

> the recent Nixon directive to cancel parity and subsidy for agriculture threatens the image of the small farmer, and paves the way for corporate farms to become the chief source of food raising, packaging and distribution. "And the rich shall inherit the earth" is within reach by gross dimensions.[20]

Ethnocentrism.   Besides its domestic conservativism, the radical right has traditionally been strongly nationalistic or, in social science parlance, ethnocentric. (An ethnocentric is someone who has

---

[20] *The Fiery Cross,* February 1973, p. 5.

an extreme distaste and suspicion of foreign cultures.) Rightists are frequently called super-patriots because they idolize American institutions and tend to equate criticism of America with treason. They are hypersensitive about national symbols such as the flag, even to the point of confusing allegiance to the symbols with allegiance to the principles of the nation itself.

They distrust foreign governments except those like South Africa, South Korea, Nationalist China, Greece, and Spain which share their animosity toward Communism. For them neutrality in the cold war is tantamount to opposition to the United States and they bitterly oppose aid to neutralist countries such as India.

And, of course, there is the United Nations. Getting the U.N. off American soil is the *cause célèbre* of the right. A passage in *American Challenge*, a right-wing paper, typifies this position:

> The U.N. has a record of crafty deceit and malevolence, and criminal performance. It is the deadly enemy of the United States. In every nation it has taken over, it has committed fearful atrocities and murdered millions of people. It awaits to do the same here.[21]

Even though the right dislikes foreign involvements, it supports a large military establishment. Rightists, like nearly everyone, have mixed feelings about the war in Vietnam. Some concede it may have been a mistake but nevertheless should be fought as vigorously as possible with whatever weapons are available. That the United States did not crush North Vietnam and the Viet Cong is taken as evidence of bungling and treason in the highest levels of government.

Prejudice.   Race prejudice, whether overt or covert, is characteristic of many but certainly not all right-wing groups. The more extremist organizations, the Ku Klux Klan, White Citizens Councils, and National Socialist White People's Party, for example, openly advocate separation and discrimination. Others, like the New Christian Crusade Church, do not engage in race baiting but are equally racist in philosophy. Still others, including the John Birch Society, disclaim any racial or religious prejudice and, in fact, make efforts to recruit minorities. Yet almost all of these groups bitterly oppose the civil rights movement. The John Birch Society *Bulletin* said at the height of the civil rights movement

---

[21] *American Challenge,* April 1973, p. 1.

The Negro Revolutionary Movement, now headed by Martin Luther King and all of the Communists with whom he has surrounded himself, is . . . the most important single part of the Communist program and strategy for taking over our country.[22]

Fundamentalism.   Within the American right there is also a strong tradition of religious fundamentalism. Some of the most prominent leaders on the right are fundamentalist ministers: Carl McIntyre (20th-Century Reformation Hour), Fred Schwartz (Christian Anti-Communism Crusade), Major Edgar C. Bundy (Church League of America), and Billy James Hargis (Christian Crusade).[23] Although these groups are ostensibly religious and not political, religion serves mainly to motivate and justify their political and social programs. Communism, for example, is damned as atheistic. And, according to many fundamentalist sects, anti-Semitism is justified by teachings in the Bible.

Along with its fundamentalism much of the radical right adheres to a rigid conventional morality. Rightists generally abhor long hair on men, X-rated movies, hippies, rock and roll, and the so-called new morality. Many of their writings reflect a fear of moral decay. They seem confused and appalled by rapid social change and, as suggested previously, they are wary of bigness, whether it is in government, unions, or industry. Since they take the Bible at its word, they oppose the theory of evolution. The right is united in its opposition to the proposed Equal Rights Amendment forbidding discrimination on the basis of sex.

The Style and Tone of the Radical Right.   Finally, harshness and truculence mark the writings of the American right. It accepts the use of force as the first and best solution for many social problems. Rightists are not very forgiving of deviance. Their prescriptions for maintaining law and order, for example, are simple and direct: capital punishment, mandatory life sentences for drug offenders, preventive detention, and sterilization for convicted rapists. They feel dissent should not be compromised but crushed. Maximum power should also be used in foreign and military affairs. Members of the radical right have difficulty understanding limited wars and

---

[22] John Birch Society, *Bulletin,* May 1965, p. 10.

[23] See Thayer, *The Farther Shores,* chap. ix, for an excellent description of these leaders and their organizations.

inhibitions about using nuclear weapons. After all, why were such weapons developed if not to be used? The enemy, they believe, should be given no quarter even if civilians are inadvertently hurt as well.[24]

Of course, not everyone in the right fits this model. There is a diversity of opinion on all of these matters. Nor are those who subscribe to these views ogres. They simply believe strictness is necessary for the preservation of society. Still, as we will see, aggressiveness is an important trait of many rightist personalities and it certainly pervades right-wing literature.

The Cognitive Style of Extremists

So far we have described the radical right by their beliefs and programs. In one sense, the content of these attitudes is the distinguishing characteristic. Yet extremists can be identified by their cognitive style. Cognitive styles refer to the way a person receives, evaluates, and acts on information.

Some social scientists believe that extremists tend to have "closed" minds.[25] Adhering rigidly and even blindly to their beliefs, they are not amenable to persuasion and fail to see inconsistencies in their own positions. Additional information about a subject cannot change an opinion because the individual refuses to accept its relevance. His beliefs are strictly compartmentalized. Furthermore, there may be a lack of differentiation between cognitive elements, as in the case of a person who refers to his opponents "radlibs." Using radlib, short for radical-liberal, suggests that the speaker believes a liberal to be no different from a radical.

Another trait of the closed mind, according to Milton Rokeach, is the acceptance of authority, rather than reason, as the final arbiter of a statement's truth or falsity. Extremists have a tendency to seek confirmation of their beliefs not from an objective appraisal of the situation but from authority figures.[26] Still another feature of extremist thinking is the categorical rejection of those holding

---

[24] When asked whether he preferred diplomacy to war with the Chinese, Robert Welch replied, "Gosh, no," and then added, "The Chinese have nothing to fight with if we want to fight them. Red China can't even feed its people." (Trenton, N.J., *Sunday Times Advertiser,* July 15, 1973, p. 17.)

[25] Milton Rokeach, *The Open and Closed Mind* (New York: Basic Books, Inc., 1960).

[26] Ibid., chap. iii.

opposing opinions. Rokeach, who calls this phenomenon "opin-ionation," gives the example, "Only a simple-minded fool would say that God exists."[27] The statement reflects the speaker's denial of God and his total rejection of those who do.

Bobby Moga, a town superviser in a midwestern city, typifies the closed-mindedness and rigidity of many extremists. He is recalling his reaction to an Anti-Vietnam War Moratorium which took place in November 1969. Although there is no indication that Mr. Moga is a member of any radical organization, his remarks are revealing:

> This is a cute little incident that happened during the Moratorium. We have some of those damned people here, even in a decent town like Aurora. Some get out here from Chicago, some of them are homegrown, those damned hippies. But nobody pays much attention to them.
>
> Anyway, this guy with greasy long hair and those granny glasses—a ridiculous-looking creep, I get mad just looking at them —anyway, he came into the township building and he started setting up a card table and some signs.
>
> I got red. God but I got mad. I walked over to him and I didn't even read his sign. I knew what the hell he was all about. I said to him, What's your problem, pal? What's with you, pal? I kept calling him pal every second breath, that's the way to keep those bastards off balance.
>
> I said to him, You ain't setting up nothing like that in here, pal, let's get movin', pal.
>
> Oh, hell yes, he started protesting, he was saying Nazi Germany and civil rights and freedom of speech and how I was no better than a German storm trooper, and I started getting madder.
>
> I reached out and grabbed him under my left arm—got a good hold on him, just like this . . . and I was holding him real tight, and he was hollering. And with my other arm—the right one, I'm right-handed, too, you know—I picked up his lousy stinking card table and his goddamned sign and I pulled the whole mess right through the door and pitched his ass out on Water Street. Don't bring that sort of crap into this building, pal, and don't make me mad, I told him. That's the only way to handle jerks like that— hustle'm right on outside. I'm not letting any goddamned hippie jerk of a demonstrator use my office for that sort of thing.[28]

---

[27] Ibid., p. 81.

[28] Joseph C. Goulden, "Voices from the Silent Majority," *Harper's Magazine,* April 1970, p. 67.

There is some debate about whether or not left-wing extremists such as Communists are as authoritarian as right-wing extremists such as Nazis, but rigid or dogmatic thinking does seem related to conservatism.[29] Gordon DiRenzo, for example, compared the cognitive styles of a sample of Republican and Democratic university students. He found that among those Democrats who bolted their party to vote for Goldwater in 1964, 64 percent scored high on a scale of dogmatic thinking. By contrast, only 28 percent of the Republicans switching to Johnson were high on the dogmatism scale. He also discovered that about half of the Republicans were high scorers.[30] Although the studies upon which these conclusions are based involve small and limited samples, they indicate that cognitive style is an important characteristic of extremism.

Summary.   We now have an idea of the meaning of right-wing extremism. It includes groups preoccupied with conspiracy, with communism, with a desire to retrieve lost values and customs. Rightists distrust change, international organizations, and government in general. They also seem to be characterized by rigid or dogmatic thinking. They are often unyielding in their beliefs, even in the face of overwhelming disconfirming evidence.

EXPLAINING EXTREMIST ATTITUDES AND BEHAVIOR

Knowing some of the values and opinions identifying the radical right is, of course, interesting but it leaves an important question unanswered: why do people support or join extremist organizations? Like any political activity, participation in right-wing causes is a complex phenomenon. Consequently, social scientists find that no single explanation satisfactorily accounts for this type of behavior. It is necessary instead to consider theories from psychology, sociology, and political science. Since many of these theories are

---

[29] H. J. Eysenck, *The Psychology of Politics* (London: Routledge & Kegan Paul, 1954); H. J. Eysenck, "The Psychology of Politics and the Personality Similarities between Fascists and Communists," *Psychological Bulletin,* Vol. 53 (1956), pp. 431–38; Richard Christie, "Eysenck's Treatment of the Personality of Communists," *Psychological Bulletin,* Vol. 53 (1956), pp. 411–30; Roger Brown, *Social Psychology* (New York: The Free Press, 1965), pp. 526–44; and Rokeach, *The Open and Closed Mind,* chap. vi.

[30] Gordon J. DiRenzo, "Dogmatism and Presidential Preference in the 1964 Elections," *Psychological Reports,* Vol. 22 (1968), pp. 1200–1201.

closely related to each other, the distinctions are somewhat artificial. But they at least demonstrate the major trends in the study of extremism.[31]

Psychological Explanations

Psychological explanations of extremism emphasize personality development and attributes. According to many psychologists, how an individual satisfies the requirements of his personality system affects his political behavior.[32] A person acts in ways that help him maintain self-esteem, control undesirable or antisocial impulses, gratify urges, and resolve deep-seated psychological conflicts. Political behavior, in short, reflects an individual's attempts to come to grips with his drives and desires.

Seen from this viewpoint, extremism results from psychopathology—that is, from a malfunction in a person's personality system. Perhaps the best study of extremism from this perspective is *The Authoritarian Personality* by T. W. Adorno, Else Frenkel-Brunswik, Daniel Levinson, and Nevitt Sanford.[33] The book tried to discover the roots of the prejudice and behavior underlying the holocaust inflicted by the Nazis on the Jews during World War II. Although the authors began by studying anti-Semitism, their research soon evolved into a thorough analysis of right-wing authoritarianism.

The Authoritarian Personality, a seminal work in the social sciences, has spawned two decades of research on the causes and meaning of authoritarianism. Many of its methods and conclusions are widely criticized, but it remains a significant source of insights into the relationship between personality and political behavior.

---

[31] The reader may notice a paradox in the following pages. Except for a few studies, most research on extremism makes inferences about activists or leaders, but relies on data based on supporters or followers. The leadership of extremist movements is often inaccessible to the social scientists who must be content to study rank and file members. Although we cannot avoid the paradox in the chapter we should at least be aware of it.

[32] Daniel J. Levinson, "The Relevance of Personality for Political Participation," *Public Opinion Quarterly,* Vol. 22 (1958), pp. 6–7.

[33] T. W. Adorno, Else Frenkel-Brunswik, Daniel J. Levinson, R. Nevitt Sanford, *The Authoritarian Personality* (paperback ed.; New York: W. W. Norton Co., Inc., 1969).

Since the study of authoritarianism is a vast undertaking—the book itself has over 900 pages—we can only consider the highlights of this type of analysis.

The Authoritarian Personality.   Authoritarianism is a personality system which is composed of a collection or syndrome of attitudes, among them political-economic conservatism, ethnocentrism, and anti-Semitism. The main trait, however, is "fascist receptivity" or a disposition to hold implicitly antidemocratic beliefs and opinions.[34] This trait has several names but for simplicity we will refer to it as *authoritarianism.*[35] Authoritarianism, in turn, consists of various components.

The principal feature is ambivalence about power and authority. On one hand, the authoritarian has belligerent, aggressive feelings toward others, particularly minorities and scapegoats, and is preoccupied with strength and weakness in his relationships with people. To the authoritarian, being a tough, dominating fellow is a virtue. Authoritarians especially feel animosity toward violators of conventional morality; they believe criminals and other deviants should be severely punished. On the other hand, the authoritarian submits to strong leadership. He feels a need which the authors call "authoritarian submission" to follow an authority, whether it is personal or impersonal, wherever it takes him, whatever it does. Authoritarian submission, in other words, is "an exaggerated, emotional need to submit."[36]

Authoritarianism involves other characteristics—cynicism and superstition, for example—but aggression, obdurate adherence to conventional morality, authoritarian submission, and idolization of power and toughness are the principal manifestations.

In addition to his ambivalence about power and obedience, the authoritarian also tends to be conservative, ethnocentric, and prejudiced. He accepts authority blindly but is eager to attack the weak and deviant members of society.[37]

---

[34] Ibid., chap. vii.

[35] Roger Brown (*Social Psychology*, chap. x) gives a discussion of the implications of the various names for this variable.

[36] Nevitt Sanford, "Authoritarian Personality in Contemporary Perspective," *Handbook of Political Psychology,* ed. Jeanne N. Knutson (San Francisco: Jossey-Bass Publishers, 1973), p. 144.

[37] Adorno et al., *The Authoritarian Personality,* p. 759.

The Origins of Authoritarianism.   What produces an authoritarian personality? The authors find the answer in Freudian developmental psychology. Authoritarianism, they say, begins in childhood and results from strict child-rearing practices. People exhibiting authoritarian traits tend to come from homes where the parents are strict disciplinarians, where love and approval are conditional upon obedience, and where concern with status is paramount. Discipline in these homes is threatening, unintelligible, traumatic, and ego-destructive.[38] The strict discipline, according to *The Authoritarian Personality,* has two consequences. First, it produces frustrations in the child which must be repressed because to express them would only invite further parental punishment. The repressed frustrations do not simply vanish but become directed against other, less threatening individuals and groups. The second consequence is a denial of faults, both in one's self and in one's parents. Individuals who have experienced severe discipline in childhood refuse to believe they or their parents have socially unacceptable desires and impulses like sex, fear, and passivity. They tend to glorify themselves and their parents. Again, however, these weaknesses which the individual refuses to accept in himself are projected on other people.[39]

Hence, frustrations engendered by parental discipline turn into aggression and the aggression is justified by attributing the repressed faults to the targets of the aggression, usually minorities. The emergence of authoritarian beliefs and attitudes, in short, represents the culmination of a long period of exposure to strict discipline and a child's reaction to it. *The Authoritarian Personality* emphasizes mainly Freudian concepts such as repression, projection, and displacement.

A Critique of The Authoritarian Personality.   Numerous studies have confirmed various aspects of *The Authoritarian Personality* theory. Scales measuring authoritarianism are related to many other indices of social and political attitudes and behavior, including dogmatism, xenophobia, nationalism, and misanthropy.[40] But in

---

[38] Else Frenkel-Brunswik, "Intolerance of Ambiguity as an Emotional and Perceptual Personality Variable," *Journal of Personality,* Vol. 18 (1949), p. 117.

[39] Adorno et al., *The Authoritarian Personality,* chap. x; and Sanford, "Authoritarian Personality," p. 145–49.

[40] Sanford, "Authoritarian Personality," p. 157. Also see John Harding,

spite of its explanatory power, *The Authoritarian Personality* has been criticized on both methodological and substantive grounds.[41] From our point of view there are two major shortcomings.

First, the book's explanations seem unnecessarily complicated. Instead of relying on Freudian developmental psychology, which is in many respects a cumbersome theory, to account for the development of authoritarianism, it is simpler to explain its growth by reference to learning theory: people simply learn authoritarian attitudes and behavior in the same way that they learn other attitudes and behavior. Someone growing up in a home or neighborhood which is prejudiced against Jews may find it rewarding to accept these opinions himself. Prejudice in this case would be instrumental in making and keeping friends and in preserving self-esteem in the community. There is evidence that prejudice, authoritarian aggression, ethnocentrism, and so forth are more common among certain social groups (e.g., the less educated) and in certain regions than in others. A child growing up in these subcultures is likely to reflect their values. Thus, learning through various socialization processes is as good an explanation of authoritarian traits as experiencing a childhood in a punitive environment.

Gertrude Selznick and Stephen Steinberg's study of anti-Semitism lends support to this argument. They find that education is the best single predictor of anti-Semitic attitudes. Furthermore, people with little schooling and who lack well-developed cognitive skills accept anti-Semitic beliefs "routinely along with other cultural beliefs. . . ."[42] Their findings strongly suggest that anti-Semitism, as well as other dimensions of authoritarianism, are merely learned as part of one's culture. The learning of these values is facilitated by an absence of much formal education.

Of course, individual learning theory does not by itself tell how a family or neighborhood developed an authoritarian climate of

---

Harold Proshansky, Bernard Kutner, and Isidor Chein, "Prejudice and Ethnic Relations," *The Handbook of Social Psychology,* ed. Gardner Lindzey and Elliot Aronson, Vol. 5 (Reading, Mass.: Addison-Wesley Publishing Co., 1969), pp. 1–76; and J. P. Kirscht and R. C. Dillehay, *Dimensions of Authoritarianism: A Review of Research and Theory* (Lexington, Ky.: University of Kentucky Press, 1967).

[41] See Brown (*Social Psychology,* chap. x) for a discussion and references.

[42] Gertrude J. Selznick and Stephen Steinberg, *The Tenacity of Prejudice* (New York: Harper & Row, Publishers, 1969), p. 157.

opinion in the first place. If a child learns prejudice from his parents, where did they learn it? They probably learned it from their parents, from their friends and co-workers, and from their immediate community. Doubtlessly, social and political circumstances facilitate the interpersonal and intergenerational transmission of these values. For example, groups concerned about their social status may find it easier to believe bad things about Jews than groups which are more secure in their social position. At any rate, learning through response-reward mechanisms is a simpler explanation of authoritarianism than the developmental psychology of *The Authoritarian Personality.*

A second, more troublesome problem is that many right-wing extremists appear to be no more authoritarian than members of conventional political movements. As was said earlier, it is misleading to assert that extremists have only one type of personality. Several studies show only a weak relationship at best between authoritarianism and membership in extremist groups. Alan Elms, for example, found that the rightists in his study, mainly John Birch Society members, were not unusually authoritarian in their relations with other people; their distinguishing characteristic seemed to be their extreme political conservatism and their susceptibility to community pressures.[43] Numerous other political scientists have arrived at a similar conclusion that extremists are not necessarily authoritarian.[44]

The conclusion that extremists are not authoritarian, at least in the sense of *The Authoritarian Personality,* rests primarily on studies of the membership of groups like the John Birch Society or of supporters of the McCarthy movement. Very little empirical research has been conducted on others such as the Nazi party, the Minutemen, White Citizens Councils, and the Ku Klux Klan. For

---

[43] Alan Elms, "Psychological Factors in Right-Wing Extremism," *The American Right Wing,* ed. Robert A. Schoenberger (New York: Holt, Rinehart & Winston, Inc., 1969), pp. 56–57.

[44] See Michael Paul Rogin, *The Intellectuals and McCarthy: The Radical Specter* (Cambridge, Mass.: The M.I.T. Press, 1967), pp. 240–2; Polsby, "Explanation of McCarthyism," pp. 811–14; Robert A. Schoenberger, "Conservatism, Personality and Political Extremism," *American Political Science Review,* Vol. 62 (1968), pp. 868–78; and James McEvoy, III, *Radicals or Conservatives? The Contemporary American Right* (Chicago: Rand McNally & Co., 1971), p. 37, for similar conclusions.

these latter groups the findings of *The Authoritarian Personality* may be more appropriate. Authoritarian aggression, preoccupation with power and toughness, projection of faults on minorities and other authoritarian characteristics are reflected in the publications of the Nazis. A National Socialist White People's Party mimeographed handbill, for instance, demonstrates opposition to school busing in the most strident terms:

> There might be school buses going up in smoke all over the country. There might be shotgun blasts into the guts of "mixmaster" principals and superintendents. There might even be hand grenades lobbed into the smelly chambers of the Supreme Court as the nine old swine go through their obscene legal hocuspocus.

Thus the theory of aggression and prejudice supplied by the authors of *The Authoritarian Presonality* probably fits some groups of extremists relatively better than others. But for a complete understanding of extremist discontent we have to turn to sociological and political explanations as well.

Social Explanations

Social explanations of extremism abound in the social sciences. That this is the case can perhaps be attributed to two causes. First, there is an assumption or bias in social science that "deviant" behavior such as extremism or violence is produced by aberrant social conditions. Since human nature is essentially good, something must corrupt men to produce deviance. What is more logical, then, than to scrutinize the social environment for the corrupting forces? Second, measuring social variables is sometimes easier than quantifying psychological concepts, particularly abstruse ones like those used in the theory of authoritarianism. To test sociological propositions one often needs to know only the subjects' occupations, incomes, and education, whereas the authors of *The Authoritarian Personality* had to develop a battery of psychological scales and indices.

Social Characteristics of Extremists.[45]   At the outset, it is useful to try to draw a social portrait of the right-wing movements. In one

---

45 In this and the following sections the propositions and data are based on members of right-wing groups such as the John Birch Society and Christian

sense, it is difficult to describe the social characteristics of the "typical" members, for none exists. Instead, membership varies with the type of organization. Yet, depending on the group we can offer a few generalizations.

According to published research, people who support the John Birch Society or Joseph McCarthy, for example, tend to be in the middle class. They are far from the lowest social strata but neither do they come from the top echelons. They are generally white, Protestant (though many Catholics supported McCarthy), small businessmen, managers, or white-collar workers. Many of them live in small towns and most have had at least some college. John Birch Society supporters, like the members of similar groups, belong to fundamentalist religious sects and claim to go to church regularly. As might be expected, they are politically conservative and usually vote Republican.[46]

Wallace supporters, by contrast, come disproportionately from lower classes. They are generally skilled and semiskilled workers; residents of small towns or farms and have less than a high school education.

Some of these points are illustrated in Table 7.2, which shows the average support scores for the John Birch Society and George Wallace *within* various social categories. (The data are the same as those appearing in Table 7.1 except that the average support scores are calculated for subpopulations of the sample. For instance, the average score for the John Birch Society among Protestants is 24.6.

Anti-Communist Crusade and on supporters of rightist political figures such as Joseph McCarthy and George Wallace. As mentioned in the text, there is little research on racist, paramilitary, and vigilante groups like the Ku Klux Klan and Nazis.

[46] See Seymour Martin Lipset, "Three Decades of the Radical Right: Coughlinites, McCarthyites, and Birchers," *The Radical Right,* ed. Daniel Bell (Garden City, N.Y.: Anchor Books, 1964), pp. 421–35; McEvoy, *Radicals or Conservatives?* pp. 47–51; Fred W. Grupp, "The Political Perspectives of Birch Society Members," *The American Right Wing,* ed. Robert A. Schoenberger (New York: Holt, Rinehart & Winston, Inc., 1969), pp. 87–107; Sheilah R. Koeppen, "The Radical Right and the Politics of Consensus," *The American Right Wing,* ed. Robert A. Schoenberger (New York: Holt, Rinehart & Winston, Inc., 1969), pp. 54–56; Martin Trow, "Small Businessmen, Political Tolerance and Support for McCarthy," *The American Journal of Sociology,* Vol. 64 (1958), pp. 273–75; Lipset and Raab, *The Politics of Unreason,* chap. vi, for descriptions of the social characteristics of the John Birch Society and related groups.

Totals are given at the bottom of the table so that a particular category can be compared with the sample as a whole.) Table 7.2, of course, refers to the public in general, not active membership in any group. What is true of the public may not be true of activists. Nevertheless, these data suggest some interesting trends.

In the first place, Wallace's sources of support are more readily identified than the John Birch Society's, perhaps because the society is less well-known. Wallace draws his greatest support from among working-class and rural individuals. He is especially well-liked among farmers, semi- and unskilled workers and among those with less than a high school education. The John Birch Society is not particularly popular among most groups in society. It receives *least* support from among professionals, city dwellers, and college graduates, though the differences are not large. Religion has the clearest relationship with support for right-wing causes: Jews are least supportive, but Protestants do not differ much from Catholics.

Superficially, at least, social class is not closely associated with public support for extremism. True, it gets more support from the little man—the shopkeeper, the factory worker, the small farmer—than from the upper crust of society. Wallace has his greatest success within the lower class while the John Birch Society's support is

Table 7.2
SOCIAL CHARACTERISTICS AND ATTITUDES TOWARD EXTREMISTS

(a)

	Religious Preference			
	Protestant	Catholic	Jewish	None
John Birch Society	24.6	23.0	10.0	16.7
	(790)	(231)	(41)	(62)
Wallace	33.9	28.4	10.6	17.0
	(983)	(271)	(42)	(67)

(b)

	Respondent's Occupation							
	Profes-sional	Managers	Clerical	Skilled	Semi-skilled	Service	Un-skilled	Farmers
John Birch Society ..	19.6	22.5	25.6	22.0	23.8	24.1	21.7	31.7
	(161)	(115)	(166)	(109)	(119)	(91)	(24)	(39)
Wallace ...	18.5	27.8	31.6	33.2	42.5	29.6	33.7	48.0
	(167)	(128)	(198)	(122)	(168)	(121)	(36)	(43)

Table 7.2 (continued)
(c)

	Education							
	7 Years or less	8th Grade	9th Grade	11th Grade	High School	High School+	Some College	College Grad-uate
John Birch								
Society ..	23.9	20.8	27.4	21.5	24.0	25.8	22.3	20.0
	(108)	(111)	(134)	(43)	(258)	(148)	(181)	(170)
Wallace ...	39.1	36.7	37.8	42.5	21.7	29.2	25.9	15.5
	(175)	(152)	(173)	(49)	(309)	(180)	(194)	(169)

(d)

	Present Residence				
	Central City	50,000 and Over	10,000– 49,000	Small Town	Rural
John Birch					
Society ...	18.7	24.5	19.9	24.7	25.3
	(132)	(236)	(187)	(242)	(360)
Wallace	19.7	26.6	28.3	33.0	38.4
	(148)	(287)	(233)	(278)	(459)

Averages for the Total Sample

John Birch Society	Wallace
23.4	31.3
(1,157)	(1,405)

Note: Figures in parentheses refer to the number of cases.
Source: *CPS 1970 American Nationl Election Study.* (See **Appendix.**)

more evenly distributed. Furthermore, these generalizations hold for radical movements in other countries as well. Radicalism in France, Germany, Austria, and Italy appeals mostly to marginal middle- and lower class individuals.[47]

But there is no clear relationship between social characteristics and extremism, and social scientists have found it necessary to develop more precise analytic concepts. One of these concepts is "status politics."

Status Politics. The idea of status politics, a term coined by Seymour M. Lipset, is quite simple.[48] If a man is laid off during a

---

[47] Seymour M. Lipset, "Social Stratification and 'Right-Wing Extremism,'" *British Journal of Sociology,* Vol. 10 (1959), pp. 346–82.

[48] Seymour M. Lipset ("The Sources of the 'Radical Right,'" *The Radical Right,* ed. Daniel Bell [Garden City, N.Y.: Anchor Books, 1964], pp. 308–32) developed the concept of status politics.

recession or cannot provide food or shelter for his family because of inflation, he can rightly or wrongly blame his troubles on the political system. Since his problems have an identifiable source—the government—he works to defeat the incumbents and replace them with men he feels will restore good times. During periods of prosperity, however, some people experience frustrations of a different kind. In addition to worrying about his economic welfare, a man might also worry about his social standing relative to other social groups. These worries involve "the not uncommon resentments of individuals or groups who desire to maintain or improve their social status."[49] In a time of rapid social mobility and change—a period during which traditional statuses are being challenged—an individual may feel threatened by those in lower statuses who are moving up. These fears would be particularly acute among people with insecure class position such as lower middle- and working-class families. Demands by blacks for better housing, schools, and employment opportunities may be perceived as threats to someone who believes he has barely been able to achieve these goals himself and who fears their loss if the blacks get their way.

Lipset contends that concern with status produces frustrations which are not relieved through "normal" political discourse and activity. The reason is that there is no clear political solution to the problem. Hence, according to Lipset, movements directed against scapegoats arise. The scapegoats are blamed for both real and imaginary crimes and so provide a convenient and satisfying outlet for pent-up status frustrations.[50] Extremist movements, in other words, provide the individual with both a cause of his worries (scapegoats) and a solution (repression of the scapegoat). Status anxiety, then, is a major reason why people join or support right-wing causes.

Status politics is really pseudo politics. Instead of looking for the solutions to concrete problems, the extremist plays on fears and resentments, creating the illusion that by attacking a scapegoat these worries will miraculously disappear. The John Birch Society, for example, sees the civil rights movement as a massive Communist conspiracy. Its literature implies that if only this conspiracy is

---

[49] Ibid., p. 309.
[50] Ibid., pp. 309–10.

crushed, every American will be more secure and free. There is little discussion in the society's literature of how ending the civil rights movement will, say, lower taxes or reduce crime.

None of this analysis should suggest status anxieties are frivolous concerns. Indeed, given the present social and political climate in Western democracies, worries about status are not entirely unreasonable. On one hand, we live in a materialistic society. Stores are loaded with good things to buy. More important, the mass media as well as other institutions seem to define success and happiness as owning a three-bedroom house in the suburbs, having two cars, color television, and going on long vacations to Hawaii or Puerto Rico. There is, in short, a prevailing consumption ethic which encourages people to own things as a measure of their success. On the other hand, the means to attain these goods and services are not available to everyone. For some individuals the "good life" is only a hope, for they cannot afford the houses, the appliances, and the vacations. Others are only marginally successful by these criteria and face the prospect of losing what they have worked hard to achieve. People who have struggled to escape congested cities do not want to return. Nor do they want the problems of the cities brought to them in the suburbs. Although many blue-collar workers hold well-paying jobs they must worry about layoffs or prolonged strikes. They also have to contend with taxes, illness, and inflation. Many individuals are in a precarious situation: they are not poor, but neither can they feel completely secure economically, especially in view of the widespread materialistic spirit in society. Seen in this light, status anxieties are easier to understand.

Lipset's contentions regarding status politics have received empirical support. Ira Rohter, for example, concludes that rightists are "disproportionately discontented with their degree of social acceptance, position, and influence," and consequently they join or support right-wing movements in hopes of enhancing "their threatened sense of importance, status, and self-respect."[51]

Another example of this phenomenon can be found in the writ-

---

[51] Rohter, "Social and Psychological Determinants of Radical Rightism," p. 223. Also see Trow, "Small Businessmen," p. 227; Lipset, "Three Decades of the Radical Right," pp. 391–446; and Walter C. Kaufman, "Status, Authoritarianism, and Anti-Semitism," *American Journal of Sociology*, Vol. 62 (1957), p. 382.

ings of rightist organizations. Consider the following passage, quoted in its entirety, from *The Fiery Cross,* the official magazine of the Ku Klux Klan:

> Recently selected by President Nixon is Negro Ronald B. Lee, to be Assistant Postmaster General in charge of the newly created Bureau of Planning, Marketing and Systems Analysis in the Post Office Dept. He will receive a yearly salary of $33,000.[52]

Quoted from a section of the magazine called "Fiery Flashes," this passage by itself probably has little interest for the average reader. It might be of great interest, however, to someone who is fearful and resentful of blacks acquiring occupations and status that have eluded him. The news story would confirm his suspicions that minorities are making progress at everyone else's expense. That they are making this progress as the result of what appears to be special efforts by government must be particularly disturbing. If one of a man's few comforts in life is thinking he is better than somebody else, imagine how galling it must be to have even that illusion shattered.

It is this kind of frustration and anger, according to Lipset, that causes people to join and support radical movements. Although this theory has critics, at this point it is a plausible explanation deserving further research.

Status Inconsistency.   Closely connected to status politics is the concept of status inconsistency. The United States and other industrial democracies have relatively open social systems. The son of a rich man no doubt has a better chance to succeed in life (at least as measured by income or education) than does the son of a poor man. Nevertheless, people can and do move up the social ladder. More specifically, it is possible for a person to advance on a limited number of status dimensions while remaining stationary on others. Although a man cannot abandon his ethnicity he can obtain a better education, income, and job than his father. Or it is possible for someone with little or no formal schooling to become quite wealthy.

Thus, members of an open society can have inconsistent or discrepant statuses. Status discrepancy or inconsistency means being high on one status and low on another. The person with little formal education (status one) and a high income (status two) has

---

[52] *The Fiery Cross,* June 1969, p. 27.

inconsistent or discrepant statuses. "The Beverly Hillbillies" of television comedy fame are a good example: through pure luck these illiterate mountain people became millionaires overnight. Conversely, two statuses are consistent if a person has the same position on each.

According to the theory of status inconsistency, people with discrepant statuses feel a certain amount of tension and pressure.[53] They occasionally have embarrassing, unpleasant, sometimes humiliating social experiences. The reason is that they are treated by others on the basis of the lower status when they wish to be treated on the basis of the higher. This differential treatment leads to disappointment and frustration as in the case of the parvenu who is denied entry into a prestigious country club because he does not come from an established family.

People apparently respond to status inconsistency in various ways. Some blame themselves or other individuals for their problems. Yet it has also been hypothesized that status discrepancy leads people to blame society and to advocate radical social changes. So they tend to support leftist or rightist political movements. These movements offer, as it were, a vicarious pleasure in getting back at the source of one's discontent.[54]

As with so many explanations of political phenomena, the evidence in support of this hypothesis is mixed. Fred Grupp finds more people with inconsistent status among the John Birch Society members he studied than among the populace as a whole.[55] Citing an unpublished study by Robert Sokol, Lipset also argues that concern with status inconsistency was related to support for McCarthy.[56]

Table 7.3 also indicates a relationship between inconsistency and right-wing preferences. Various types of inconsistencies are presented along the top of the table.[57] The first column, for instance, includes only those individuals with an eighth-grade edu-

---

[53] Gerhard E. Lenski, "Status Crystallization: A Non-Vertical Dimension of Social Status," *American Sociological Review*, Vol. 19 (1954), pp. 405–13.

[54] Ibid., pp. 412–23.

[55] Grupp, "Political Perspectives of Birch Society Members," p. 97.

[56] Lipset, "Three Decades of the Radical Right," p. 403. For additional evidence, see Gary B. Rush, "Status Consistency and Right-Wing Extremism," *American Sociological Review*, Vol. 32 (1967), p. 91.

[57] This classification of status inconsistency was suggested, in part, by McEvoy, *Radicals or Conservatives?*, pp. 37–40.

cation or less but who earn more than $10,000 a year. Their average support scores for the John Birch Society and Wallace are 34.2 and 59.0, respectively, considerably above the averages for the total samples. In general, status discrepancy is related to support for the John Birch Society and especially to support for Wallace. Although the number of cases is not large, people in status inconsistent positions are more favorable to rightist groups and candidates than the populace as a whole. (Note, however, that even within these categories support for the extremists is not very high.)

Table 7.3
STATUS INCONSISTENCY AND ATTITUDES TOWARD EXTREMISTS

		Average Scale Scores for:		
Status 1: Status 2:	$\leq$ *8th Grade* $>$ *$10,000*	$<$ *High School Managers or Professionals*	$>$ *$15,000 Semiskilled or Less*	*Average Scores for Total Sample*
John Birch Society ...	34.2 (12)	25.6 (131)	29.4 (27)	23.4 (1,157)
Wallace	59.0 (23)	37.5 (183)	47.7 (30)	31.3 (1,405)

Key: $\leqq$— has or earns less than or equal to
   $<$— has or earns less than
   $>$— has or earns greater than
   $\geqq$— has or earns greater than or equal to
Note: Figures in parentheses refer to the number of cases.
Source: *CPS 1970 American National Election Study.* (See Appendix.)

In spite of these findings, a number of authors conclude status inconsistency is only weakly associated with right-wing extremism. Based on a review of several studies plus his own data, James McEvoy decided the hypothesis has little explanatory value and other variables are better predictors of rightist behavior.[58]

Social Mobility.   Another closely related concept is social mobility. There is some evidence that extremists may be more socially mobile, particularly in a downward direction, than is the public as a whole. It is well known that prejudice is related to downward mobility,[59] and Rohter finds rightists more mobile than nonright-

---

[58] McEvoy, *Radicals or Conservatives?*, pp. 37–40.

[59] Bruno Bettelheim and Morris Janowitz, *Social Change and Prejudice* (New York: The Free Press, 1964), chap. ii.

ists.[60] But again there is counterevidence. James Barber, for example, finds that mobility has little impact on voting preferences. More specifically, downwardly mobile individuals are not much more conservative than people who are stationary.[61]

Mass Society and Extremism. Finally, the concept of mass society supplies another explanation of extremism.[62] According to the theory of mass society, a nation's economic and political development can drastically alter or even cause the breakdown of traditional social institutions and values. Among the hardest hit are the family, the church, and the local community. In traditional societies, these institutions give individuals a sense of belonging and worth. People feel they know their place in society. Moreover, they can cope with what goes on in the world not only because they feel secure but also because existing social institutions help to make events intelligible.

Various trends contribute to the decline of traditional social institutions and values: urbanization, industrialization, the division of labor, political development including universal suffrage, rapid social change and even domestic crises produced by depression, inflation, or war. With the decline of traditional society some individuals have difficulty adjusting. They become isolated and estranged; they cannot find satisfactory and meaningful social relationships. Not having ties to any social institutions, they drift in what is to them a chaotic world, a world they feel incapable of understanding and are powerless to affect.

Not everyone will feel this way, of course, but the theory states that as economic and political modernization continue, increasingly large numbers of people are adversely affected. Society then becomes impersonal and autonomous, and many individuals feel little or no attachment to one another or to traditional values and customs.

---

[60] Rohter, "Social and Psychological Determinants of Radical Rightism," p. 221.

[61] James Alden Barber, Jr., *Social Mobility and Voting Behavior* (Chicago: Rand McNally & Co., 1970), chaps. vi–vii.

[62] The theory of mass society is developed in the writings of Erich Fromm (*Escape From Freedom* [paperback ed.; New York: Avon Books, 1965]) and Hannah Arendt (*The Origins of Totalitarianism* [New York: Harcourt, Brace & Co., 1951]), but perhaps the best description of the theory and its implications is William Kornhauser, *The Politics of Mass Society* (Glencoe, Ill.: The Free Press, 1959).

In this situation, the mass society theorists assert, people turn to mass movements for gratification. The mass movement in a sense assumes the role of traditional society. Its followers have something to belong to, to identify with and to support. They derive a sense of worth from it. The movement is a matrix holding people together. It gives them common goals and also helps them understand the world by explaining events in terms of the movement's ideology and programs. Thus, the theory of mass society explains the acceptance of extremism as the consequence of a breakdown in traditional social relationships and their replacement with relationships based on a mass movement.

Although this theory and variations of it are widespread in the social sciences, the theory is somewhat difficult to operationalize and test. The most common practice is to study the behavior of individuals with relatively few social ties—people who do not belong to any clubs or organizations, who live in isolated areas, who work on their own, who do not take part in community affairs—in short, people who seem cut off from society. Probably the most extensive study along these lines is William Kornhauser's *The Politics of Mass Society*. Kornhauser shows that Fascist and Communist parties in Europe derived more support from alienated and isolated groups than from people who were more integrated into society. For example, he contends that isolated intellectuals (e.g., free-lance writers) were more likely to join the Nazi elite in Germany than were intellectuals with institutional affiliations, such as university teachers.[63]

Kornhauser also cites small businessmen who, he feels, are not well assimilated into the industrial order of capitalist countries. In particular, he refers to them as "marginal" because they lack any "realistic possibilities for improving [their] long-run economic position in a world increasingly dominated by large-scale organization."[64] The small businessman is especially apt to feel powerless and estranged and thus finds partial fulfillment in mass movements. Some evidence supports these contentions. Right-wing groups, both in America and elsewhere, do attract a disproportionate number of proprietors and managers of small businesses.[65]

---

[63] Kornhauser, *The Politics of Mass Society*, p. 193.

[64] Ibid., p. 202.

[65] Ibid., chap. xi; Trow, "Small Businessmen," pp. 274ff.

In sum, there is considerable theorizing and research on the impact of psychological and social variables on political extremism. These propositions have been explored and tested in a wide variety of areas. But like many explanations of social phenomena, they have critics, especially among political scientists. Social psychological explanations, the critics say, are deficient on two grounds. First, these approaches do not entirely explain extremist behavior. As Wolfinger and his associates remind us, rightists are not necessarily "social or psychological cripples."[66] Nor can their behavior be entirely attributed to social aberrations such as status anxiety or inconsistency. Based on an extensive review of research on Mc-Carthyism, Nelson Polsby argues that social-psychological variables have little explanatory power.[67]

A second shortcoming of social-psychological theorizing is that simpler, more direct explanations are available. More specifically, one can account for right-wing attitudes and behavior in terms of *political variables*.

Political Explanations

Instead of relying on elaborate social or psychological theories, some political scientists believe we should take rightist political movements at face value. That is, we should attempt to understand their political causes as well as their political programs. If people join or support right-wing causes, we should not immediately assume that they or society are maladjusted. Perhaps these people find the radical right satisfying simply because they believe in its values and ideology.

Actually, several studies have demonstrated the utility of looking at extremism as a political phenomenon. Polsby's work, mentioned above, discounts authoritarianism and status anxiety as plausible explanations of McCarthyism. Instead, he finds that the variables most closely associated with support for McCarthy are political

---

[66] Wolfinger et al., "America's Radical Right," p. 285.

[67] Polsby, "Explanation of McCarthyism," pp. 811–14; also see McEvoy, *Radicals or Conservatives?*, chap. ii; Elms, "Psychological Factors," pp. 151–54; and Rogin, *Intellectuals and McCarthy*, pp. 240–42. In addition, see Alejandro Portes ("Political Primitivism, Differential Socialization, and Lower-Class Leftist Radicalism," *American Sociological Review*, Vol. 36 [1971], pp. 820–35) who discounts the mass society theory as an explanation of left-wing extremism.

preferences on issues and parties: McCarthy supporters tended to be politically conservative and Republican.[68]

Other research has produced similar conclusions. Michael Rogin, who also doubts psychological and status explanations, sees the rise of the McCarthy movement as the result of specific political circumstances, rather than social factors. And, although a disproportionate number of lower class individuals endorsed McCarthy, the main characteristic of his backers was Republicanism. Republicans supported McCarthy to a far greater extent than did Democrats.[69] Likewise, members of the John Birch Society and other groups are mostly staunch Republicans and political conservatives. Robert Schoenberger's study of upstate New York conservatives, for example, shows that they do not fit the stereotype of right-wing extremism—they seem as socially and psychologically well adjusted as anyone. What distinguishes them is their extremely conservative attitudes toward unions, welfare, and big government.[70]

Table 7.4 gives further evidence for these generalizations. It indicates a relationship between political preferences on parties, candidates, and issues and support for the John Birch Society and George Wallace. As mentioned before, the public is not especially fond of either Wallace or the John Birch Society but certain groups have more positive feelings than others. In particular, Republicans and Wallace voters feel more favorable toward the Birch Society than do Democrats and Humphrey voters. Political conservatives, as defined by the questions on Vietnam policy and the role of the federal government, favor the rightists more than do the liberals. These relationships are not strong but they are at least consistent with previous research.

In short, people may join or endorse extremist movements simply for political reasons. They find the ideology of the right consistent with their own views and can support it. This is a parsimonious explanation, one which avoids complicated social and psychological interpretations of human behavior. Yet it leaves unanswered the question of *why* certain people come to hold extremist attitudes in

---

[68] Polsby, "Explanation of McCarthyism," p. 819.

[69] Rogin, *Intellectuals and McCarthy,* passim.

[70] Schoenberger, "Conservatism, Personality and Political Extremism," pp. 868–77.

Table 7.4
POLITICAL EXPLANATIONS OF EXTREMISM

(a)

	Political Party Preference						
	Strong Democrat	*Democrat*	*Leaning Democrat*	*Indepen- dent*	*Leaning Republican*	*Republi- can*	*Strong Republican*
John Birch Society.	21.4	21.6	23.9	23.6	25.4	23.3	29.2
	(225)	(260)	(131)	(137)	(95)	(179)	(120)
Wallace .	27.5	31.9	31.9	35.0	38.2	29.9	28.6
	(283)	(337)	(147)	(173)	(109)	(212)	(132)

(b)

	Vote 1968		
	Humphrey	*Nixon*	*Wallace*
John Birch Society	17.3	25.0	32.6
	(349)	(436)	(79)
Wallace	19.6	28.1	79.0
	(419)	(491)	(105)

(c)

	Vietnam Policy		
	Pull Out Immediately	*Continue Fighting*	*Escalate War*
John Birch Society	20.6	24.2	25.0
	(369)	(381)	(292)
Wallace	26.2	28.0	41.3
	(455)	(452)	(350)

(d)

	Is Federal Government Getting Too Powerful?	
	Yes, Too Powerful	*No, Not Too Powerful*
John Birch Society	24.2	21.6
	(398)	(386)
Wallace	34.4	28.2
	(450)	(480)

Note: Figures in parentheses refer to the number of cases.
Source: *CPS 1970 American National Election Study.* (See **Appendix.**)

the first place. It is one thing to say John Birch Society members are chiefly distinguished by their conservativism. It is another thing to explain why they are conservative. The political approach maintains that social and psychological variables are unnecessary or do not work in explaining the conservatism but it does not suggest a plausible alternative.

Furthermore, political scientists have mainly studied the most "respectable" end of the right-wing spectrum—the John Birch Society, the Christian Anti-Communism Crusade, the Wallace movement, and the like. Little systematic research has been on other types of rightist groups such as racist organizations (e.g., Ku Klux Klan, White Citizens Councils), the hatemongers (e.g., Nazis), or the Vigilantes (e.g., Minutemen). For these groups, authoritarianism, status anxiety, status inconsistency, and mass society may be more plausible explanations.

CONCLUSION

The radical right, like any social or political movement, is neither easy to describe nor explain. From the various theories and countertheories presented in this chapter, it should be apparent that social science still has a considerable way to go in understanding radicalism. No single approach presently seems adequate to the problem.

Ironically, relatively little research is carried out in this area. This absence no doubt reflects the belief that there are more important problems to study. Yet as we know, radicalism has considerable influence on politics, both in America and abroad. In order to preserve democratic institutions and practices we should undertake greater efforts to understand the concerns, needs, and motives of political extremists.

8

Unconventional Politics: Political Violence

Marquette Frye and his brother, Ronald, were feeling good as they drove home in their mother's 1955 Buick.[1] They had spent the afternoon at a friend's house drinking screwdrivers, and Marquette, a 21-year-old black, had consumed enough vodka to make him temporarily forget his problems. Marquette's problems were similar to those of many blacks living in the Watts section of Los Angeles: he was unemployed and did not have a salable skill, he had a police record, and his girl friend, Gloria, was pregnant.

When they were only two blocks from home a California Motorcycle Patrolman, Lee Minikus, halted the Buick. He had just received a tip by another motorist that the driver of the Buick "might be drunk or something." Marquette failed the Patrol's

---

[1] This account of the Watts riot is based mainly on Robert Conot, *Rivers of Blood, Years of Darkness*, copyright © 1967 by Bantam Books, Inc. (New York: William Morrow & Co., Inc. and Bantam Books, Inc.). For a more academic discussion of the Los Angeles riot, see Nathan Cohen, *The Los Angeles Riots: A Socio-Psychological Study* (New York: Praeger Publishers, 1970); and David O. Sears and John B. McConahay, *The Politics of Violence* (Boston: Houghton Mifflin Company, 1973).

standard sobriety test so Minikus radioed for a car to take Marquette to jail and a tow truck to haul his car away. Up to this point, Marquette had been in a jovial mood, bantering with the arresting officer, although he was apprehensive about going to jail.

Since it was a warm August evening, many people were on the street and soon a small crowd formed. Someone, recognizing the Fryes, went to get their mother.

Minikus, who was writing the ticket, was joined by another motorcycle patrolman and the tow truck operator. Although the crowd grew in size it was basically friendly, mostly kidding Marquette about his predicament. Then just as the tow truck was about to hook onto the Frye's car, Marquette's mother arrived. After first berating her son for drinking, she asked if she could drive the car home. The officers agreed.

Meanwhile, Marquette drifted into the crowd. His mood had plunged to despair. He could not face the thought of going to jail. As the two policemen who were assisted by still another officer tried to get him into a patrol car, Marquette began sobbing and shouting. With his arms waving wildly and his feet dragging he was not easy to manage. The three patrolmen succeeded in wrestling Marquette into the car, but then had to face an angry Mrs. Frye who felt they had been unnecessarily rough on her son. A scuffle developed in which she accidentally tore a patrolman's shirt. She, too, was arrested along with her other son, Ronald, who for no apparent reason had been clubbed by a newly arrived motorcycle patrolman.

During the fracas the crowd suddenly became more menacing. Attracted by police sirens and the commotion of the fight with the Fryes, people began jamming the sidewalks and street. Those who had just arrived were told that the police had beaten Marquette and his mother.

After Marquette, Ronald, and Mrs. Frye had been driven away the remaining officers prepared to withdraw. Before they could leave, however, one of them was allegedly spit on by a girl wearing pink hair curlers. Rushing into the crowd, two policemen dragged Joyce Ann Gaines back to their car where she was handcuffed and placed under arrest. Miss Gaines, a lady barber working in her father's shop, looked pregnant because she was wearing a white smock. A rumor quickly spread that the police had brutalized a pregnant woman.

As the police withdrew they were showered with rocks and bottles.

The crowd did not disperse but grew in size and anger. The police soon began receiving reports of vandalism and rock throwing. Motorists, both black and white, were pulled from their cars and beaten. Several fires were started. The crowd quieted down later in the evening but by the next day the situation was out of hand.

The Los Angeles riot of 1965 had begun.

Before the riot was over it had taken a terrible toll. Thirty-four people died; more than 1,000 were injured. Almost 1,000 buildings were damaged or destroyed by arson and looting. Property losses exceeded $40 million. During the six-day riot, the police and National Guard arrested over 3,000 people.

In addition to the destruction of lives and property, the riot had serious political implications. The Los Angeles riot disrupted the political life of the country. It precipitated a debate about national priorities and the adequacy of domestic policies. Along with disturbances in other cities, it undoubtedly brought changes in many federal programs. Urban violence caused a searching examination of race relations, of the condition of America's cities, and of the national government's ability to meet these problems.

On the negative side, riots like the one in Los Angeles contributed to a domestic "backlash," to a retrenchment against civil liberties, to a call for law and order. In short, the riots seemed to polarize Americans on social issues. For a while the stability and tranquillity of political life seemed threatened.

Violence is, of course, a fact of life. It always has been and some say it always will be. Although a few nations avoid violence for long periods of time, it crops up nearly everywhere in one form or another. True, the democratic creed encourages us to believe that disputes should be settled peacefully. Yet the events of the 1960s demonstrate that violence is possible even in "stable" democracies such as the United States. In the past few years we have witnessed riots, assassinations, bombings, and hijackings.

In many areas of the world, violence is even more common and serious. Politics are frequently disturbed by terrorism and assassination. Guerrilla war is an important means of political change in some countries while in others political grievances are expressed by demonstrations and riots. Indeed, there are times when violence seems more commonplace than peace.

In this chapter we will explain the occurrence of political violence. We want to know more than just the immediate causes but the underlying conditions as well. We will look also for causes common to different types of violence. Does a riot have anything in common with a guerrilla war? Is an assassination motivated by the same forces as a fire bombing? Is there, in brief, a set of causes applicable to many kinds of violence in many contexts?

Answering these questions requires us to use knowledge from sociology, psychology, anthropology, history, and political science. This eclecticism is necessary since no one field adequately explains all the facts. Furthermore, political violence is a general phenomenon. But although we will mention different types, most of our time will be spent discussing riots. Also, we will deal only with collective violence and ignore individual acts such as assassinations. The social sciences have accumulated much information about riots, so it seems advantageous to limit our analysis to them.

Before continuing, one should be aware of two biases in the study of violence. First, social scientists almost always study violence of the masses, looking for its causes and cures. Yet legitimate authorities (like the police or military) sometimes use violence, even when other alternatives are available. Except for research on war, however, we seldom study "elite" violence, and our knowledge of its causes is meager. This chapter is no different in this respect, but we should at least keep in mind that violence is not confined solely to the discontented masses.

A related bias is the view that violence represents an individual or collective pathology. Starting from the assumption that violence has no place in a democratic society, many social critics study violence in the same way someone analyzes a disease: its causes have to be found and eliminated. This view is occasionally challenged, however. In many instances, one could argue, violence is a useful, even necessary tool to bring about social change. Some scholars, perhaps in a minority, think violence—even spontaneous uprisings like riots—can be a reasonable, rational response to intolerable political, economic, or social conditions. Violence, they assert, should be studied as a form of political participation; instead of seeing it as an aberration whose causes must be expunged, it should be studied from the perspective of the participants by studying their motives and goals. We will return to this point at the conclusion of this chapter and in the last chapter.

SPARKS THAT LEAD TO VIOLENCE

There is almost always an immediate "cause" behind group violence such as riots and lynchings. The arrest of the Fryes touched off the Los Angeles riot. The Detroit riot of 1967 started after the police raided a private drinking club (a so-called blind pig). The Washington and Chicago riots of the following year were precipitated by the assassination of Martin Luther King. The alleged raping of a white woman by a black has sparked many lynchings. And, as every school child knows, the American Civil War began with the firing on Fort Sumter.

The immediate "causes" of collective violence have common properties. First, they are highly visible. They bring people together into an emotional atmosphere, thereby creating interpersonal communications networks. These imperfect networks facilitate the spread of rumors. In the case of Watts, rumors of police brutality spread through the crowd. Second, there is an emotional and sometimes bloody confrontation between groups, most often between a crowd and authorities. Finally, the happenings provide a rationale for subsequent actions. The Watts rioters, for example, justified their attacks on police and white motorists as retaliation for the alleged brutality inflicted on the Fryes and Miss Gaines.

Although we can almost always uncover an immediate cause (or a "spark") for many acts of collective violence, these should not be mistaken for the primary causes. Violence usually arises from complex circumstances. The "spark" is simply the last straw, the event which activates underlying conditions. So in order to understand political violence, we need to probe further than the events immediately preceding the violent outburst.

Discovering the causes of violence, however, is not easy. There are almost as many theories as there are people investigating the problem. Some scholars believe violence results from frustration while others regard it as a product of social learning. Still others hold that violence, especially organized violence, is simply a form of political participation and should be analyzed as such. We will look at each of these arguments in turn, but before doing so, something needs to be said about "popular" explanations of violence.

POPULAR EXPLANATIONS OF VIOLENCE

Instinct Theory

One commonly hears that men are instinctively aggressive and that we can always expect to have violence in society in one form or another. At best, man can only mitigate its consequences. This view has been popularized and to some extent supported by data in the works of ethologists such as Robert Ardrey, Konrad Lorenz, and Anthony Storr, among others.[2] Generalizing mainly from studies of animals, these authors conclude that the sources of aggression lie primarily in man's nature, not his environment. They believe aggression is a natural drive, one which motivates behavior much as hunger and thirst do. In these respects men are essentially analogous to wild animals. These thinkers reject the notion that violence is always the consequence of social conditions. Aggressive behavior, they say, is inherited and cannot be expunged from human beings any more than it can be erased from tigers or cobras. So we might as well get used to the fact that humans have an innate tendency to be combative.

Perhaps the extremist expression of this position is Freud's belief in "death instincts."[3] Part of everyone's personality, death instincts are manifested in many forms of destructive behavior, according to Freud. Men have an urge to destroy as well as create and preserve. These impulses cannot be transcended, only contained and mitigated. In fact, the development of culture represents a continuous struggle between life and death instincts.

This view has been popularized in many ways. For example, some people claim that Americans' fascination with football exemplifies man's aggressive nature. The game attracts fans precisely

---

[2] Robert Ardrey, *The Territorial Imperative* (London: Collins, 1967); Konrad Lorenz, *On Aggression,* trans. Marjorie Wilson (New York: Harcourt, Brace & World, Inc., 1966); Anthony Storr, *Human Aggression* (New York: Bantam Books, Inc., 1970).

[3] Sigmund Freud, *Civilization and Its Discontents,* trans. and ed. by James Strachey (New York: W. W. Norton and Co., Inc., 1961), pp. 58 ff.

because it is a brutal sport. The rougher the contest, the more the spectators enjoy it. And, one of the commonest cheers heard at a football game is "Hit 'em again—harder, harder." There are other aspects of contemporary society which also seem to indicate an inherent aggressiveness in man: other contact sports such as boxing and ice hockey, the fascination with guns and the success of television and movie violence are examples.

Although some of these ideas have received empirical verification, particularly in studies of animal behavior, they have been challenged on numerous grounds. Some social scientists question the analogy with animals, arguing that many species (including those used to document instinct theory) are less aggressive than commonly supposed. Ethologists such as Ardrey claim that baboons which fight over territory and status are innately aggressive. But as David Pilbeam points out, the studies on which these conclusions are based have been done on baboons living in the semicaptivity of game preserves. Their confinement to game parks has an "unnatural" effect on their behavior. Baboons living in the wild, Pilbeam maintains, are actually quite placid and unwarlike.[4]

Furthermore, the argument that man is inherently aggressive seems too simplistic, given our knowledge of human behavior. The argument ignores the complexity of human drives and motives. In particular, it underestimates the extent to which these drives are susceptible to conditioning or training.[5] As we will see, learning can play an important role in the acquisition of aggressive behavior. Why, for example, is it not possible that Americans *learn* to like football, much as they learn to like other sports? And besides, many people find football abominable or boring. Variations in people's reactions to violence, in other words, imply that aggressiveness is not a universal trait, but one which is learned. Thus, although aggression may acquire the status of a drive, many feel it is too misleading and simplistic to blame violence solely on instinct.

---

[4] David Pilbeam, "The Fashionable View of Man as a Naked Ape Is . . .," *New York Times Magazine,* September 3, 1972, pp. 28–30. For an excellent discussion and critique of the instinct theory of aggression, see Leonard Berkowitz, *Aggression: A Social Psychological Analysis* (New York: McGraw-Hill Book Co., 1962), chap. 1.

[5] Elton McNeil, "Psychology and Aggression," *Journal of Conflict Resolution,* Vol. 3 (1959), pp. 209–18; and Berkowitz, *Aggression: A Social Psychological Analysis,* chap. 1.

Riffraff Theory

At the other end of the spectrum are those who take an opposite approach to violence. They see it as the product of small bands of troublemakers who lack widespread support. These groups use violence for their own devilish purposes. According to this interpretation, people who participate in, say, riots are criminals, malcontents, drifters, outside agitators—in short, the riffraff of society. This line of thinking is especially popular among certain politicians because it directs attention away from other causes of violence. One congressman said, for example, "A majority of the rioters are hoodlums, looking for trouble, seeking a living without working for it and demanding something for nothing from the government."[6]

Acceptance of the riffraff explanation absolves the officials from responsibility for the underlying conditions. It also suggests that the cure for violence is simply to get tough. After all, it is easier to talk about law and order than it is to change malfunctioning social and economic structures.

Like other popular explanations of violence, the riffraff theory contains a grain of truth, but it oversimplifies and distorts the causes of collective violence. Data on urban riots show, for example, that large numbers of blacks supported and participated in the disorders. The rate of participation was certainly higher than would be expected on the basis of the riffraff theory. David Sears and John McConahay report that about 15 percent of the inhabitants in the curfew zone of Los Angeles were active participants in the riot while another 31 percent were close spectators. This means that about 30,000 people took part directly while another 60,000 or 70,000 looked on.[7] Even if these people represented a minority of the inhabitants of the area, they can hardly be classified as a small group of troublemakers.

---

[6] Quoted from Jason Epstein, *The Great Conspiracy Trial* (New York: Vintage Books, 1971), p. 44.

[7] David O. Sears and John B. McConahay, "Participation in the Los Angeles Riot," *Social Problems*, Vol. 17 (1969), p. 9. Similarly, Robert M. Fogelson's review of riots in 11 metropolitan areas finds that participation varied from 2 to 14 percent of the people in the riot zones. (Robert M. Fogelson, *Violence as Protest: A Study of Riots and Ghettos* [Garden City, N.Y.: Anchor Books, 1971], pp. 37–38). Also see Benjamin D. Singer, Richard W. Osborn, and James A. Geschwender, *Black Rioters* (Lexington, Mass.: D. C. Heath & Co., 1970).

Nor do all the blacks living in urban areas condemn riots. Angus Campbell and Howard Schuman's survey of 15 cities found widespread support and justification for riots; many blacks thought they were a necessary protest against white discrimination.[8] Finally, rioters are not drawn from the worst elements of society but seem to be fairly representative of their communities. If many rioters have police records it is because many people living in ghettos have police records. If many come from broken homes it is because there are many broken homes in the inner city. All in all, the participants seemed typical of the people living in the areas in which the riots occurred, at least in terms of economic and social characteristics. The riots, in short, drew support from all of the socioeconomic segments within the riot areas. The participants were not, as many politicians would have it, totally atypical of the communities.[9]

Closely related to the riffraff theory is the stress on the mental sickness or pathology of the individuals engaging in violence. Acts of violence are often described as the work of madmen. In many cases, the perpetrators *do* seem insane. Many assassins appeared to have had serious mental disturbances.[10] Arthur Bremer, the man who shot Governor George Wallace in 1972, apparently had severe emotional problems. His diary, for instance, reads like the work of an egomaniac and a man in desperate search for immortality.[11] Lynching, riots, and guerrilla wars no doubt attract deranged individuals. Still, most instances of collective violence are too broadly based and complex to be explained solely by reference to psychopathology.

---

[8] Angus Campbell and Howard Schuman, *Racial Attitudes in Fifteen American Cities* (Ann Arbor, Mich.: Institute for Social Research, 1968), pp. 57–62.

[9] Anthony Oberschall, "The Los Angeles Riot of August 1965," *Social Problems*, Vol. 15 (1968), p. 329. Also see Sears and McConahay, "Participation in the Los Angeles Riot." But for evidence that rioters were more "deprived" than nonrioters, see Singer, Osborn, and Geschwender, *Black Rioters;* and James A. Geschwender and Benjamin D. Singer, "Deprivation and the Detroit Riot," *Social Problems*, Vol. 17 (Spring 1970), pp. 457–63.

[10] James F. Kirkham, Sheldon G. Levy, and William Crotty, *Assassination and Political Violence*, A Report to the National Commission on the Causes and Prevention of Violence, Vol. 8 (Washington, D.C.: U.S. Government Printing Office, 1969), pp. 62–70.

[11] Arthur H. Bremer, "An Assassin's Diary," *Harper's Magazine*, January 1973, pp. 52–66. It is interesting to note that Bremer did not seem to care much about whom he killed as long as his act brought him notoriety.

If man's instincts or society's riffraff or psychopaths do not account for violence, what does? One explanation is the frustration-aggression hypothesis.

FRUSTRATION AND AGGRESSION

The basic idea of the frustration-aggression hypothesis, which is probably the most widely known and accepted explanation of violence, is quite simple: frustration causes aggression.[12] Frustration results from interference with a goal-directed behavior. Suppose that a young man trying to make a decent living for his family is refused a job because he is black. In social science parlance, we say his goal-directed behavior (i.e., the earning of a livelihood) is interfered with or blocked by discrimination. The interference produces frustration which in turn produces aggression. Aggression, in this case, simply means doing harm to someone or something. Actually, aggression is a slippery concept to define,[13] but for our purposes we can equate aggression with violence.

From the time that the frustration-aggression approach was originally proposed, it has undergone numerous changes and refinements. For one, it is not so much the behavior itself but the anticipated satisfactions associated with the goal that produce frustration. If a person expects to be rewarded by a particular behavior, interference with that behavior will produce frustration. A man who is denied the employment he feels will give him the things other people have will be especially disappointed by its denial. Similarly, the closer a person is to his goal the greater will be his frustration if he is blocked from attaining it.

Some psychologists think that aggression acts as its own reward. "Releasing pentup anger," McNeil writes, "gratifies the need for aggression and acts to restore an emotional equilibrium."[14] This is,

---

[12] John Dollard, Leonard Doob, Neal Miller, O. H. Mowrer, and R. Sears, *Frustration and Aggression* (New Haven, Conn.: Yale University Press, 1939); Leonard Berkowitz, "The Frustration-Aggression Hypothesis Revisited," *Roots of Aggression,* ed. Leonard Berkowitz (New York: Atherton Press, 1969), pp. 1–28.

[13] Dollard et al., *Frustration and Aggression,* chap. 1; Arnold H. Buss, *The Psychology of Aggression* (New York: John Wiley & Sons, Inc., 1961), chap. 1; Albert Bandura and Richard H. Walters, *Social Learning and Personality Development* (New York: Holt, Rinehart & Winston, Inc., 1963), chap. iii.

[14] McNeil, "Psychology and Aggression," p. 207.

of course, the familiar idea that after we "blow off steam" we feel better. Hence, aggression may act as a *catharsis*. Laboratory experiments on the cathartic effect of aggression yield mixed results, however, and in fact the expression of aggression may lead to further aggressive outbursts, especially if the aggression is rewarding or goes unpunished.[15] It seems safest to say that whether or not aggression acts as a catharsis depends upon the circumstances.

In the original version of the theory, aggression was described as the natural and inevitable outcome of frustration.[16] Frustration always produced aggression and aggression always resulted from frustration. These assertions were immediately challenged and now aggression is believed to be only one of several possible responses to frustration. Its occurrence depends on a variety of conditions. For example, if an individual accepts the legitimacy of a frustrating agent he is less likely to respond aggressively. Furthermore, as we will see, aggression can occur in the absence of frustration.

Thus, the occurrence of frustration-induced aggression is determined by the situation. In order to explain collective violence we need to know what conditions produce public frustrations and what conditions facilitate their expression in violence.

Conditions Which Produce Collective Frustration

Deprivation. It is widely thought that violence is bred by poverty. If living conditions are unbearable, if a man has no way to feed or clothe himself and his family, he becomes desperate. In such a situation he may turn to violence, supporting or participating in riots or revolutions. This reaction is all the more probable if he feels his deprivation is not his fault but society's. In the language of the frustration-aggression hypothesis, deprivation causes widespread frustration, which in turn produces a readiness to resort to violence.

Political turmoil appears more frequently in underdeveloped than in developed countries where living conditions are less des-

---

[15] Shabaz Khan Mallick and Boyd R. McCandess, "A Study of Catharsis of Aggression," *Journal of Personality and Social Psychology*, Vol. 4 (1966), pp. 591–96. Also Leonard Doob and Lorraine Wood, "Catharsis and Aggression: Effects of Annoyance and Retaliation on Aggressive Behavior," *Journal of Personality and Social Psychology*, Vol. 22 (May 1972), pp. 156–62.

[16] Dollard et al., *Frustration and Aggression,* chap. i.

perate. True, industrialized Western democracies are not completely stable—the recent history of the United States belies that
argument. But incidents of violence are apt to occur more often,
for longer periods, and with greater intensity in less developed
nations.[17]

Even within the United States violence is somewhat related to
economic deprivation. Lynchings took place mainly in rural areas,
especially in the South, where the standard of living was low.[18]
Similarly, studies dealing with the ecology of riots show that the
disorders tend to occur in cities having high concentrations of
blacks. These places are usually characterized by crowding, substandard housing, poor health and sanitation, unemployment—in
short, the very conditions which aggravate and frustrate people
trying to live a decent life.[19] Urban rioters in the 1960s tended to
have lower occupational statuses and incomes than nonparticipants.
They were also more likely to have experienced greater unemployment in the year before the riot.[20] Although rioters were in many
ways representative of their communities they seemed somewhat
more deprived than the bystanders.

Although deprivation per se is related to violence, most social
scientists believe the relationship is more complicated than has
been indicated. We saw in an earlier chapter that extreme deprivation leads to apathy, not violent activity. In addition, contrary to
some of the above-mentioned studies, other research finds that
violence is only weakly related to socioeconomic status. Sears and

---

[17] Ted Robert Gurr, *Why Men Rebel* (Princeton, N.J.: Princeton University
Press, 1970), chap. 3.

[18] Hadley Cantril, *The Psychology of Social Movements* (New York: John
Wiley & Sons, Inc., 1963).

[19] Seymour Spilerman, "The Causes of Racial Disturbances: A Comparison
of Alternative Explanations," *American Sociological Review*, Vol. 35 (1970),
pp. 627–49; Seymour Spilerman, "The Causes of Racial Disturbances: Tests
of an Explanation," *American Sociological Review*, Vol. 36 (1971), pp. 427–42;
Bryan T. Downes, "Social and Political Characteristics of Riot Cities: A Comparative Study," *Social Science Quarterly*, Vol. 49 (1963), pp. 504–20; Milton
Bloombaum, "The Conditions Underlying Race Riots as Portrayed by Multidimensional Scalogram Analysis: A Reanalysis of Lieberson and Silverman's
Data," *American Sociological Review*, Vol. 33 (1968), pp. 76–91.

[20] Geschwender and Singer, "Deprivation and the Detroit Riot," p. 465.
Also see Conot, *Rivers of Blood, Years of Darkness*, and Singer, Osborn, and
Geschwender, *Black Rioters*.

McConahay's data show that "Every stratum of the ghetto contributed its share of rioters."[21] Therefore, the concept of deprivation has been replaced by a more complicated but also more useful term, "relative deprivation."

Relative Deprivation. People have needs and desires which they feel must be satisfied in order to be happy. As long as these requirements are met, they are content. When, however, there is a gap between what they want or feel they deserve and what they get, they feel deprived. We call this feeling *relative deprivation*. Relative deprivation involves comparative, not absolute, standards.

One standard of comparison is what others are getting. If I want the same life-style or standard of living as the people I see on television and yet I do not even begin to approach that level, I may feel deprived. Of course, there will always be a gap between what one wants and what one gets. But if the "want-get" gap grows too large, it produces tension or frustration. Hence, relative, not absolute, deprivation is believed to be the major source of societal frustration.

To see how relative deprivation explains collective violence, look at Figure 8.1.[22] In a society as a whole, the level of demands and needs and their satisfaction may gradually rise over time. As long as both needs and satisfactions rise at roughly the same rate, the populace remains content and there is little collective frustration. At some point, though, there may occur a sudden change in either the total level of needs or in the society's ability to satisfy the existing needs. Consider each possibility.

Suppose nearly everyone in a country suddenly wants considerably more material goods than he presently possesses. Then there would be a sharp increase in needs. If the level of need satisfaction stayed constant—that is, if production could not keep pace with the demands—an "intolerable gap" would soon develop.[23] (See Figure 8.1a.) The gap represents collective frustration: there are many individuals who want goods but cannot receive them because of inadequate supply. As a result, the citizens become frustrated.

---

21 Sears and McConahay, *The Politics of Violence,* p. 25.

22 This analysis is based primarily on James C. Davies, "Toward a Theory of Revolution," *American Sociological Review,* Vol. 27 (1962), pp. 5–19; and Gurr, *Why Men Rebel,* pp. 46–56.

23 Davies, "Toward a Theory of Revolution," p. 6.

Figure 8.1
RELATIVE DEPRIVATION AND FRUSTRATION

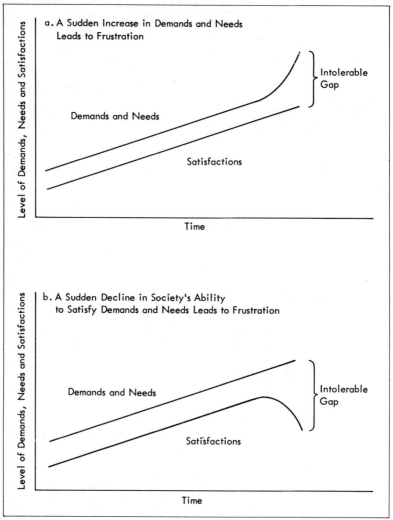

Sources: Figure based on James Davies, "Toward a Theory of Revolution," *American Sociological Review*, Vol. 27 (1962), pp. 5–19; and Ted Robert Gurr, *Why Men Rebel* (Princeton, N.J.: Princeton University Press, 1970), pp. 46–56.

Given the right conditions (to be discussed in a moment) their anger may turn to violence.

Some observers wonder if this is not what happened in the United States during the late 1960s. The civil rights movement, the proclamation of the Great Society, and the general affluence depicted on television may have raised the expectations of many black Americans. They may have expected to start receiving the benefits of the fantastically wealthy economy. Tragically, the political and economic system was unable or unwilling to cope with these rising expectations, causing hope to plunge into despair and bitterness. The resulting frustration, exacerbated by unemployment, discrimination, and the misery of ghetto life, needed only a spark like the arrest of the Fryes to produce violent outbursts.

As in the United States, rising expectations may account for political unrest and violence in other parts of the world, particularly in those countries which are rapidly modernizing. The introduction of education and mass communications in these societies leads to sharp increases in demands which the governments and economies cannot meet. The revolution in communications makes citizens aware of what people in other nations are getting; they want and demand some of these things for themselves. Yet unless these demands can be met, at some point disappointment is inevitable, creating widespread frustration. Whether this frustration causes violence depends largely on the effectiveness and responsiveness of the political system.

Another way collective frustration occurs is shown in Figure 8.1b. Although the level of demands and needs may rise at a constant rate, there may be a precipitous drop in society's ability to meet these needs. A drop of this type could result from a depression, a national catastrophe, or a war. In any event, a gap develops between what people want or feel they should have and what society is able to give them. The intolerable gap is likely to be severe if it follows a period of prosperity and economic expansion.

Crane Brinton believes many revolutions are caused by relative deprivation of this sort.[24] For example, the French economy in 1789 suffered a sharp reversal after several years of growth and prosper-

---

[24] Crane Brinton, *The Anatomy of Revolution*, rev. ed. (New York: Vintage Books, 1965), chaps. ii–iii.

ity. The frustration produced by the economic downturn, Brinton hypothesizes, underlay the storming of the Bastille. He explains other events like the Russian Revolution and the American Civil War in similar terms.[25]

Like many concepts in social science, relative deprivation has both supporters and critics. A simple and convincing idea, relative deprivation seems to explain a great deal of data. And yet it contains ambiguities and is difficult to measure empirically.

Although relative deprivation supposedly produces frustration in individuals, most studies attempting to measure and test the deprivation model have dealt with nations as a whole, not with individuals. These studies, in effect, make inferences about individuals from aggregate data. Even measuring relative deprivation at an aggregate level is difficult and, some critics claim, it has not been done very well.[26] (Of course, simply because a concept is hard to measure does not necessarily mean it, or theories based on it, are useless.)

Perhaps more devastating to the adherents of relative deprivation are the findings that deprivation does not always lead to violence and that violence frequently occurs in the absence of deprivation. David Snyder and Charles Tilly collected data on collective "disturbances" in France for the period 1830 to 1960.[27] (They defined a disturbance as any incident involving 50 or more persons in which people or property were seized or damaged.[28]) Their investigation found that the number of disturbances and the number of participants in them were unrelated to measures of economic hardship. Based on these data, they conclude the "link-

---

[25] Also see Lawrence Stone, "Theories of Revolution," *World Politics,* Vol. 17 (1966), pp. 159–76; Davies, "Toward a Theory of Revolution"; Gurr, *Why Men Rebel,* chaps. ii–v; and Ivo K. Feierabend and Rosalind Feierabend, "Aggressive Behaviors within Politics, 1948–1962: A Cross-National Study," *The Journal of Conflict Resolution,* Vol. 10 (1966), pp. 249–71.

[26] Peter A. Lupsha, "On Theories of Urban Violence," *Urban Affairs Quarterly* (1969), pp. 273–96; Peter A. Lupsha, "Explanations of Political Violence: Some Psychological Theories versus Indignation," *Politics and Society* (1971), pp. 89–104; and Edward N. Muller, "A Test of a Partial Theory of Potential for Political Violence," *American Political Science Review,* Vol. 66 (1972), pp. 928–59.

[27] David Snyder and Charles Tilly, "Hardship and Collective Violence in France," *American Sociological Review,* Vol. 37 (1972), pp. 520–32.

[28] Ibid., p. 522.

age between relative deprivation and collective violence . . . can be safely rejected."[29] Other scholars arrive at similar conclusions.[30]

In spite of these shortcomings, theories based on relative deprivation are still among the most persuasive explanations of collective violence. Nevertheless, there are still other sources of collective frustration.

Racial and Religious Discrimination. Discrimination can lead to frustration if it blocks goal-directed behavior. The effects of discrimination will be most severe when the victims do not accept the discrimination as rightful or legitimate. Until recently, a strict caste system dominated Indian social life, making it difficult for a person to advance upward from one caste to another. Yet the frustrations produced by this social system were probably mitigated to a large extent by general acceptance of the class lines.

The deleterious effects of discrimination are most apparent in nations having deep ethnic or religious cleavages. In many of these countries discriminatory treatment is not passively accepted. When a person is victimized by discrimination his frustrations may accumulate and possibly find expression in violence. Bitter hostility and competition between Protestants and Catholics underlie much of the violence in Northern Ireland.

Social Change. Rapid social change can disrupt family and community relations, especially in traditional societies. Change leads to a breakdown of old customs and norms. If new values and practices come too rapidly, they are difficult to absorb. Hence, social change and social mobility cause tension and frustrations. These frustrations are sometimes expressed in extremist movements or in social and political violence.[31]

This is another reason why violence frequently breaks out in modernizing countries. Industrialization, urbanization, economic modernization and growth, population explosion, political and social awakening—all of the correlates of development—put enormous strains on traditional institutions, norms, and customs. The frustrations produced by these pressures invariably affect individ-

---

[29] Ibid., p. 526.

[30] Muller, "A Test of the Partial Theory of Potential for Political Violence," pp. 953–54; Lupsha, "Explanations of Political Violence," p. 97ff.

[31] Karl W. Deutsch, "Social Mobilization and Political Development," *American Political Science Review,* Vol. 55 (1961), pp. 493–514.

uals who may—if the conditions are ripe and leadership is available —react by taking part in demonstrations, strikes, riots, or uprisings.

These, then, are the main social conditions producing collective frustration. Undoubtedly others can be identified but our purpose is merely to see what sort of factors underlie frustration. These conditions are present to some degree in every society. When they become acute, however, mass discontentment is apt to rise. As we have said, frustration does not always lead to violence; frustration can be controlled or released in nondestructive ways. Let us look, therefore, at some circumstances which encourage or discourage the expression of frustration in violence.

Conditions Which Encourage Frustration-Induced Violence

The Amount and Duration of Frustration.   Generally speaking, the more a person is frustrated, the more likely he is to respond aggressively.[32] Years of deprivation and second-class citizenship which affect nearly every aspect of a man's spirit will have a deeper impact than a few temporary setbacks. You occasionally hear someone say, "I had to make it the hard way, but I didn't riot. Why can't colored people do the same?" Part of the answer lies in the magnitude and duration of the frustrations faced by blacks. They have simply endured more deprivation and discrimination than whites.

The Legitimacy of the Frustrating Agent.   We are often prevented from doing what we would like without being overly upset. Jaywalking may be convenient, but most of us will quietly follow a policeman's command to cross at the corner. We do so because we accept his authority. When the frustrator acts arbitrarily or without authority, however, we find his interference less tolerable. Illegitimate or undeserved frustration is more likely to produce anger and aggression than frustration which is accepted as legitimate.[33]

The Attributes of the Situation.   The presence of the Los Angeles police increased the excitement and anger of the mobs early in the riot. In the minds of the residents of Watts, the police symbolized the oppressive, discriminatory aspects of American life. Their con-

---

[32] Dollard et al., *Frustration and Aggression,* chaps. 1–3; Buss, *The Psychology of Aggression,* chap. ii; McNeil, "Psychology and Aggression," pp. 203–4.

[33] Berkowitz, *Aggression: A Social Psychological Analysis,* chap. v.

duct, their attitudes, their paraphernalia—all were cues which further aroused the rioters.[34] Leonard Berkowitz believes that attributes of the frustrator or of the target of aggression (e.g., his appearance, his name, his deportment) can encourage the expression of aggression.[35] Police cars, for example, are more inviting targets for rock throwers than store windows with "SOUL BROTHER" painted on them. Cues or attributes of the situation may increase the probability that aggression will occur after frustration.

Alternatives, Rewards, and Punishment. Alternative courses of action will lower the risk that frustration will turn into violence. A government whether it is local, state, or national that listens and responds to the legitimate complaints of its citizens will have less violence to deal with than one which turns away from its constituents. If there is a lesson in the Kerner Commission Report which assessed the causes of urban disorders, it is that the American political system is insensitive to the needs of the black community.[36] Life in the ghetto leaves a man with little else but violence. Urban violence takes many forms: gang fights, wife or child beatings, muggings, assaults, vandalism, even riots. But in view of the massive frustrations of the ghetto and the absence of alternative modes for its reduction, one can understand the pervasiveness of violence in inner cities.

Similarly, if aggression is believed to be rewarding, its occurrence is all the more likely. We have already seen that people learn by reinforcement: reinforced behaviors occur more readily than non-reinforced behaviors. (See Chapter 3.) The same principle applies to aggression. A person expecting reward from his aggression will be more aggressive than a person who expects punishment, other things being equal.[37]

Punishment is also strongly related to the expression of aggression, though in peculiar ways. The threat of punishment deters

---

[34] Conot, *Rivers of Blood, Years of Darkness,* passim.

[35] Berkowitz, "The Frustration-Aggression Hypothesis Revisited," pp. 15–20. Also see Leonard Berkowitz and Russell G. Geen, "Film Violence and the Cue Properties of Available Targets," *Journal of Personality and Social Psychology,* Vol. 3 (1966), pp. 525–30.

[36] *Report of the National Advisory Commission on Civil Disorders* (New York: Bantam Books, 1968).

[37] Buss, *The Psychology of Aggression,* pp. 28, 53–58.

aggression. Liberals may not like to admit it but a strong, determined, even brutal military or police force may be the best short-
term solution to violence. The Los Angeles riot seemed to subside
shortly after the National Guard arrived in force. True (as we have
just seen), the police or National Guard may aggravate a situation,
but their presence in overwhelming numbers probably outweighs
this disadvantage, at least for a while. Cross-national study seems
to indicate that strong punitive forces limit the scope and magnitude of civil disorders. Snyder and Tilly's study, cited above, argues
essentially that countries with strong internal security forces
experience less collective violence than nations that are weak in
these respects.[38]

On the other hand, punishment itself may act as a source of
frustration which further raises anger and hostility. Numerous
laboratory experiments demonstrate that punishment can produce
aggressive responses, though these responses may be displaced or
directed against scapegoats or may be expressed in ineffective, non-
functional ways.[39] Faced with punishment from outside sources,
the members of a group may simply be aggressive toward one
another.

If, in short, people believe violence is both rewarding and beyond
punishment, they are more likely to behave violently than if they
see no value in it or do not fear retribution.

Norms and Violence.   Most of us live in a social environment
which unequivocally condemns violence. Since childhood we have
been constantly exhorted to settle our personal differences peacefully, to work through the system to solve our problems, to trust
reason and goodwill rather than bullets or bombs. If we resort to
aggression we are chided and punished.

Sometimes, however, the norms of a group or subculture encourage the use of violence. Where permissiveness exists frustration will
likely lead to aggression. Norms favoring violence are a reinforcement for the individual's behavior. They indicate to him that
instead of being punished for his actions he will be rewarded.

Studies of rioters support these ideas. In most of the cities
investigated, researchers find an interesting ambivalence in blacks'

---

[38] Snyder, and Tilly, "Hardship and Collective Violence in France," pp.
526–30; also see Gurr, *Why Men Rebel,* chap. viii.

[39] See Gurr, *Why Men Rebel,* pp. 241–42, for references.

attitudes toward the riots. Most blacks claimed they would not take part themselves and they deplored the bloodshed and destruction of property. But neither were they very critical of those who did riot. In fact, many ghetto dwellers justify violence as a necessary protest against an intolerable, degrading existence. Bystanders at the Watts riot, Sears and McConahay find, formed a "permissive audience" for those who took an active part.[40] Although these spectators condemned the bloodshed and destruction, they sympathized with rioters who they felt had been badly mistreated by society.

The crowd as a "permissive audience" is a significant concept to which we will return. For now, it is important to remember that riots do not take place in a vacuum. Like the Sears and McConahay study, research shows that black communities are tolerant if not supportive of riot behavior even though they may have the most to lose.[41]

Favorable community attitudes toward violence underlie many instances of its occurrence. Blacks are not alone in this respect. Listen to the reactions of some whites to the lynching of a black man in Leeville, Texas in 1930:

> *A farmer:* The officers was to blame. When they seen the mob at the trial, they should of started back to jail with the nigger. Then the mob could have lynched him.
>
> *A salesman:* Believe me, those damn niggers were sure good after that. They just bowed and scraped around. You got to do something occasionally to keep them in their place or they'll get too smart.
>
> *A member of the PTA:* Only one man was sentenced for burning that courthouse, and he shouldn't have been.
>
> *A waitress:* The Negro deserved to die and burning was too good for him.
>
> *A wife of a café owner:* We did a grand business that day. The officers should have started to the jail with the Negro. Then the mob could have got him without burning the courthouse.
>
> *A physician:* The deputy sheriff should have just shot the bastard without ever arresting him.

---

[40] Sears and McConahay, "Participation in the Los Angeles Riot," p. 10.

[41] Also see Campbell and Schuman, *Racial Attitudes in Fifteen American Cities*, pp. 47–52; J. R. Feagin, "Social Sources of Support for Violence and Nonviolence in a Negro Ghetto," *Social Problems*, Vol. 15 (1968), pp. 434–35.

A shoe repairman: The nigger got what he deserved. They will get a little smart if you don't keep them in their place.

A photographer: Before the troops stopped us from selling them, we made about $300 on our flashlight picture of the burned nigger.[42]

Whenever collective frustration is present, then, favorable social norms may aid the transition of the frustration into aggression. In this sense, the climate of opinion is an important determinant of violence.

Let us summarize. Violence is precipitated by an immediate cause, or "spark." But there are antecedent conditions. One is frustration. Several factors produce collective frustration, among them absolute and relative deprivation, racial and religious discrimination, and social changes. No doubt others could be found, but these seem to be the most important. Frustration does not always lead to violence. Whether it does or not depends on the nature of the situation, the climate of opinion, expectations about rewards and punishments, and so forth. These latter conditions are called intervening or mediating variables and they partially determine the scope and magnitude of violence.

These concepts are summarized in Figure 8.2, which shows some of the conditions producing frustration and facilitating its expression in violence.

Although the frustration-aggression model is probably the most popular and widely researched approach to the study of mass vio-

Figure 8.2
FRUSTRATION-AGGRESSION AND COLLECTIVE VIOLENCE

Social Conditions Producing Frustration	Conditions Facilitating the Translation of Frustration into Violence	"Spark" or Precipitating Incident
Deprivation Relative deprivation Discrimination Social change } Frustration	Amount and duration of frustration Legitimacy of frustrating agent Situational factors Alternatives Rewards Punishment Norms	Collective violence

---

[42] Cantril, *The Psychology of Social Movements,* pp. 108–9.

lence, it does not describe the total picture. For a fuller explanation we need to add social learning theory.

SOCIAL LEARNING AND VIOLENCE

Aggression sometimes occurs in the absence of frustration. This may happen if a person learns to aggress in order to satisfy his needs or if he imitates the behavior of others. In either case, frustration may play only a secondary role.

People can learn aggression just as they learn other types of behavior. Learning takes place when a response is rewarded or reinforced. In many cultures or subcultures a child develops aggressive responses to various situations because he has found that aggression is rewarded in one way or another. By acting tough he may win the attention of his parents or the respect of his friends. Being a good fighter allows him to get his way at school or in the neighborhood. A person soon comes to regard violence as instrumental. In this connection, Edward Muller finds that blacks in his sample who believe in the efficacy of violence are much higher on a scale of potentiality for violence than those who do not believe in its effectiveness.[43]

Imitation, another form of learning, is especially important in collective behavior. People learn by observing what others do. Besides learning *how* to respond, an individual may expect some form of direct or indirect reward for his actions. When seeing someone throw a rock at a police car, the members of a crowd may not only observe his behavior but also experience his sense of excitement and exhilaration. If excitement and exhilaration have reward value for the individuals in the crowd, they too are apt to start throwing rocks.

Imitation also facilitates learning because the model "disinhibits" previously undesirable responses.[44] In the faceless crowd it is easy to rationalize one's behavior by saying that everyone else is doing the same thing. Thus, the crowd, acting as a model, encourages individuals to do acts they would not otherwise do.

---

[43] Muller, "A Test of a Partial Theory of Potential for Political Violence," pp. 953–54.

[44] Bandura and Walters, *Social Learning and Personality Development,* chap. iii.

Neal Miller and John Dollard analyze lynch mobs in terms of imitation.[45] One effect of a mob, they say, is "interstimulation." The members reinforce each other's behavior and reduce inhibitions against unlawful behavior. As a result, the ferocity and extent of the mob's brutality exceeds what any one individual would do on his own. Lynchings often go beyond the hanging of the victim to include torture and mutilation.

Another example of the effects of imitation is shown in this episode in the 1965 Los Angeles riot:

> Twenty-three-year-old Calvin Joe Jones was coming from the opposite direction in his Volkswagen. He was up early because a friend, Lawrence Charles Jacques, had spent the night at his house, and had to go to work. As Jones drove down Vermont Ave., a fellow on the street hailed him. "Hey, man!" he said. "Go get yourself a free TV!"
>
> Jones continued on. He was a hard-working young man who had graduated from high school at the age of 17, and supported himself ever since. Even though he was the father of two children he had no serious financial problems—he was making $475 a month as a cook in an hotel, and his wife earned $275 a month working in an electronics plant. He was active in his church, and everyone thought well of him.
>
> When he came to the store that was being looted, he could not resist pulling the car into the Shell Service Station next door, just to watch what was going on. The show room was rapidly being stripped, color television sets, radios, and pieces of furniture rushing by him and disappearing in all directions. He would not, ordinarily, have stolen 50¢, but there was an excitement to all of this; the stigma of theft was being removed because everyone was thieving. It seemed to him that, "with all the confusion and the flowing of merchandise, I had a chance to get something for nothing."[46]

Here, Calvin Jones, imitating the crowd, appears to discredit frustration-aggression explanations of riots. But, in fact, his behavior only shows that riots, like most social movements, are complex phenomena attracting individuals with a wide range of motives and needs. No single explanation can account for *all* of the behavior in a riot.

---

[45] Neal E. Miller and John Dollard, *Social Learning and Imitation* (New Haven, Conn.: Yale University Press, 1941), chap. xv.

[46] Conot, *Rivers of Blood, Years of Darkness*, p. 291.

Despite the considerable controversy about the effects of television on violence, the mass media do seem to be important agents of social learning. Of course, a few studies show children are not greatly affected by television programs depicting violence.[47] Nevertheless, other research indicates children imitate and learn aggressive behavior from media like filmed cartoons, even in the absence of frustration.[48] And still other investigators find that the media heighten or facilitate the display of aggression.[49] These studies, based mainly on laboratory experiments, show that aggressive behavior can be learned via the media. (See Chapter 4 for a more thorough discussion.)

There is additional evidence that the media, particularly television and radio, contribute to violence in the real world. In the urban riots of the 1960s, the media played several roles. First, they were a cue informing people that a riot was taking place. During the Los Angeles riots, Conot reports that whenever people heard of a store being looted, they went to get in on the action; whenever they recognized a burning building on television, they headed for that area.[50] Also referring to the Los Angeles riot, Oberschall says that television coverage "acted as a significant clue for the collection of crowds in the vicinity of the original arrest location. . . ."[51]

Perhaps more important, television can arouse individuals. Singer reports that blacks in Detroit were "angry or disturbed by what they had seen."[52] He cites another effect of television: it offered "routine 'instructions' on how a riot is conducted *when it arrives*."[53] These effects, together with the disinhibiting nature of

---

[47] See Joseph Klapper, *The Effects of Mass Communications* (Glencoe, Ill.: The Free Press, 1960), chap. vi; and Walter Weiss, "Effects of the Mass Media of Communication," *The Handbook of Social Psychology,* ed. Gardner Lindzey and Elliot Aronson, Vol. 5, 2d ed. (Reading, Mass.: Addison-Wesley Publishing Co., 1969), pp. 127–41, for references.

[48] *Television and Growing Up: The Impact of Televised Violence,* Report to the Surgeon General (Washington, D.C.: U.S. Government Printing Office, 1972).

[49] Berkowitz, *Aggression: A Social Psychological Analysis;* Leonard Berkowitz, "The Effects of Observing Violence," *Scientific American,* Vol. 210 (1964), pp. 35–41.

[50] Conot, *Rivers of Blood, Years of Darkness,* p. 244.

[51] Oberschall, "The Los Angeles Riot of August 1965," p. 334.

[52] Benjamin D. Singer, "Mass Media and Communication Processes in the Detroit Riot of 1967," *Public Opinion Quarterly,* Vol. 34 (1970), pp. 236–45.

[53] Ibid., pp. 244–45. Italics his.

riot coverage in the media, contributed to a "riot readiness" among many blacks in the Detroit area.

Radio and television, then, can be effective socializers. Their most important effect is in providing cues and models which people imitate. Showing scenes of looting and burning, rock throwing, and vandalism may be good journalism, but, given certain preconditions it may inadvertently lower inhibitions against violence and give people violent models to copy. We need more evidence before we can be sure—and certainly before we can recommend curtailment of the coverage of episodes of collective violence—but there is nevertheless a strong suspicion that the media may inadvertently encourage or exacerbate violent outbursts.

The finding that aggression is sometimes produced by learning and does not always result from frustration leads some scholars to reject the frustration-aggression model and its derivatives (e.g., relative deprivation).[54] But these two approaches, learning theory and frustration-aggression, complement as much as contradict each other. Frustration may encourage the expression of previously learned aggressive behaviors. Social learning predisposes an individual to react in characteristic ways in various situations. Frustration may trigger or intensify these previously learned responses.[55]

CONCLUSION: VIOLENCE AS POLITICAL PROTEST

These theories of violence may satisfy social scientists but they are apt to leave the activist or even the political philosopher a bit cold. So far, we have assumed that collective violence is caused by social and psychological factors, many of which the participants are probably not aware of. The explanations have a deterministic quality: they do not recognize the volition or will of the actors. Instead, violence is seen as the almost inevitable outcome of "objective" conditions. Since these objective conditions motivate behavior, there is little room for consciously selected goals. Thus, even if we have not treated violence as a social pathology, neither have we approached it as a rational, considered, purposive behavior directed to the achievement of specific goals.

---

[54] See, for example, Lupsha, "Explanations of Political Violence," pp. 96–97.
[55] McNeil, "Psychology and Aggression," pp. 209–18.

Much violence does seem senseless. Some cases of lynchings, assassinations, terrorism, mobs, and so on are spontaneous outbursts not related to any discernible purpose. In other cases, though, there may be more rationality than first meets the eye. After all, psychologists admit that one of the strongest instigations to aggression is self-defense or defense against "noxious stimuli."[56] Self-defense usually does not have to be explained by elaborate social and psychological theories.

A few social scientists describe collective violence as a rational (and, perhaps, the only) response to intolerable social and political conditions. Furthermore, violence may arise from simple outrage. Peter Lupsha argues, for instance, that indignation, rather than deprivation, accounts for many instances of violence.[57] As an example, consider students protesting the treatment of minorities. The students themselves are not suffering hardships or deprivation, but they are outraged by what they have seen and heard of living conditions in ghettos or on Indian reservations. Their indignation in certain circumstances could lead them into violent confrontations with political authorities.

Even mobs and riots can be interpreted as a form of collective protest. Although urban disorders are not planned, some feel they do represent protest over the unbearable conditions of the inner cities. Jeffrey Paige suggests that it is useful to describe ghetto rioting as a "disorganized political protest" and rioters as people who both distrust conventional political processes and yet wish to express their grievances.[58]

Furthermore, behavior in many forms of collective violence often displays a coherence, a rationality, that is not immediately apparent. The rioters in Los Angeles, for example, ". . . observed certain *bounds* . . . directed their aggression at *specific targets,* and . . . selected *appropriate means* for the ends they intended to obtain."[59] In other words, certain riots may be far from the random outbursts of violence that they at first sight appear to be. Although crowd dynamics can stimulate people to violate his own sense of

---

[56] Buss, *The Psychology of Aggression,* pp. 30–31.

[57] Lupsha, "Explanations of Political Violence," pp. 99–103.

[58] Jeffrey M. Paige, "Political Orientation and Riot Participation," *American Sociological Review,* Vol. 36 (1971), p. 819.

[59] Oberschall, "The Los Angeles Riot of August 1965," p. 337. Italics his.

right and wrong, we should not neglect the reasons why they seek out the crowd in the first place, join it and continue to give it support. The members of a riot or mob share an anger, and this anger largely determines what the crowd does.

Other types of violence, notably guerrilla war, have more explicitly political purposes. Although guerrilla war may attract malcontents and psychopaths and is rooted in the complex social and economic conditions we have described, it usually has clear political goals. Since the participants are aware of the objectives—indeed, for many of them the objectives are the reason for their involvement—we must examine these goals in order to understand fully the war. We should not let social and psychological theory obscure the political meanings of mass movements.

In conclusion, then, probably the best way to explain mass political violence is to examine the interplay between situational and historical factors, on the one hand, and social-psychological forces on the other. No doubt there are deep-seated causes underlying every form of violence. And yet, those who take part do so for their own reasons. If we are to comprehend collective violence we cannot forget the motives of the participants. But we should also examine underlying conditions because people frequently do things for reasons they themselves are unaware of. Therefore, we require two pieces of information: first, what are the economic, social, and psychological circumstances surrounding an act of violence and second, what are the intentions of those taking part in it. With this knowledge we can gain insights into both the causes and merits of political violence.

9

The Common Man and Public Policy

By most standards President Nixon's 1972 reelection campaign was a dramatic success. Carrying every state except Massachusetts and the District of Columbia, the President won a near record 61 percent of the popular vote. The margin of his victory in the electoral college, 521 to 17, was also almost unprecedented. Both the campaign and the election itself gave the appearance of overwhelming public support for the President and total rejection of his opponent, George McGovern.

After the election, the President as well as many other commentators began referring to the victory as a "mandate." It was tempting to see his reelection as an endorsement of all the programs and proposals of the Nixon administration's first four years. President Nixon claimed at one point that

> Last November, the American people were given the clearest choice of this century. Your votes were a mandate . . . to complete the initiatives we began in my first term and to fulfill the promises I made for my second term.
> This Administration was elected to control inflation, to reduce

the power and size of government, to cut the cost of government so that you can cut the cost of living, to preserve and defend those fundamental values that have made America great, to keep the nation's military strength second to none, to achieve peace with honor in Southeast Asia and bring home America's prisoners of war, to build a new prosperity, without inflation and without war, to create a structure of peace in the world that would endure long after we were gone.[1]

The President's is a familiar argument. The winning side in most elections usually claims to have a mandate from the people to do what it wants.[2] Implicit in this line of reasoning are the assumptions that voters are aware of and care about issues, that they see differences between candidates, and that they are motivated primarily by a concern with issues. There is a further assumption that people who vote for a candidate are united across a wide spectrum of issues.

These assumptions, in turn, rest on the fundamental belief that the will of the people can be and is expressed through the conventional forms of political participation such as elections. Whatever a democratic government does—its laws, court decisions, administrative rules—flows from the needs and demands of its citizens. The enactment of the public will is, in theory at least, the essence of democracy.

Quite obviously government cannot be run like a town meeting with each person participating fully and equally in the deliberations. Modern government is too big, too complex, and involves too many technical decisions for that to happen. Generally, it is not worthwhile for a man to become too deeply involved in decisions which hardly affect him. A blue-collar worker is not likely to be affected by rural electrification programs except perhaps in the most indirect way.

Clearly, then, the practical problem of democracy is to aggregate and translate the popular will into public policy without stifling creativity and efficiency. The principal means for accomplishing this goal is the delegation of authority to public officials. Holding

---

[1] *New York Times,* August 16, 1973, p. 26.

[2] Ironically, on the same day President Nixon made this statement a Gallup poll showed that his popularity had dropped to 31 percent, the lowest figure for a president in 20 years. About 70 percent of the sample did not approve of the way he was handling his job (*New York Times,* August 16, 1973, p. 24).

this authority temporarily, these officials serve at the pleasure of the public which reviews and approves their actions and behavior. Various institutions for monitoring and controlling the activities of political leaders have evolved over the years, among them elections, political parties, lobbies, public hearings, referenda, recall petitions, protest demonstrations, and even public opinion polls.

These institutions and practices theoretically have common properties. For one, they communicate to decision makers the desires of the people. For another, they ensure that policy conforms to the public interest. Since these institutions are accessible to everyone, they do not consistently favor one group over another; each citizen, in other words, has an equal opportunity to influence the decision-making process. And, by the same token, public officials do not manipulate them to create the appearance of serving on behalf of the public when in fact they are serving in the interests of a few. Thus, through institutions and procedures such as elections, the public can express its will.

This is how an ideal democracy works. The goal of empirical democratic theory, however, is to determine how well these ideals are met in actual practice. Does public policy really represent the will of the people? Is an election a mandate? Does public opinion control the activities of elected officials? Or do elites control public opinion?

This is the type of question we take up in this chapter. It is not possible to discuss the matter fully, for to do so would require a separate book. Instead, we will simply sketch some of the problems of popular control of public policy, concentrating mainly on elections but touching on other institutions as well. But first in order to see the limits of the public's control over decision making in a democracy, it is fruitful to examine the characteristics of the decision-making process itself.

DECISION MAKING IN A DEMOCRACY

Since it is impossible to describe governmental decision making in detail, we will state a few generalizations which show how hard it is for the public to control policy making on a day-to-day basis.[3]

---

[3] For an excellent general introduction to decision making, see Charles E. Lindblom, *The Policy-Making Process* (Englewood Cliffs, N.J.: Prentice-Hall, Inc., 1968).

Most decisions are made in private, well-hidden from public scrutiny. The privacy of decision making results more from necessity than from a conspiracy to deceive or defraud the public. Each level of government has to make literally thousands of decisions. Many of them are trivial, others are quite technical. They cannot all be the subject of public debate because their numbers would overwhelm the public's capacity to deal with them. Hence, most decision making in a democracy is left to relatively few individuals. These authorities may be accountable, either directly or indirectly, to others, but within their areas of responsibility they have wide discretionary powers. Furthermore, much of what they do goes unnoticed by most citizens.

Although the majority of decisions made in this manner are more or less inconsequential for the common man, many of these matters have broad ramifications. Price rates for natural gas, for example, affect millions of homeowners and businessmen. Yet the rates are regulated by the Federal Power Commission, a group whose membership, structure, and operation are largely unknown to the public. Only a few groups, notably oilmen and consumer advocates, become sufficiently familiar with the Commission's activities to have much influence on its deliberations. Of course, the FPC, like other regulatory agencies, is ultimately responsible to Congress and hence to the people. But as a practical matter it operates in semi-obscurity, and its daily operations are influenced mostly by a limited number of interest groups.

The example of the FPC leads to another, closely related generalization: policy making is not affected by the public as a whole so much as by *attentive publics*. Governments engage in numerous types of programs. Some programs directly affect only certain groups while other programs affect still other groups. Naturally, those groups immediately concerned with a policy will be more interested in its formation than groups less directly affected. There is a tendency, then, for policy making to be followed most closely by the people who feel they have the most to win or lose.

In this respect Gabriel Almond presents an interesting breakdown of public opinion on foreign affairs. First, he identifies an apathetic and indifferent "general public."[4] The second element is

---

[4] Gabriel A. Almond, *The American People and Foreign Policy* (New York: Frederick A. Praeger, Inc., 1960), p. 138.

a much smaller "attentive public" which is interested and informed and actively follows the decisions of the policy elites. Finally, there is the foreign policy elite consisting of individuals both in and out of government who make policy. To the extent that public opinion affects foreign affairs at all, it does so mainly through the attentive public. Since the masses are simply not involved they influence policy (if at all) only indirectly.[5]

The notion of an attentive public applies to all aspects of politics. What the Department of Agriculture does about farm subsidies, for example, affects every consumer in the long run, but it has an immediate impact on farmers. Farmers and farm organizations pay close attention to the Agriculture Department because they believe their livelihoods depend on its policies. The rest of us know very little about acreage allotments, price supports, commodity controls, and the like.

Therefore, according to many political scientists, we should refer to attentive publics rather than to the public as a whole when discussing popular control of policy. The implication is that at any point in the decision-making process a relatively small number of individuals will be involved. This is not to say the people have no voice, only that they exercise it in a limited fashion.

Another factor affecting the public's influence is the decentralization of decision making. Theoretically, the legislative branch of government enacts laws and the executive branch enforces them. Yet, as everyone knows, the division of labor is not that simple. Both bureaucracies and judiciaries frequently make policy. Quite often Congress will pass a bill setting general guidelines but will leave the executive branch wide discretionary powers to implement the program. Consequently, bureaucracies at the federal and local level have created a vast body of "administrative law." Such bureaucratic rules and regulations are as enforceable as any laws passed by Congress.

By interpreting and applying these regulations, the courts also make decisions. For example, when a court orders immediate school desegregation, it is in effect determining what a community's policy on integration will be. More important, policies made in one branch of government are sometimes altered or even reversed in

---

[5] Ibid., pp. 138–39.

another, as when a president refuses to spend money appropriated by Congress. In short, public policy is seldom made in one easily identifiable location and at one point in time. Rather, policy making goes on continuously in various places.

Because policy making is decentralized in this manner, the citizen's power to control it is at once expanded and curtailed. On one hand, he has several opportunities to affect decisions. If he does not succeed in one place he may try in another. Having failed to prevent the passage of a law, he may attempt to nullify it in the courts or to prevent its implementation in the bureaucracy. There are multiple points of access which one may use to exert influence. On the other hand, this decentralization makes it difficult to assign responsibility for policies that are not working. Who is to blame for inflation? Is it the president? The Congress? The state and local governments? It is very hard for the citizen to blame one person because that person can (often with truth) blame someone else. As long as no institution or unit of government has the sole responsibility for a program, the public's control of it is weakened.

Policy making is also *incremental*.[6] Not very often is a policy boldly announced and carried out. Most major programs represent years of debate and study. Changes in them are usually small, occurring in bits and pieces. When social security was first enacted, it left millions uncovered and its benefits were relatively meager. Over the years it has slowly expanded, but at no point were there radical departures from what went before. The majority of policies like social security became law only after considerable wrangling and compromise. Changes come slowly even when public opinion seems to want more drastic action.

Richard Harris' narrative of the enactment of Medicare provides an example of public opinion clearly and overwhelmingly favoring a program long before Congress voted it into law.[7] Organized efforts to pass a federal program of health insurance began as early as 1912. Yet Medicare was not signed into law until 1965, 53 years later. During most of this period polls showed consistent desires for some type of health insurance program. In a 1961 Gallup poll, for in-

---

[6] See Lindblom, *The Policy-Making Process,* pp. 26–27.

[7] Richard Harris, *A Sacred Trust,* rev. ed. (Baltimore: Penguin Books, 1969).

stance, 67 percent favored Medicare, but it was four years later before the bill passed both houses and was signed by President Johnson.[8] Given this type of performance Harris concludes that it ordinarily "takes a generation or more for Congress to approve a major piece of social legislation."[9]

There is, then, a bias in the political system against sweeping change. The defenders of the status quo have an easier task than the advocates of bold new programs. The public normally has to be quite persistent before major alterations in public policy can be achieved.

Part of this phenomenon can be explained by the fact that policy choices are often limited by other decisions. C. Wright Mills, a sociologist, introduced the term "global decision" to refer to a decision of such magnitude and importance that many other policies are shaped by it.[10] And surprisingly, global decisions are often made in the highest levels of government, far from the public's eye. Some of them seem to happen without a full awareness of all of their ramifications. America's nuclear strategy is an example.

During the Eisenhower administration, the United States relied on a "finite deterrent" strategy in which we maintained just enough nuclear weapons including warheads and delivery systems to survive an enemy's first strike and still retaliate. Since the retaliation can inflict unacceptably high losses on the enemy, a force of this type will presumably deter or prevent an armed attack. The advantage of finite deterrence is its relatively low cost: a nation needs to maintain only enough nuclear weapons to forestall an attack by its enemies. Its principal disadvantage is that it leaves decision makers with few options. Suppose, for example, that an enemy does not launch an all-out attack, but instead starts a "brush fire" war against

---

[8] Ibid., p. 130.

[9] Ibid., p. 35.

[10] C. Wright Mills, *The Power Elite* (New York: Oxford University Press, pp. 11–15. Mills's arguments, particularly as expressed in his *The Power Elite* have been hotly debated by social scientists. What troubles most scholars is Mill's contention that all global decisions are made by a single elite composed of a few politicians, industrialists, and military men. That claim is not being made here. The only point is that some decisions are vastly more important than others and that once these decisions have been taken they limit what can be done in other areas.

an ally. The only alternatives would then be to do nothing or to retaliate with an all-out nuclear strike. Neither option seems appropriate to the situation.

Partly as a consequence of this disadvantage, the United States shifted during the Kennedy presidency to a "counterforce" strategy, also called a no-cities or damage limitation strategy. Counterforce, requiring a large and sophisticated nuclear arsenal, provides several options in the event of an enemy attack. In theory, it permits a controlled response appropriate to whatever the enemy does. Instead of unleashing an all-out attack, for instance, a nation could try to destroy only the enemy's military forces, sparing his cities for at least the time being. Or, part of the weapons could be launched in the expectation that the remaining weapons will deter any further enemy moves. Even though a counterforce strategy gives more alternatives it is much more expensive to build and maintain. In addition to an elaborate command and control system, it requires a large stockpile of warheads and delivery systems.

The point is not which of these strategies is superior. It is only to demonstrate that in choosing counterforce, the Kennedy administration effectively determined what *other* programs could be. A counterforce arsenal is so expensive that it is not possible to fund it and other programs as well. It simply requires too many missiles, submarines, planes, and warheads. Therefore, even though the public may favor more spending on health care, education, and pollution control, what can be done in these areas is limited by the size of the defense budget.

Public policy really involves a hierarchy of decisions. Once a global decision like the choice of a nuclear strategy is made, it forecloses alternatives in other areas.

Many global decisions seem to evolve over time and are not decided by a single election or vote in Congress. In fact, many are not subject to public debate at all. The debate over counterforce was conducted mainly among foreign policy and military specialists and a few scientists and intellectuals in the government, on university campuses, and in think tanks. Even Congress was on the periphery of the decision. Although the Democrats raised the question of a missile gap in 1960, counterforce versus finite deterrence was never debated by the two presidential candidates, nor by any candidates for the House or Senate. And, more significant, nuclear strategy was formulated in an absence of debate about its relationship to other national priorities.

The last sentence raises another point about policy making in America. Decisions are often made independently and serially and without regard to their impact on one another. Since democracies react to crises rather than plan for them, public policy tends to be directed toward the solution of immediate problems. Consequently, the nation frequently stumbles into programs which endure until a new crisis upsets them. Thus, it is hard for the public to know and evaluate the interrelatedness of different governmental activities.

Given these constraints and problems of decision making in a democracy, we may wonder what effect public opinion has or can have. Perhaps the best way to answer this question is to look at voting.

ELECTIONS AND PUBLIC POLICY

Do Elections Control Public Policy?

According to conventional wisdom, voting is the most obvious and direct way for people to affect public policy. Voting is frequently viewed as a panacea for many social and political problems: if a corrupt political machine is holding up progress, then throw the rascals out at the next election. If a minority is the victim of discrimination, then just give them the right to vote so they can force an end to their subservience. So enamoured are Americans of the power of the ballot that they have tried for decades to export it to other nations. Throughout the war in Vietnam, American advisors pleaded and cajoled the South Vietnamese to "hold elections" as if these elections somehow proved that democracy was flourishing there.

Do elections really provide effective controls over decision makers and hence over decisions themselves? There seems to be agreement that choosing a "government" is not the same as choosing "governmental policies."[11] Elections, in other words, are not a direct expression of desires of the electorate. Robert Dahl explains why.

[11] Gerald M. Pomper, *Elections in America* (New York: Dodd Mead & Co., 1968), p. 51.

He argues that elections reveal very little about the preferences of a majority. Applying his analysis to a recent case, consider again President Nixon's landslide victory in 1972. He won over 60 percent of the votes cast. Yet, in another sense, he is a minority president because only about 55 percent of those eligible to vote did vote. This means that Nixon won far less than a majority of the eligible electorate.[12] This type of victory is not uncommon in American politics. In several instances, a president has even been elected with less than a majority of the popular vote. (This has happened twice out of the last four presidential elections: in 1960 with Kennedy and in 1968 with Nixon.) Similarly, most congressmen and other elected officials are "minority" representatives.

The upshot is that even if all of the people who voted for the winner had the same preferences they would not necessarily constitute a majority. To see if a majority exists we would have to examine the opinions of the nonvoters. Generally, their opinions are not the same as those of the voters. Chapter 5 showed, for example, that nonparticipants differed significantly from participants. Hence, the winner of an election, even if he wins by a landslide, is not always justified in claiming a mandate for his programs.[13]

Another problem cited by Dahl is the heterogeneity of preferences among the winning candidate's supporters. Suppose that half of the people who voted for Nixon favored raising social security benefits but voted for Nixon on other grounds. Then even though Nixon won in a landslide it would be incorrect to assert that he had a mandate to keep social security payments at their current level.[14]

Elections, then, do not automatically ensure majority rule on public policy questions. In a few instances, of course, citizens have a direct voice, such as votes on bond issues, referendums, city ordinances, and state constitutional amendments. But for the most part, however, the people must exercise control indirectly by voting for lawmakers instead of the laws themselves. Whether or not the people *can* control the making of policy in this manner depends on several conditions.

---

[12] Robert A. Dahl, *A Preface to Democratic Theory* (Chicago: University of Chicago Press, 1956), p. 125.

[13] Ibid., pp. 125–56.

[14] Ibid., pp. 127–31.

First, voters must be aware of and motivated about policy questions. They must know the issues and how they relate to their own needs, aspirations, and values.[15] Moreover, they must take issue positions into account when voting. If a candidate favors a cut in federal spending, then, other things being equal, voters with similar views should vote for that person. To do so requires them to see policy differences between the candidates.

At the same time, voters must be offered a meaningful choice between candidates standing for specific policies. And once elected, these representatives must behave as they promised during the campaign. If the candidate says he favors cutting spending, then he should vote for cuts in appropriations.[16] Finally, if the voter is to have any chance to discipline errant representatives, then betrayals must be relatively easy to detect. For how else will the voter know if he has been fooled?

How well are these conditions met in American politics? Not very well, according to most political scientists. But there is sharp disagreement over who is at fault.

Some observers blame the people. As seen in Chapter 6, there is a school of thought which holds that the typical voter is not well informed, does not particularly care about issues, does not know where the candidates or parties stand, and votes primarily according to his party identification or his partisan attitude. In a study of the 1958 congressional election, Donald Stokes and Warren Miller found many voters to be unaware of or unconcerned with the issue positions of both parties or of congressional candidates. For example, a sample of 1,700 respondents were asked their likes and dislikes of the two major parties. Fewer than 12 percent of the answers had anything to do with the parties' legislative records or positions on

---

[15] Ideally, citizens themselves would decide what issues are important enough for debate and action. In practice it appears that issues, or the agenda of political discourse, are determined at least as much by elites as by the public. See Peter Bachrach and Morton S. Baratz, *Power and Poverty: Theory and Practice* (New York: Oxford University Press, 1970), chap. iii, for a further discussion of this point.

[16] See John L. Sullivan and Robert E. O'Connor, "Electoral Choice and Popular Control of Public Policy: The Case of the 1966 House Elections," *American Political Science Review*, Vol. 66 (1972), pp. 1256–68; and Richard W. Boyd, "Popular Control of Public Policy: A Normal Vote Analysis of the 1968 Election," *American Political Science Review*, Vol. 66 (1972), pp. 429–49, for a discussion of some of these points.

issues.[17] They also discovered that perceptions of congressmen are "almost barren of policy content."[18]

The failure on the part of the voter to connect parties or candidates with policy questions has been highlighted by John Sullivan and Robert O'Connor. They find that since congressional candidates generally have different attitudes, the public is usually offered a meaningful choice. Furthermore, the elected representatives vote according to their attitudes. Hence, in Sullivan and O'Connor's opinion, as well as that of many other political scientists, the electorate fails to take advantage of the opportunity to control policy through voting: the voter has a meaningful choice among candidates, but he does not vote his policy preferences.[19] This generalization is probably more true for congressional than presidential voting because there is usually less information available about candidates for Congress. At any rate, if elected officials fail to represent the interests of their constituents, this school feels the fault lies with the people, not their leaders.

Yet this position is not without its challengers. We also saw in Chapter 6 that voters are not necessarily stupid, that they care about issues, and, more important, that they have beliefs about where the parties and candidates stand on issues and they take these beliefs into account in voting. As we saw, there are numerous exceptions but enough people seem to vote rationally to make us wonder if public officials are doing all they can to facilitate the public's task of choosing the right leaders.

In this vein we may ask how easy it is for the voter to act rationally. It is well known that politicians are masters of obfuscation when it comes to talking about sensitive problems. Richard Scammon and Ben Wattenberg, in *The Real Majority,* elevate this tendency to a scientific principle.[20] They caution candidates against taking extreme positions on issues because to do so risks votes. The

---

[17] Donald E. Stokes and Warren E. Miller, "Party Government and the Saliency of Congress," *Public Opinion Quarterly,* Vol. 26 (1962), pp. 531–46, cited in *Readings in American Political Behavior,* ed. Raymond E. Wolfinger (Englewood Cliffs, N.J.: Prentice-Hall, Inc., 1966), pp. 69–83.

[18] Ibid., p. 80.

[19] Sullivan and O'Connor, "Electoral Choice and Popular Control of Public Policy," pp. 1264–65.

[20] Richard M. Scammon and Ben J. Wattenberg, *The Real Majority* (New York: Coward-McCann, Inc., 1970), chap. vi.

smart candidate, they say, is the one who moves to the "center," to the middle of the road where he will not lose votes to his opponents. The best way to do this is not to talk about issues at all, or if one is forced to say something, say as little as possible. Be noncommittal and above all do not say anything that can be used against you later. The result is that even if candidates do have definite ideas and opinions about current events they feel they must state their views carefully. But if the candidates keep their cards close to their vests, how are voters to judge their qualifications? They, the voters, must use other evaluative criteria such as the candidates' images and personalities.

A good example of the problem confronting voters can be found in the 1968 presidential campaign. Benjamin Page and Richard Brody carefully examined Richard Nixon and Hubert Humphrey's campaign speeches on the war in Vietnam.[21] They found that Nixon and Humphrey differed very little, if at all. If there was an "absence of Vietnam policy voting," the authors concluded, it can be attributed to the fact that "in reality there was little difference between the candidates."[22]

Or consider national party platforms, which are often as ambiguous and evasive as any document can be. Furthermore, they are not binding on anyone. There may, of course, be sound reasons why platforms are noncommittal on issues. As Nelson Polsby and Aaron Wildavsky say, a platform is designed to achieve party unity.[23] If it proposed explicit programs and doctrines it might splinter the party. Consequently, the platform is a mild declaration of principles and goals. Now, all of this may be true, but the fact remains that a platform does not make the voter's job of choosing between two candidates any easier. Indeed, it even makes his task harder because the real issues become clouded.

Another factor limiting the public's control of policy is the nature of the news media, which thrive on events or happenings. Although there is no systematic study of the topic, it seems reason-

---

[21] Benjamin I. Page and Richard A. Brody, "Policy Voting and the Electoral Process: The Vietnam War Issue," *American Political Science Review,* Vol. 66 (1972), pp. 984–86.

[22] Ibid., p. 985.

[23] Nelson Polsby and Aaron B. Wildavsky, *Presidential Elections,* 2d ed. (New York: Charles Scribner's Sons, 1968), pp. 234–42, 252–55.

able to say that the media are more concerned with politics—that is, who did what to whom—than with issues. Needless to say, issues are discussed on television and in newspapers and magazines. Nevertheless, two factors stand out in the treatment of issues by the media. First, they play second fiddle to events such as the endorsement of one candidate by another or a giant political rally. George McGovern no doubt answered more questions about his dismal showings in the polls than about his defense or welfare proposals. Similarly, the media seem at least as impressed with the size of a man's crowd as with what he is saying to it. The second point is that issues are often treated superficially. A newspaper study may briefly explain a candidate's position on issues but it is seldom possible to relate these positions to one's own needs and interests.[24]

Finally, another factor discouraging the use of elections to control policy is the unrewarding nature of politics. There is a disconcertingly widespread distrust of government and political parties. The data in Table 9.1 are revealing in this respect. Taken

Table 9.1
PUBLIC SKEPTICISM AND CYNICISM ABOUT GOVERNMENT

Over the years, how much attention do you feel the government pays to what people think when it decides what to do?

A good deal	24.5%
Some	50.4
Not much	25.1
Total	100.0%
	(1,468)

How much attention do you think most congressmen pay to the people who elect them when they decide what to do in Congress?

A good deal	30.6%
Some	46.3
Not much	23.1
Total	100.0%
	(1,460)

I don't think public officials care much what people like me think.

Agree	48.7%
Disagree	51.3
Total	100.0%
	(1,457)

---

[24] For an interesting if polemical treatment of some of these topics, see Robert Cirino, *Don't Blame the People* (Los Angeles: Diversity Press, 1971).

Table 9.1 (*continued*)

Generally speaking, those we elect to Congress in Washington lose touch with the people pretty quickly.

Agree	62.0%
Disagree	38.0
Total	100.0%
	(1,442)

How much of the time do you think you can trust the government in Washington to do what is right?

Always	6.6%
Most of the time	48.1
Some of the time	45.0
None of the time	0.3
Total	100.0%
	(1,471)

Do you think that quite a few of the people running the government are a little crooked, not very many are, or do you think hardly any of them are crooked at all?

Hardly any	16.5%
Not many	50.9
Quite a lot	32.7
Total	100.1%
	(1,445)

Parties are only interested in people's votes but not their opinions.

Agree	55.7%
Disagree	44.3
Total	100.0%
	(1,450)

Would you say the government is pretty much run by a few big interests looking out for themselves or that it is run for the benefit of all the people?

For benefit of all	42.6%
Few big interests	52.2
Other, depends	5.2
Total	100.0%
	(1,435)

Note: Figures in parentheses refer to the number of cases.
Source: *CPS 1970 American National Election Study.* (See Appendix.)

from a study of the 1970 congressional election, they indicate widespread skepticism about political parties and candidates. Over half of the respondents believe that parties are only interested in votes and that elected officials quickly lose touch with their constituents after an election. Many doubt whether the government listens to the people. And, perhaps most disturbing, about half of the sample feels the government can be trusted only "some of the time." These data reflect a deep suspicion of the electoral process as a means of controlling policy.

Distrust of government has been increased by the Watergate scandals. Citing a Louis Harris poll, the *New York Times* concluded that "Most Americans have lost confidence in government and other institutions that affect them day by day . . ."[25] Only 19 percent of the sample had a great deal of confidence in the executive branch of government. The corresponding percents for the Senate, the House of Representatives, and the Supreme Court were 30, 29, and 33, respectively. Citizens, the survey showed, were disillusioned, disenchanted, and cynical about politicians and political institutions.[26]

Where do these attitudes come from? At this point we can only speculate. Nevertheless, one source clearly seems to be broken campaign promises. During any campaign many more promises are made than can be kept. Most candidates for state and national office favor lower taxes, safe streets, less air and water pollution, higher employment, and the good life for one and all. They make claims about their ability—and their opponent's lack of ability—to achieve these goals. Yet life goes on much as before. Changes do occur, but they come about slowly, grudgingly. To the man on the street, political rhetoric must sound hollow indeed, for he has learned that a single person cannot do everything he says he will. Thus, many people probably find it unrewarding to follow issues closely. They sense that the time and trouble devoted to learning where the candidates stand may be wasted.

More important perhaps is the difficulty of convincing people that politics is not both futile and corrupt. As we noted in Chapter 7, many Americans lead "marginal" lives. They face unemployment, economic insecurity, illness, overcrowding in many aspects of their lives, and shortages. Government seems unable or unwilling to solve or even mitigate these problems. At the same time, politicians everywhere appear rapacious, uncaring men intent on lining their own pockets. They worry more about their personal needs

---

[25] *New York Times,* December 3, 1973, p. 34.
[26] Ibid.

than the public's. This is, at least, how many citizens have come to view government.

The preceding paragraphs contain some sweeping generalizations. There are important differences between the two political parties and between many candidates, differences which many people recognize and act on. The point has only been to emphasize that if elections do not control public policy, then only part of the blame should be put on the voter. We hear countless tales of the irrationality, myopia, and ignorance of the American voter and many observers want to blame him for the shortcomings of public policy. Yet political elites are not without fault. They, too, must assume responsibility for the proper functioning of the electoral process.

The Functions of Elections

To recapitulate, we have said that elections in theory are important means of public control of policy. Yet nearly everyone agrees that elections perform this function poorly. Before entirely dismissing elections, however, we can ask if they serve other purposes.

Clearly in some instances elections are an expression of the policy preferences of the voters. This effect is most likely where an issue is both highly visible and salient in a constituency. In many American communities civil rights legislation is an important matter: how a congressman votes on these issues may affect his chances for reelection.

Warren Miller and Donald Stokes provide an interesting example of the potential importance of voting as a control on public officials and hence on public policy.[27] Representative Brooks Hays of the Fifth District in Arkansas acted as an intermediary between the White House and Governor Orville Faubus in the Little Rock school integration crisis of 1956. As a result of these efforts, Hays was perceived as a moderate on civil rights and was handily defeated by a write-in opponent. School desegregation was such a sensitive issue in the District that every person in the Miller and Stokes sample had read or heard about both candidates. The authors

---

[27] Warren E. Miller and Donald E. Stokes, "Constituency Influence in Congress," *Elections and the Political Order*, ed. Angus Campbell et al. (New York: John Wiley & Sons, Inc., 1966), pp. 369–70.

conclude that ". . . Hays was regarded both by his supporters and his opponents as more moderate than Alford [his opponent] on civil rights and that this perception brought his defeat."[28] In this case, there is a direct connection between constituency pressures and elite behavior.

Although these types of situations may be relatively rare, there is widespread belief in the ability of the electorate to punish those who run counter to public opinion. Elections, as with other expressions of public opinion, can serve as potential sanctions: if an elected official does not perform as his constituents want, he is turned out of office. Incumbents usually have an advantage over their opponents—about four out of five incumbent congressmen, for example, successfully retain their seats in an average election—but most officials seem to feel the public's eye is constantly on them. They believe that if they step out of line their opponents will seize the opportunity to mobilize opinion against them. The assumption, which may or may not be true, is that people vote against rather than for someone. In any event, even though voters might not take policy considerations into account, elected officials frequently act as if they did. This may explain their apparent preoccupation about their standing in public opinion polls. And as long as these officials fear losing their power they will adjust their behavior to conform with their perceptions of public opinion.

In this way, the public limits policy alternatives that decision makers feel free to consider. During the early Kennedy administration there was some interest, both in and out of government, in relaxing America's policy of nonrecognition of Communist China. Yet according to David Halberstam the idea was dropped for fear of arousing hostile domestic opinion.[29] Similarly, it is quite common for decision makers to postpone making an especially sensitive decision until after the next election.

Robert Dahl suggests still another, perhaps the most important, function of elections. Recall that Dahl believes elections tell little about the policy preferences of a majority. Nevertheless, he believes them to be essential to democracy because they expand the scope of

---

[28] Miller and Stokes, "Constituency Influence in Congress," p. 370.

[29] David Halberstam, *The Best and the Brightest* (New York: Random House, Inc., 1972).

political conflict.[30] His reasoning has two elements. First, decision makers respond to pressure; they listen when a group vehemently argues its case. Second, an election is one means by which a group can exert pressure. If the group organizes and mobilizes its membership it can form a significant block which has to be reckoned with in an election. Now, the key to Dahl's argument is that nearly any group can take advantage of elections to advance its cause. The electoral process, then, does not ensure "majority rule" on policy questions, but it helps to establish "minorities rule."[31] Elections also prevent the political system from being inaccessible or closed to the masses. Therefore, the chief virtue of the ballot is that it promotes equality of opportunity in the policy-making process.

Voting is all the more important in this respect since most elections are not won by more than a few percent. A candidate cannot risk losing a winning margin by alienating any sizable block of voters, even if it is a minority, and he thus has to be sensitive to the policy demands of at least some of his constituents.[32]

On the other hand, Dahl's critics believe that not all groups in society are equally able to mobilize for electoral activity. Some groups such as the poor are too disorganized and have too few resources to compete effectively against more established groups like unions or business organizations. Elected officials can safely ignore poor people's policy demands because the poor are too weak and fragmented to form a cohesive block. Therefore, they are not part of anyone's winning coalition. If sufficient numbers of them could be attracted to the polls, decision makers would become more responsive to their needs. But as was seen in Chapter 5, poor people generally do not participate in politics.

On another plane, elections have an additional function: they reduce political conflicts and cleavages. They do this by encouraging people to compromise in return for a chance to share political power. In order to win an election a candidate must form a winning coalition. Coalition building involves bringing together groups with diverse goals and needs. If everyone is to profit from

---

[30] Dahl, *A Preface to Democratic Theory,* chap. v.

[31] Ibid., p. 132.

[32] Miller and Stokes, "Constituency Influence in Congress," p. 368.

the coalition he has to make sacrifices so that the candidate or party can win. Making these sacrifices means differences are resolved and bargains made. The result is a lessening of conflict. People compromise for the sake of winning.[33]

Elections, then, can help preserve social and political tranquillity. But needless to say, they do not always produce this result. Extremists sometimes rise to power through the electoral process as Hitler did in 1932. And in the United States demagogues have often achieved remarkable success at the polls. Nevertheless, a "winner-take-all" system like ours provides inducements for cooperation. To be elected, a presidential candidate has to have a broad spectrum of support. He cannot do it by appealing only to a limited segment of the population.

Finally, we can also look at voting from a different perspective. Murray Edelman feels participation in politics has a meaning quite different from that expressed in traditional democratic theory.[34] Whereas democratic theory sees mass participation as a means to an end, namely the control of leaders and policy, Edelman believes participation may be an end in itself. He argues that many public policies really benefit small groups. What gives these programs legitimacy is the appearance that the masses have played some role in their enactment. Elections, he says, provide satisfactions to the individual who is reassured by his participation and by the feeling that he has a voice in government. Political participation "reinforces the impression of a political system designed to translate individual wants into public policy."[35] So even if the system works for the benefit of a few, it has the appearance of working for all.

Edelman's position is not drastically different from Dahl's. Dahl believes that policy is determined by minorities competing against one another. Any particular policy may thus be the product of a relatively small group. The system is democratic, though, because everyone has a chance, by elections and other forms of participation, to take part in this process. Edelman adds to this the idea that although the masses may in fact have little effect on policy most of

---

[33] See, for example, the discussion in Polsby and Wildavsky, *Presidential Elections*, pp. 279–80.

[34] Murray Edelman, *The Symbolic Uses of Politics* (paperback ed.; Urbana, Ill.: University of Illinois Press, 1967), chap. i.

[35] Ibid., p. 17.

the time, their involvement in politics gives them psychological satisfaction: they think they are part of the policy-making process and thus they accept it.

In summary, voting affects public policy, but not in the direct manner suggested by democratic theory. Rather, its significance is indirect. The public disciplines, legitimizes, and sets limits on public policy. It remains for future scholars to find ways to make policy even more responsive to the electorate.

THE POLITICAL CONSEQUENCES OF VIOLENT PROTESTS

According to classical democratic theory people should express their policy preferences through conventional modes of political participation. If people want a law passed they should write their congressmen, petition, organize a lobbying group, and vote. These are the "accepted" means for translating public preferences into policy.

Throughout this book, however, it has become evident that people accept nonconventional methods for expressing their grievances and promoting their causes. With few exceptions unconventional politics—boycotting, demonstrating, protesting, rioting, and rebellion—are the tools of disadvantaged, deprived groups seeking to alter the status quo. Higher status individuals are in a better position to take advantage of the opportunities offered by traditional political practices. Still, involvement in nonconventional political activities is widespread, and in concluding the discussion of popular control of public policy it is useful to speculate about the effectiveness of such behavior.

To narrow the topic, we will consider only riots. Many social scientists feel riots are a form of protest. Clearly they have numerous possible causes, some of which the participants are not even aware of. But it is also true, as we saw in Chapter 8, that it is misleading to view riots solely as anomic, mindless outbursts of violence. They have at least some attributes of collective protest movements. Although urban disorders may be unplanned and leaderless, they are a form of protest against genuine grievances.[36]

The riots in American cities in the 1960s shared many character-

---

[36] Robert M. Fogelson, *Violence as Protest* (Anchor Books ed.; Garden City, New York: Doubleday & Co., 1971), p. 21.

istics of political protest movements. The participants who were representative of their communities[37] had well-known complaints: substandard housing, inadequate health and sanitary facilities, inferior schools, high unemployment, and poor police protection—all of which they blamed partly on social, economic, and political discrimination. More important, rioters expected an improvement in their situation as a result of the disorder. David Sears and John McConahay report that a majority of the black participants and observers of the 1965 Watts conflagration were optimistic about the aftermath of the riot.[38] Nor did they feel they were engaged in senseless destruction, but rather were making a positive protest against unfair conditions.[39]

Furthermore, riot behavior itself is often purposive. Superficially, the rioters seemed to act wantonly, indiscriminately, and without restraint. But they frequently showed compassion toward the police, firemen, and bystanders and were selective in their choice of targets.[40] They vented their rage against the symbols of oppression such as police cars and stores that charged excessive prices or sold inferior merchandise. Churches, schools, homes, and recreation facilities were generally left untouched or only accidentally damaged.

Riots can thus be interpreted in Robert Fogelson's words as "articulate protests against genuine grievances in the black ghettos."[41] In accepting this view we may then ask if violent protest does any good. Do riots help or hurt the drive for equality of opportunity? What conditions make protest of this type effective?

Reactions to Violent Protest

Some of these questions can be answered by looking at the immediate reactions produced by urban riots like the Watts disorder. On

---

[37] See Chapter 8.

[38] David O. Sears and John B. McConahay, *The Politics of Violence* (Boston: Houghton Mifflin Co., 1973), pp. 160–62.

[39] Fogelson, *Violence as Protest*, pp. 16–17.

[40] Ibid., p. 16. It is worth noting that the principal victims of riots are the rioters themselves. The number of dead and injured among the participants greatly exceeds the casualty rate among law enforcement officers.

[41] Ibid., p. 4.

the positive side, they usually create a dialogue between the protesting group and representatives of the power structure. For those who feel themselves on the outside this is not a small accomplishment. It may, in fact, be the first step toward establishing permanent access to important policy makers.

Riots also produce action on a number of fronts though this action may be mainly symbolic. A violent outburst frequently encourages state and federal authorities to set up employment and youth-related programs. Perhaps the most significant results of a riot are symbolic. Various public officials are prompted to declare their sympathy, to promise improvements and to set up commissions of inquiry to study the problems and make recommendations. Symbolic rewards are not insignificant because they may eventuate in concrete action, but neither are they an immediate solution to pressing hardships. In any event, another hoped-for result of violent protest is a crystallization of public sentiment on the side of the protesters. Among blacks riots seem to have this effect. They encourage feelings of group solidarity and purpose.[42]

On the negative side, though, riots create a short-run backlash inasmuch as the majority of whites react with hostility. Table 9.2 compares the attitudes of whites and blacks. It shows in particular a distrust and hostility toward riots that contrasts sharply with the generally positive feelings of blacks. Certainly one of the most pronounced outcomes of the 1960s has been a repressive approach to dissent and law and order. Many cities have turned into armed camps.

Measured against the expectations of the participants, the results of riots seem meager indeed. State and federal governments have begun some programs but by and large there has been no enduring effort to redistribute wealth and end discrimination. Violent protests may even create a retrenchment of the status quo as the majority determines to preserve its position. Believing compromise will inevitably produce more demands, many public officials have adopted an unyielding stance toward black militancy.

Although sustained protest can disrupt a nation's political life by creating tension, interfering with economic and communications systems and overburdening decision-making processes, it seldom

---

[42] Sears and McConahay, *The Politics of Violence,* chap. xi.

Table 9.2
REACTIONS OF WHITES AND BLACKS TO URBAN RIOTS

	Whites	*Blacks*
Beliefs about the causes of riots		
Discrimination	41%	83%
Discrimination and blacks themselves	9	5
Only blacks themselves	50	12
	100%	100%
	(2,285)	(2,669)
Were riots planned in advance?		
Planned in advance	51%	21%
Some planning	38	41
Not planned at all	11	39
	100%	100%
	(2,535)	(2,837)
Have riots helped or hurt the cause of Negro rights?		
Helped	14%	36%
No difference; helped and hurt	20	39
Hurt	66	25
	100%	100%
	(2,578)	(2,988)
Sympathy with black protest movement		
Low sympathy	40%	—
Medium sympathy	17	—
High sympathy	17	—
	100%	—
	(2,656)	—

Note: Figures in parentheses refer to the number of cases.
Source: Angus Campbell and Howard Schuman, *Racial Attitudes in Fifteen American Cities.* (See Appendix.)

achieves this goal. It certainly has not done so in the United States. The accomplishments of violent protest are limited, and it is worth inquiring into the conditions making it a more or less effective political weapon.

Conditions of Successful Protest Behavior

Obviously, successful protest depends on numerous situational factors such as the establishment's capacity to inflict punishment and its willingness to use it, the adaptiveness of the political system and the quality of leadership. But above all, the nature of the protester's *demands* is crucial. Demands can be analyzed in several ways.

First, governments dispense both symbolic and material rewards, but, generally speaking, symbolic benefits are less costly and hence easier to provide than substantive ones. Consequently, protests often meet with symbolic success. After a riot, for example, a government may be willing to appoint a committee to listen to grievances. The naming of a committee after all, is easy and cheap. It does not require reallocating resources or reordering priorities. Very often demands are satisfied by symbolic rewards because the protesters obtain reassurance that their efforts have been fruitful.

When people insist on material changes such as greater public expenditure for housing or health they have less chance for success, especially if meeting their demands requires taking from another group. The civil rights movement in America has been successful up to a point. The movement encouraged the federal government to outlaw the most blatant (but not necessarily the most pernicious) forms of racial discrimination. Civil rights legislation banned segregated schools and public accommodations, and outlawed discriminatory voting and employment practices. Unfortunately, these acts have been largely symbolic because they did not materially improve the status of blacks. The achievement of the latter goal requires redistributing material resources. And needless to say, the redistribution of wealth is exceedingly hard to accomplish.

Symbolic rewards are not meaningless, for they may ultimately bring real changes. The point is only that protests will be most successful if the demands involve symbolic rather than material rewards.

Similarly, the salience and visibility of policy demands affects outcomes of protest movements.[43] If a majority considers a policy unimportant it will usually be willing to yield on it. Requests for black studies programs in secondary schools and colleges have been granted partly because they are perceived to be unimportant—at least to the white majority. The same generalization applies to the visibility of a program. Reorganizing an obscure housing authority is easier than passing an open housing ordinance of which everyone is aware.

It is also simpler to demand changes in governmental policies

---

[43] William R. Keech, "Some Conditions of Negro Influence over Public Policy through Voting," Paper delivered at the 1966 Annual Meeting of the American Political Science Association, New York, N.Y., September 6–10, p. 8.

than in private practices.[44] A state can order and enforce an end to discriminatory hiring practices in its own bureaus. Making industry do the same is much harder.

Another consideration in this regard is the discrepancy between prevailing norms and actual practices. The egregious gap between our democratic creed and our treatment of blacks doubtlessly contributed to the success of the early civil rights movement. Beliefs and behavior were so out of alignment that it was difficult to resist calls for an end to discrimination. Now, however, the more visible and blatant signs of discrimination have largely disappeared making it easier for the majority to resist protests. In other words, pointing to all the civil rights legislation passed in the 1960s, politicians can say "The legal barriers have been removed. Now it's up to each person, white or black, to make of himself what he can." Of course, the obstacles to self-fulfillment are just as formidable as ever but at least our laws do not glaringly contradict our constitutional principles.

In the end, successful protest behavior depends on communication.[45] A protest, even a violent one, has to communicate with three groups: the protest's followers (e.g., the black community), the target (e.g., the government and community leaders), and interested third parties who might be enlisted as allies. In order to succeed, the protest must speak to all three. Ideally it pressures the target group without at the same time alienating the other two. Again, drawing on the experience of the civil rights movement, one sees that in earlier stages its leaders created a wide range of support by communicating with previously neutral groups such as college students. The recent emergence of black militancy and especially its violent rhetoric has been a double-edged sword. Black solidarity and pride have been enhanced, but only at the expense of support from third parties.

The point, in summary, is not to cast judgment on any particular social movement. It is instead to assert the general proposition that protest as a type of political participation depends heavily for its success on communications. Some movements manage, some do not.

---

[44] Ibid., p. 9.

[45] For a discussion of the importance of communications as a part of protest behavior, see Michael Lipsky, "Protest as a Political Resource," *American Political Science Review*, Vol. 57 (1968), pp. 1144–58.

Appendix: A Note on the Sources of Data

The data used in this book have been supplied for the most part by the Inter-University Consortium for Political Research (ICPR) of the Institute for Social Research, the University of Michigan. Most of these studies are based on representative cross-section samples of citizens who are 18 years or older living in the United States. Samples range in size from 1,000 to 3,000 respondents. In addition, several cross-national samples have been used. These studies also involve representative samples ranging from 1,000 to 8,000 respondents. Finally, a few special purpose data sets have been utilized. The particular studies, together with the sample sizes and principal investigators, are listed below. (SRC means Survey Research Center and CPS means Center for Political Studies.) Two sets of data were supplied by the Lou Harris Political Data Center of the University of North Carolina. These studies are also listed below.

Neither the ICPR nor the Lou Harris Center is responsible for any interpretation placed on these data. Their assistance in providing them is gratefully acknowledged, however.

Data supplied by the ICPR:

SRC 1968 American National Election Study (1,673)
CPS 1970 American National Election Study (1,694)
CPS 1972 American National Election Study (2,705)
David Butler and Donald E. Stokes, *Political Change in Britain 1963–1970* (2,922)
John Meisel et al., *1965 Canadian Election Study* (8,193)
Philip E. Stouthard et al., *Dutch Election Study, 1970* (1,838)
M. Kent Jennings, *Student-Parent Socialization Study* (2,099)
Charles L. Taylor and Michael C. Hudson, *World Handbook of Political and Social Indicators II* (136)
Angus Campbell and Howard Schuman, *Racial Attitudes in Fifteen American Cities* (5,759)

Data supplied by the Lou Harris Political Data Center:

The 1972 Detroit Survey of Attitudes Toward Busing and Other Attitudes (1,078)
David Kovenock et al., *Comparative State Election Project* (7,676)

Index

This book has been set in 11 and 10 point Baskerville, leaded 2 points. Chapter numbers and titles are in 36 and 18 point Optima. The size of the type page is 26 x 43⅔ picas.